ABOUT THE AUTHOR

Professor Keith Ward is a Fellow of the British Academy, and Professorial Research Fellow at Heythrop College, London. He was formerly Regius Professor of Divinity at the University of Oxford, and is one of Britain's foremost writers on comparative theology and Christian issues. Notable works written by Keith Ward and published by Oneworld include *Christianity: A Beginner's Guide, God, Chance & Necessity, God: A Guide for the Perplexed,* and *God, Faith, and the New Millennium.*

Morality, Autonomy, and God

Keith Ward

ONEWORLD

A Oneworld Book

First published by Oneworld Publications 2013

ISBN 978-1-78074-317-2
ISBN 978-1-78074-318-9 (eBook)

A version of Chapter 8 was given as a paper to the
Oxford University McDonald Centre for Theology,
Ethics and Public Life Conference in May, 2013.

A version of Chapter 14 was given as a paper to the
International Conference on Persons at Lund University
in August, 2013.

Typeset by Cenveo Publishing Services, India
Printed and bound by CPI Group (UK) Ltd, Croydon, CR0 4YY

Oneworld Publications
10 Bloomsbury Street
London WC1B 3SR
England

This book was written during my tenure of a Professorial Research Fellowship at Heythrop College, London, and the research for it was largely undertaken in Heythrop College library. I am very grateful to my colleagues there for their friendship and academic stimulation.

CONTENTS

Introduction   xi

PART I: FROM NATURALISM TO THEISM

1 BEING A MORAL AGENT   3
   Some senses of moral autonomy   3
   The Ionian enchantment   6
   The Platonic alternative   9
   Just discernment and evaluative commitment   13

2 REASON AND SENTIMENT: A PHANTOM BATTLE?   18
   Reason and desire   18
   The rationalist case   20
   Hume on virtue   22
   Doing the reasonable thing   25
   Being reasonable about feelings   28
   An uneasy truce   31

3 HYPOTHETICAL AND CATEGORICAL MORALITY   35
   Virtue and human flourishing   39
   Distinctive human goods   40
   Love of the Good   43

4 NATURALISM AND ITS DISCONTENTS   46
   Enriched naturalism   46
   Basic goods and human flourishing   51
   The pursuit of happiness   53
   Ideals of universal fulfilment   55
   The idea of the Good   59
   Perceiving value   61

5 NATURAL LAW   65
   Natural law and divine law   65
   Natural and personalist purposes   68
   The Enlightenment Project   71
   Quasi- and real realism   75

6 THE OBJECTIVITY OF THE GOOD   80
   The naturalistic fallacy   80
   Moore and Platonism   82
   Knowing the Good   84
   The demand of the ideal   86
   Contemplating the Good   88
   The world viewed *sub specie aeternitatis*   90
   Morality and purpose   92
   Art and beauty   94

7 TOWARDS THEISTIC MORALITY   97
   From the Platonic Good to a personal God   97
   A morally conditioned God   101
   The divine-command theory   103
   Divine perfection   107
   A concept of God   109

PART II: AN OUTLINE OF A THEISTIC MORALITY

8 MORAL COMMITMENT AND MORAL PURPOSE   115
   Kant's notion of creative rational will   115
   The moral purpose: happiness in accordance with virtue   119
   The *summum bonum*   123
   A Kantian 'moral argument'   126

9 KANT, EVIL, AND REDEMPTION   129
   Kant and autonomy   129
   Radical evil   131
   The limits of autonomy   134

10 THE RELIGION OF HUMANITY   141
    God and human well-being   144
    God and human rights   147
    Justice and desert   150
    The virtues and God   153

11 THE ANTI-MORALISTS   156
    Nietzsche and the will to power   156
    Affirming life   160

12 THE OPTION FOR THE POOR   164
    Marx and liberation   164

13 SARTRE AND AUTHENTIC LIFE   173
    'Existence precedes essence'   173
    Choosing for all humanity   175
    Morality and meaning   177
    Authenticity and religion   180

14 PHILOSOPHICAL IDEALISM AND RELIGION   183
    Well-being and purpose   183
    Absolute Idealism   186
    Personal Idealism   190
    The end of morality   193
    Morality and world religions   195
    The beatific vision   197

15 SOME CHRISTIAN DOCTRINES   201
    Sin and atonement   201
    A theistic morality   207

    Conclusion   213

    Bibliography   216

    Index of Names   220

    Index of Subjects   221

INTRODUCTION

This book aims to lay out a philosophical defence of a theistic basis for morality. The argument proceeds in four main stages: first, it is argued that views of morality have metaphysical presuppositions; second, that one convincing metaphysical view is that of 'enriched' or 'expansive' naturalism, rooting moral beliefs in the existence of objectively existing values, which are parts of the 'fabric of reality'; third, that a Platonic account of objective value is a coherent form of such an enriched naturalism, and the best way of avoiding 'ontological queerness', as Mackie calls it; and fourth, that theism is not an optional supernaturalist addition to moral belief, but a metaphysical revision of Platonism, underpinning an objective, authoritative, and efficacious view of morality.

A SUMMARY OF THE ARGUMENT

Chapter 1: Being a Moral Agent

Humans are free agents who (partly) self-determine their acts by reason. This chapter introduces some main themes of the book. It outlines two views of the autonomy of moral discourse: that moral discourse contains an irreducible and distinctively moral element, not reducible to natural or metaphysical facts; and that moral discourse does not depend upon any metaphysical beliefs. I accept the first view, and reject the second, and the whole book can be seen as an argument for the importance of metaphysical beliefs to understandings of morality.

Then I outline a view of the autonomy of moral agents, as the view that moral agents are self-determining, in at least partly determining their own behaviour by moral reasons, which are thereby seen as having causal power. This is contrasted with reductively naturalist accounts of moral belief, like that of E.O. Wilson.

Referring to work by Peter Strawson and Iris Murdoch, I argue that, when forming basic beliefs about human morality and human nature, description, interpretation, evaluation, and commitment are inextricably intertwined. Morality is as much a matter of 'ways of seeing' as of prescription.

Any adequate account of moral commitment presupposes seeing humans as agents self-determined by reasons.

Chapter 2: Reason and Sentiment: A Phantom Battle?

Moral reasons essentially relate to human inclinations and desires. The chapter explores the nature of moral reasons, referring to Samuel Clarke and David Hume as finding moral reasons in a realm of eternal and necessary moral truths, or as founded on contingent human sentiments, respectively. It is suggested that morality is primarily about discovering reasonable choices for partly rational, passionate, social, and free agents, and that Clarke and Hume agree at least on this.

Chapter 3: Hypothetical and Categorical Morality

Moral reasons aim at worthwhile states, which constitute human flourishing or well-being. A worthwhile state (a 'good' or value) is a state reasonably choosable by an affective intelligent agent. Using a presuppositional argument developed from Philippa Foot, I argue that there are basic states that all rational agents have a good reason to want. Four such states are understanding, appreciation, creativity, and empathy, and together they can be taken to define important constituents of human flourishing.

Chapter 4: Naturalism and its Discontents

Basic values are objective, parts of the fabric of reality, not simply inferences from the existence of actual desires in individuals. By reference to the 'enriched naturalism' of John McDowell, and the 'expansive naturalism' of James Griffin, I argue that values are not 'subjective' – they do not depend upon desires people happen to have. They are matters of perceiving what is the case, and legislate what desires people ought to have.

Chapter 5: Natural Law

The appeal to reason, human inclinations, human flourishing, and the objectivity of values is characteristic of traditional Christian 'natural law' ethics. This raises the question of how far such a morality requires metaphysical foundations. I argue that even an expansively naturalist view of morality has difficulty in upholding the universality and categorical force of an ethic of human flourishing. Aristotelian views of a moral teleology may need revising, but there may be some need for a meta-physical underpinning for beliefs about human flourishing. Discussions of Alasdair MacIntyre and Simon Blackburn ground an argument for a deeper metaphysical foundation to underwrite the objectivity and authority even of an apparently naturalistic ethics.

Chapter 6: The Objectivity of the Good

The idea of a supreme moral ideal ('the Good') can provide a home for the objectivity of moral truths and the authority of moral obligations. G.E. Moore, Iris Murdoch, and Stewart Sutherland have spoken of 'non-natural properties', of 'the Good', and of 'the Eternal', as founded on a quasi-Platonic supreme ideal, which can be a motivating object of moral contemplation. As in Plato, there is unclarity about whether or how far causality and purpose, or even real existence, may be involved in positing such an ideal. Nevertheless, 'Platonic enchantment' engenders the idea of an objective focus for moral vision and commitment, which alleviates John Mackie's fear of ontological 'queerness'.

Chapter 7: Towards Theistic Morality

The addition of Mind to the Good provides a principle for selecting actual goods (that is, for creating a cosmos), an existent focus of devotion, reverence, and imitation, and a hope for the future triumph of good, that a purely conceptual 'Ideal' cannot. This could be called 'God'. Platonism can generate (as in Augustine, for instance) a theistic base for morality that dissolves the Euthyphro dilemma, and provides a firm metaphysical foundation for moral objectivity and authority.

Chapter 8: Moral Commitment and Moral Purpose

God as the most adequate metaphysical foundation for a morality of human flourishing and universal justice and benevolence. Immanuel Kant's so-called 'moral argument' for God is widely dismissed. I aim to show that it is central to his Critical philosophy to hold that reason is essentially creative and purposive, aiming at the rule of goodness, and that hope for moral success is vital to moral commitment. Moreover, his key argument is that, in certain conditions, it is reasonable to make a practical moral and epistemological commitment in face of theoretical uncertainty. I defend his view.

Chapter 9: Kant, Evil, and Redemption

Kant saw that there is a moral gap between obligation and achievement, and that divine help is needed to overcome human moral failure. This is an important and neglected feature of Kantian morality. John Hare has drawn attention to the 'moral gap' that Kant sees between duty and possible achievement. One advantage of theistic morality is that it perceives this gap as a feature of the human situation, and therefore sees morality in a wider context of ideal goal, failure to achieve it, and some remedy for this failure. For a theistic morality, that is a distinctive part of what morality is.

In this chapter, I also draw out further very different meanings of 'autonomy' – inventing moral law; working the moral law out for oneself; personally recognizing what is right; being free to criticize moral authorities for good reason; and being free to choose good or evil. I argue that, taken in the three latter senses, autonomy is compatible with revelation – though revelation is always subject to moral critique.

Chapter 10: The Religion of Humanity

Another way in which theism can strengthen naturalistic moral beliefs is that it provides an objective basis for giving all human life special regard, and for cultivating a sense of unity with and reverence for all sentient life, and indeed for all creation. J.S. Mill and Nicholas Wolterstorff have both written positively of these possibilities, and I argue that theistic morality gives the most adequate possible grounding for an objective, authoritative, and invincible morality. When properly understood, it therefore strongly supports a humanistic morality, while deepening and extending that morality beyond the realm of the human and beyond the reach of natural human capacities.

Chapter 11: The Anti-Moralists

Theistic morality, properly interpreted, entails the affirmation of life, concern for the poor and underprivileged, and creative freedom. Three influential recent writers have denied this, and have denigrated both belief in objective morality and God as unworthy of belief. I try to see the strength in their critiques, while stressing important things they have missed, and defending the entailments I have mentioned. First is Friedrich Nietzsche. Nietzsche wanted beliefs that would be life-affirming, joyous, and creative. That is what belief in God should give, since God creates life for the sake of the fulfilment and joy it should bring. Nietzsche's own commendation of the 'will to power' and of eternal recurrence is not in fact life-affirming for the vast majority of suffering humanity, 'the herd'.

Chapter 12: The Option for the Poor

Karl Marx wanted all, especially the poor and oppressed, to be able to exercise their potential creatively. That should be the aim of theism too. But the natural dialectic of history is unlikely to make this possible, and theism seeks to keep the idea alive, while acknowledging continual failure to attain it.

Chapter 13: Sartre and Authentic Life

Jean-Paul Sartre argued that humans should be free and live authentically. This is an aspiration of theism too, but freedom must be for the sake of good, not unconstrained and desire-led action. Sartre saw this, but was unable to see any alternative to absurdity and despair. That is precisely where a passionate commitment to God as the ultimate cosmic wisdom and moral hope in objective uncertainty is reasonable, as both Kant and Kierkegaard argued.

Chapter 14: Philosophical Idealism and Religion

One important element of theistic morality is the hope of union between human and divine, which makes the moral life a journey to union with invincible love. Taking themes from Aristotle, Bradley, Whitehead, Aquinas, and William James, I try to show how theistic morality culminates in the hope of beatific vision, and in the full actualization of the objective Ideal in and through the lives of finite creatures. I distinguish the Absolute Idealism of Hegel and Bradley from the more personal Idealism of theism, and argue for the greater coherence and rationality of the latter view.

Chapter 15: Some Christian Doctrines

Though I have defended theism in general, I conclude by addressing four problems that are specific to Christianity, as most of the philosophers I have discussed have interacted with that faith. Is Christian morality a matter of obeying divine commands? Does original sin not render morality irrelevant anyway, since we cannot do what we ought? How can it be just for one man (Jesus) to be punished for the sins of other people? And how can someone who believes in a God of love believe in Hell?

These are the four questions I address, suggesting ways in which some Christians, anyway, could respond positively to them.

I conclude with the claim that theism gives an objectivity, authority, effectiveness, and hope to morality that no secular view can match. Nevertheless, humans can know what is good without believing in God, and morality can exist without religion. My claim is that there is not just one thing, morality, agreed by all, to which some would add peripheral religious beliefs. Rather, theistic morality is in principle different to secular morality, and may reasonably claim to incorporate a peculiarly penetrating view of human nature and its ills. That does not mean that this 'proves' there is a God. But it is one powerful reason for moving the mind towards thinking of God. It is, for some, even a reason for seeing that in the demands of morality one hears the voice of a transcendent reality of supreme value. As Kant said, then one might see one's duties as divine commands. I have tried to provide a context in which some of the implications of that way of seeing may be clearer, and some of the objections to such a morality may dissolve away.

Part I

FROM NATURALISM TO THEISM

1

BEING A MORAL AGENT

SOME SENSES OF MORAL AUTONOMY

In modern moral philosophy, there has come to exist a widespread view that ethics is autonomous. That is, as characterized in the *Oxford Dictionary of Philosophy*, views of ethics do not depend upon divine commands, the dictates of pure reason, or facts of nature. Moral principles 'stand on their own feet', and are arrived at by intellectual processes that are proper to purely ethical thought. This is the sort of view advocated by Ronald Dworkin in *Justice for Hedgehogs*, when he argues that ethics cannot be supported by metaphysics or by God.

There is probably some sense in which this is correct, but the idea of autonomy is a very complex one, and there are some important senses in which ethics is not autonomous. My own belief is that there is an irreducible moral element to some widely held human beliefs. However, it would not be reasonable, when thinking about ethics, to ignore alleged divine commands, considerations of 'pure reason', or facts of nature, especially of human nature. I further think that it would be entirely reasonable to take the existence and nature of God, if there is a God, as a foundation for ethical thinking, in which case ethics would not be autonomous in the sense of being completely independent of metaphysical beliefs, and in particular of belief in God. I also believe that there is a specific and defensible view of the nature of morality as irreducible, objective, and authoritative, which is one justifying reason for positing the existence of God.

Those who speak of the 'autonomy of ethics' do not, of course, mean that we should ignore any question of fact when thinking about ethics. They usually mean that such questions, though relevant to ethical decision making, do not decide ethical issues. It would be ridiculous to say that, when enquiring into what I ought to do, I must not refer to what I am capable of doing – that is, to my capacities, desires, and feelings. I am an animal of a certain sort, with specific capacities, and I live in an environment which makes some actions easy, some difficult, and some impossible. In some sense, if I ask what I ought to do, I need to know what it is possible for me to do, what my capacities are, and I need to believe that I could, but need not, do certain things. I need to think of myself as a being that has knowledge, ability to envisage future possibilities, and the freedom to choose between them because of reasons that I am able to formulate.

These considerations prompt a different but closely related view of autonomy, concerned not with the nature of moral discourse but with the nature of moral agency. Humans, it may be said, are distinctively moral agents who can act for reasons that they themselves formulate, and who are not wholly determined by physical or social necessities. This sense (autonomy as self-determination) allows for the existence of many influencing factors and constraints on personal choice, but insists on an ineliminable element of personal choice, where the individual must take responsibility for what they do. I believe this to be a defensible view of autonomy.

It could well be said that being a self-determining rational and free agent is a 'fact of nature'. It states a truth about what sorts of being humans are, and, since humans are part of the natural world, these seem to be straightforwardly natural facts. In that case, facts of nature would include reason-directed processes, free actions, and moral purposes. Some tough-minded philosophers would be unhappy about this, believing that in the end nature is just what the natural sciences talk about, no more and no less. What this signals is the ambiguity of the words 'nature' and 'natural'. They could be taken to refer to purely physical entities and properties, which could be investigated by the natural sciences, or even by the most basic natural science, physics. Or they could be taken to refer more generally and unsystematically to the natural world in which humans live, including humans, animals, plants, and rocks, as well as desires, thoughts, intentions, and values. If one is going to include values in the natural world, there is no reason in principle why God should not be thought of as playing a role in the natural world too. It may be simple prejudice that excludes such a possibility, but the fact is that most philosophers who call themselves naturalists mean to exclude God, especially as a super-natural moral authority, in principle.

This latter sense is what James Griffin has called 'expansive natural-ism' (Griffin, 1986, ch. 3). One way of marking the difference between these two interpretations of 'nature' is to say that the first is a reductive proposal that would see all genuine explanations as explanations in natural science, and all existent entities as in some sense physical or material and nothing more. The second interpretation would not insist on such reduction, and might even think it impossible to carry out. It would be more sympathetic to there being many levels of explanation, and with there being emergent properties (most obviously, such things as desires, thoughts, and feelings) arising from a complex integrated material substratum. The force of the word 'natural' on this interpretation is hard to pin down, but is probably meant to stress the fact that there is only one world, one reality, not two distinct worlds, one of matter and the other of spirit, connected in some mysterious way. Furthermore, the material substratum is probably seen as the primary causal generator of all other properties, however emergent they may be. That addition would rule out God, though belief in the causal primacy of the material must be more a theoretical hypothesis than an experiential observation.

If one says that humans are autonomous, in the sense of self-determining, this looks like an anti-reductionist move – not all human behaviour is explicable purely in terms of physics, for example. At the same time, 'being self-determining' can be seen as a perfectly 'natural' feature of the natural world, since in it many beings may be self-determining to a lesser or greater extent. I suppose that, for moral autonomy to be meaningfully asserted, it would have to be said that there is a level of interpretation and explanation of the natural world that needs to employ irreducibly moral concepts. And it may turn out that, in this sense, humans, though fully part of the natural world, are truly autonomous and morally self-determining.

There are interpretations of what it is to be self-determining that I would regard as implausible. For instance, if someone thought that humans could completely determine what they are to do, without regard to independent and pre-existing standards of goodness or obligation, that would be thought by some to undermine the idea of morality altogether. Or if someone argued that each person should decide for themselves what to do, without depending on any authority and without being influenced by any socially accepted values, that might seem to be unduly individual-istic or even arrogant. So, the idea of self-determination stands in need of analysis before one can happily commit oneself to it.

THE IONIAN ENCHANTMENT

There are philosophers who would deny autonomy, even in the 'self-determination' sense of having a capacity for free and responsible moral action. They might deny that reasons can have a causal role in what happens, or that I am free to choose between future alternatives. In this respect, there are contested factual beliefs, beliefs about 'facts of nature', that are proposed by believers in autonomy as necessary conditions of thinking about ethics, in the sense of seriously thinking what I ought to do, how I ought to act, or what sort of person I ought to be. For believers in moral autonomy in this simple sense, the existence of moral obligation presupposes the fact of human freedom and the causal efficacy of reason, or reflective thinking. Those who say that all human acts are determined by laws of physics, that there are no alternative futures, and that, even if there are, reasoning plays no causal role in which possible future becomes actual must think of ethical reflection as an essentially non-causal epiphenomenon of human brain activity.

Such a belief embodies a particular view of what ethical thinking is. It could be, for example, thinking about the general rules of social conduct, which have been genetically programmed by their adaptiveness to the environment in earlier stages of hominid evolution. This appears to be the view that the originator of sociobiology (now often called evolutionary psychology) E.O. Wilson, in his more reductionist moods, takes in his book *Consilience*. It entails that, if I now ask the ethical question 'What should I do?', I am reflecting in consciousness the behavioural routines that form part of my largely inherited mental suite of behaviours, and their physically caused resolution into one specific activity. He writes, 'rational choice is the casting about among alternative mental scenarios to hit upon the ones which, in a given context, satisfy the strongest epigenetic rules' (Wilson, 1998, p. 199). There is a sort of 'casting about' going on, though this is actually a series of causal processes in the brain, which are not in fact consciousness -led or -directed. The conscious elements of this process are epiphenomenal, or not true causes. The process proceeds by purely physical causal principles, and is not directed to any end, much less a consciously formulated one. The 'chosen scenario' will be the one that satisfies the strongest epigenetic rules. An epigenetic rule is a hereditary bias of mental development (ibid., p. 275), which predisposes brains to act in various ways (ibid., p. 166). Thus, a process of rational ethical decision making is in reality a purely physical brain process whereby the most strongly established neural pathway – established in the far past of the species by genetic processes that were randomly generated and have been selected by the environment – becomes actuated.

Consciousness, intention, evaluation, and free choice are eliminated from this process. Or, if not eliminated, they are identified with physical brain processes, which proceed in accordance with non-conscious, non-intentional and physically determined laws, the nature of which can be clarified by an understanding of evolutionary adaptiveness. Conscious reflections and decisions have no contributory causal role in the process.

Ethics is still possible, and perhaps inevitable, as a matter of psychological fact. However, it is clear that ethics would not, on this view, be autonomous, since no human being is truly self-determining. Ethics would, in principle, depend upon, and indeed be reducible to, scientific laws, which are facts of nature. It would be wholly caused by physical processes and could be completely explained in terms of adaptive behaviour and conscious rationalization. Wilson writes that '"ought" is just shorthand for one kind of factual statement' (ibid., p. 280), a statement about what society has chosen. Such choices have themselves been codified and selected by evolutionary pressures for survival. And those pressures are explicable in the end by fundamental laws of physics, which would show what behaviours are likely (or certain) to be selected in environments that are themselves physically constituted.

Interestingly, there are good reasons for thinking that a belief in human free decision making is strongly adaptive and therefore genetically deep-rooted in human nature. In other words, if the theory of genetic determinism is true, we will have, and will be determined to have, good reasons for thinking it is false. The theory will tell us that we are probably determined to believe that we are not wholly determined. I will then believe that I am determined (I believe X) to believe that I am not determined (I believe -X). I cannot rationally believe both these things at the same time. That, of course, is no problem for the theory, which entails that having good reasons for action is causally irrelevant, so it makes no difference whether it is incoherent or not. However, for those who think that incoherence matters, something will have to give.

In asking what might give, we might point to what are probably the weakest points of the reductionist theory – the claim that I am wholly determined to believe whatever I do believe, and that new information or thought can make no difference, as meaningful information or logical thought, to what I believe. It seems more plausible to think that I may have genetically based predispositions to form certain sorts of beliefs, but that new sensory information, consciously considered, can modify or direct these predispositions in various ways.

Wilson concedes that it seems implausible to suppose that all our beliefs are determined by purely physical laws. Though he sometimes advocates such a view, and says that he wishes it were true, usually he does not. He states the view a couple of times: 'All tangible phenomena, from the birth of stars to the workings of social institutions, are based on material processes that are ultimately reducible . . . to the laws of physics' (ibid., p. 297). And 'nature is organised by simple universal laws of physics to which all other laws and principles can eventually be reduced' (ibid., p. 59).

This strong reducibility thesis is, however, subject to immediate quali-fication by Wilson. In the first statement, the expression 'based on' allows for weaker interpretations, such that there may be other factors in addition to laws of physics, though the laws of physics must form their basic substratum. In the case of the second statement, he admits that it is an oversimplification, but he still hopes that the strong thesis will turn out to be correct in some form.

If this is a hope, rather than a matter of established fact, then it is proper to question whether it is a fruitful, helpful, or commendable hope. I can see why it could be commended. What drives Wilson's argument is a hope that science will turn out to provide one unitary explanation of how things are. This 'Ionian enchantment', as he calls it, incorporates a strong belief in the unity of knowledge, and in the capacity of the human mind to achieve such unity. 'The world is orderly and can be explained by a small number of natural laws' (ibid., p. 3). No 'spooky mysteries' will remain, but a seamless web of causal explanations will provide a complete understanding of this one natural world of which we humans are part.

This is undoubtedly faith, in the sense that it is a belief that goes well beyond the evidence, and may indeed be impossible, for all we can tell. That impossibility only incites Wilson to embrace it more fully, for he says that he loves 'the challenge and the crackling of thin ice', and the thrill of pursuing an exciting, grand, and intellectually bold ideal. I see the attraction of elegance, simplicity, and mathematical rigour in the Ionian enchantment. However, it can hardly be denied that this is a grand story of the universe as a whole, whose main function is the pragmatic one of inspiring scientific work and commitment, and which mainly exists as an ideal that is supremely worth striving for, even if in the end it turns out to be false. Thus it is that, as Wilson says, 'science is religion liberated and writ large' (ibid., p. 5).

It is a reductive story, leading us to reduce beliefs about human desires, consciousness, and thoughts to beliefs about material particles behaving in accordance with impersonal laws of physics. It leaves no room for the objective and real existence of beauty, truth, and goodness as elements of reality. It is therefore ironic that it claims to reveal the objective truth about the universe, a truth that is mathematically elegant and beautiful, and that is good (rationally choosable) largely because of the intrinsic satisfaction of understanding and appreciating that truth and beauty. The moral commitment to truth at any cost, to the importance of understanding the universe, and to eliminating superstition and ignorance is unmistakeable. This is a deeply paradoxical thought, though it is difficult to turn it into a formal contradiction. It is more like a conflict of opposing intellectual tendencies, one prioritizing analytical understanding, and the other focused on moral and humane commitments.

The Ionian enchantment is a faith, based on the huge success of the natural sciences, but facing major problems of working out just how to reduce most of our ordinary beliefs about human thoughts and desires to laws of physics. Like many faiths, it has some good evidence in its favour (largely in terms of pragmatic success), but faces major conceptual problems when one attempts to work it out in detail. If it seems inspiring to reduce all knowledge to simple, universal, and precisely quantifiable terms, it may also be seen as (literally) demoralizing and dehumanizing to reduce all ethical, artistic, and philosophical beliefs to theories in mathematical physics.

THE PLATONIC ALTERNATIVE

Maybe – and this is very much the theme of this first chapter – this is an evaluative matter, and not just a purely descriptive matter. Opposed to the Ionian enchantment is another, just as ancient and honourable, and strongly embedded in classical philosophical thought, the Platonic enchantment. It is not denied that the physical world is orderly and can be explained by mathematical laws. But it is asserted that beneath this physical world – not in another world but at the heart of this world and as its inner and true reality – there is a reality of truth, beauty, and goodness, of value and purpose. These elements are irreducible. They cannot be reduced to other simpler sorts of reality. They are ultimate constituents of reality. They in no way undermine the unity and intelligibility of the physical world, and indeed they underpin and guarantee that unity and intelligibility by grounding them in one ultimately intelligible reality from which they flow.

If there is, as Wilson desires, a consilience between the natural sciences and the humane sciences, it is more likely to be found in a view which embraces both without annihilating either. Whereas reductive naturalism has difficulty in explaining how consciousness, rationality, freedom, and purpose can be given a reductive explanation, the thought that elegant and unified laws of nature are physical expressions of one beautiful, elegant, intelligible reality is not at all paradoxical – though to the determined naturalist it introduces a superfluous and unnecessary (naturalists tend to call it 'spooky', to make it seem odder than it is) dimension to reality. We need to recall that, if the naturalist is a quantum physicist, spooky elements (from a classical materialist point of view) are already there in good measure. In addition, if we are 'expansive naturalists', there seems no insuperable obstacle to seeing quasi-mental properties as irreducible parts of the natural world. When we have got that far, it seems only a limitation of imagination to decree that some sorts of value or mind-like properties could not possibly exist as the 'veiled reality' that underlies what appears to us as a physical three-dimensional linear-time-like world of solid physical objects.

However, I am not concerned here with explorations of such a directly metaphysical nature. I am concerned with the roots of moral perception, and with how they interact with views of human nature. My point is that it is very hard to give an account of morality in reductionist terms, which does not undermine, even while it presupposes, a commitment to aiming at what is good (for instance, understanding of truth) for its own sake. If we have a choice between an Ionian ideal, which challenges the independent reality of goodness, and a Platonic ideal, which makes goodness foundational to all existence, that is probably not resolvable by appeal to 'bare facts'. It is a choice that already involves evaluation, and an orientation of life in a specific way.

Of course, Ionianism and Platonism are extreme ends of a wide spectrum of conceptual possibilities, and there are all sorts of reservations that people would make about committing themselves wholeheartedly to either. The central question remains, however, of whether an interpretation of human existence and of the place of morality in human life does not already involve an evaluative element, which, as such, is not susceptible to straightforward value-free empirical verification. This is perhaps a matter of intellectual, not moral evaluation, but it is evaluation nonetheless. It would be absurd to say that all reductive naturalists are immoral, treating people as mere machines, and that all non-reductive naturalists are morally just, treating others with respect as rational agents. I have suggested that reductivists usually have a high evaluative commitment to seeking truth, however unpleasant it may be. And non-reductivists may well theoretically regard others as rational agents, while not caring about them at all. The perils of moralism are well known, and seeing others as responsible moral agents can lead to judgemental, censorious, and self-righteous behaviour, which may be more harmful than treating others as machines that cannot really help what they do.

The connection between a commitment to seeing the world in a certain way and a commitment to actually treating others with respect and compassion is not as simple as that. Nevertheless, if persons are seen as machines without responsibility, and if this is thought through rigorously, one of the main intellectual presuppositions of respect for others may well be undermined. So, it is important to note that one main argument against a ruthlessly reductive view is that, while it actually expresses a real evaluative commitment (to truth), that commitment is in the end less morally supportive than a commitment to a more expansive naturalism that allows intentions, reasons, values, and purposes a real and causally effective place in nature. Where neutral 'purely factual' verification fails to resolve the issue, there is an evaluative reason for adopting a non-reductivist ontology. It seems to be the case that our most basic theoretical perspectives cannot rid themselves of irreducibly evaluative elements. I shall call the view that theoretical and evaluative elements are tied together in this way 'perspectivalism', to make the point that we see things most basically from a specific historical and cultural perspective, not, as Thomas Nagel has put it, 'from nowhere'.

The arguments Wilson adduces in his book do not in fact support a strong Ionian thesis. The very expression 'epigenetic rules', on which he places much weight, implies that there is a 'gene-culture co-evolution', whereby cultures affect the expression of genetic dispositions, even while genes lay down constraints on human capacities, including tendencies to believe certain sorts of things. Wilson in fact mentions three different elements in the development of morality: hereditary dispositions, socially established practices, and intelligent choices. There is a corresponding three-stage process in the evolution of morality – though whether evolving humanity actually passed through these stages successively, or whether they represent logical distinctions rather than historical ones, would be extremely difficult to establish.

At the earliest pre-rational stage, animals act randomly, and some of these establish action-patterns that are laid down in the descendants of more successfully adapted individuals. At a later, social stage, societies adopt rules, some of which enable their societies to flourish and survive, and these rules become culturally (but not genetically) coded into society members. At a later stage still, intelligent choices can be made between possible behaviours – as Wilson says, we are now able to 'fashion a wiser and more enduring ethical consensus' (1998, p. 267). Rational choice between envisaged futures becomes possible.

It looks as though we have to say that our genetic predispositions can be overridden by new evidence, and by arguments that depend on that evidence. If so, we cannot be completely genetically determined. In practice, we must assume that our moral beliefs can be changed by new evidence or arguments. Facts about evolutionary adaptiveness may contribute valuable insights into how humans came to have the basic moral predispositions – to limited altruism and reciprocal benevolence – they have. However, they will not answer the question of how we should now act.

All this implies that there is no basic agreement on what ethics is (or morality – I am using these words as equivalents, and, though I have no objection to giving distinct meanings to 'ethics' and 'morals', different writers disagree on what these distinct meanings are, and I would not wish to enter those disputes). To say that ethics is autonomous already incorporates a contested view of what sort of thing morality is. It would deny that ethics is a set of behavioural routines that are to be adequately explained in terms of evolutionary mutation and adaptation, and, ultimately, in terms of laws of physics. It is to say that there is human consciousness, knowledge, freedom, and causally operative reason. It seems to be a presupposition of moral reflection that humans have an 'inner life' of feeling and consciousness, that they are rational beings, exercising 'final causality', able to envisage non-existent (possible future) states and select some of them as 'good', as goals to be sought, and that they are free, able to exercise causal influence on events that might have been different without that influence. These are weighty metaphysical claims, and, to that extent at least, one central view of what morality is depends on metaphysical postulates. To put it more pointedly, the view of autonomy as self-determination, and as a *sui generis* and self-contained field of enquiry, implies a non-reductive metaphysical view, so that it is not autonomous in being independent of wider metaphysical beliefs.

JUST DISCERNMENT AND EVALUATIVE COMMITMENT

The exact nature of the postulates implied by belief in moral autonomy as self-determination is difficult to spell out. Peter Strawson, in his influential paper 'Freedom and Resentment' (1974), distinguished between objective and reactive attitudes towards other persons. Objective attitudes treat persons as physical objects, their existence determined by physical laws, and their behaviour changeable, in principle, by physical interventions, such as surgery, brain manipulation, or genetic engineering. Reactive attitudes treat persons as centres of consciousness, thought, and choice, as we think of ourselves when trying to decide what is true or how to act.

As we can tell ourselves to concentrate, try harder, think logically, decide rationally, and act circumspectly, so we can tell other persons the same things, praise them when they do such things, and blame them when they do not. Just as we have to see ourselves as faced by alternative possibilities, and able to determine the future to some extent by thinking and deciding, so we see others in the same way when we treat them as persons, not as objects. If I think about what I ought to do, I presuppose that my thought will make some difference to what I do, and that my directed thoughts will bring about whatever physical brain-states correlate with the more or less rational decisions I make. Whatever sophisticated theories I may adopt with regard to brain–mind identity or lack of it, in practice, I must act as if my consciously directed thinking will produce physical brain-states that might not have occurred if I had not done any thinking. So it will be in the case of my attitudes to other persons. I presuppose that, in normal cases, if and only if they think hard, they will make decisions (and thus put their brains and bodies into physical states) that would not have obtained had they not thought, or if they had thought differently. To regard others as persons is to assume this is true, and to hold them responsible for actions that they consciously chose.

Wittgenstein and others have argued that this is not a matter of moving from my own case, of which I am sure, and inferring that other persons must have feelings and thoughts like mine, though I can never be sure. For my thoughts and the language in which I express them have been learned from others, and shaped by a long history of social change and interaction. I know that others (in the first case, those who teach me to speak) are reasoning and responsible beings, who elicit from me my free responses to their consciously directed acts towards me. I inhabit a world of persons with their own inner lives, their own thought processes, and their own social interactions, and it is in realizing this that I learn that I am a member of a community of reasoning agents.

I am not, in other words, self-determining in the sense that I make up all my language and my ways of thinking and acting for myself. I am from the first someone who has learned ways of thinking and choosing from my society. Even to think of myself as an autonomous and free rational agent is something that would be foreign to me if I was born and lived as a slave in a rigidly hierarchical society. There are people who would not think of freedom as a value, and who would regard personal reflection on how to act as a useless and irrelevant activity.

Of course, if one believes that it is important to being a mature person that one should always have an area of moral responsibility, then one will say of such people that they are in fact free to some extent – they can, for instance, work gladly and happily, or glumly and reluctantly, they can care for one another compassionately, or ignore their fellows. Moral choice always exists, and moral decisions for good or ill are always made. But that is something of an *a priori* assertion, which the facts just have to fit. There are people who will deny ever having knowingly made a moral choice, and who see themselves as wholly determined to be the way they are.

Indeed, this is the default position of those who believe in predestination. They may accept that they do whatever they do necessarily, and carry on doing it. Believers in predestination, historically, have usually thought that some being – probably God – determines things for good, and so they are fairly content with how they are. In modern times, people are more likely to think that things are determined by accident or blind necessity, and that considerations of justice or goodness are not relevant to what happens to them.

They can say, with the ancient Greek lyric poet Pindar, 'Be true to yourself' (Pythian 2,72), by simply going on being the way they are – perhaps they can take Ibsen's spin on Pindar, which he formulates in the play *Peer Gynt* as the Troll motto: 'Be true to yourself, and to Hell with the world'. If they begin to wonder whether they should interpret 'self-realization' in this way, they are indulging in useless morbidity. They should just get on with it, doing what comes naturally to them. 'Be what you are, and do not worry about changing what you are' – because there is no alternative anyway.

If you thought that, by realizing the truth of the reductive theory, you could change your way of life, you would be assuming that beliefs have a causal role in behaviour – which would undermine the reductive theory.

However, if there were such a thing as moral freedom, and the possibility of changing what one is, then to adopt a deterministic attitude might plausibly be seen as a responsibly willed denial of moral responsibility – which would be immoral.

Thus, what might be called by many a presupposition of morality, and of being a moral agent, is partly already a value judgement. It is an interpretation or evaluation of what it is to be properly human, and not a completely value-free description. Yet it is meant to be a description. This suggests that the most basic descriptions of what it is to be a human being cannot avoid evaluations, or basic ways of seeing and acting towards human beings. Ways of seeing and commitments to acting are bound together in such a way that what one thinks it right to do follows from the way one sees one's situation. Yet that way of seeing already embodies a certain sort of personal commitment, to being-in-the-world in a specific way.

This is not too strange in ordinary human affairs. We know that a person in a bad mood will tend to see the most depressing side of things, whereas a happy and cheerful person can be in the same situation, but find something uplifting or inspiring about it. Human perceptions reflect and express human moods and attitudes. Even in biology, some evolutionary psychologists find nature to be 'red in tooth and claw', without purpose or point. But others can see the same data as showing the development of integrative organization that leads progressively to the emergence of intelligence and understanding.

This means that even attending to the facts involves a cognitive attitude, a conceptual interpretation, which is not value-neutral. To see oneself and others as moral agents is a genuinely basic interpretation – it is not inferred from some other piece of knowledge. But that basic interpretation is already value-laden.

This seems to imply that values are not all consciously chosen, but many of them exist before one consciously chooses anything. I think that, in a sense, that is true, and the situation is something like this: one learns an interpretation of the world from others, and the perceptions one has embody values learned from one's culture. But as one continues to learn, to encounter new experiences and come across new concepts, one begins to modify or reinforce those learned perceptual evaluations.

The first moral choices may occur in youth for most people, and even at quite an early stage offer the choice of either respecting others as free agents with their own interests and values, or regarding them as means to one's own satisfaction. The elements of moral character may be laid down very early. But they will always be reinforced by one's immediate community, and also by one's own developing consciousness of the objects and persons one meets.

If this is so, then to regard others as free reasoning agents is a basic natural evaluative interpretation. But it is always liable to be countered by regarding some others as less than free reasoning agents – simply by ignoring their reasons and decisions in favour of one's own.

However, there is an obvious objection. Can we not admit that others are free reasoning agents, but choose to ignore that fact, and treat them as objects? Yes, of course; we all do that to some extent. Yet that means we are not attending to their real natures and needs. Really perceiving, really knowing, is responding to their true natures, and that is already adopting a stance of giving value to the nature of things. Giving value is not deciding to put value on them, when the value is not there. It is recognizing the value that is there.

Iris Murdoch puts this well in *The Sovereignty of Good*, when she says that 'goodness is connected with . . . a refined and honest perception of what is really the case, a patient and just discernment and exploration of what confronts one' (1970, p. 38). Such perception is a matter of effort and discipline. It is not some sort of instantaneous intuition. 'When M is just and loving she sees D as she really is' (ibid., p. 37). One has to learn to see justly, which means that one has to be just and loving in order to see what is really there. There is 'the progressive attempt to see a particular object clearly' (ibid., p. 23). Virtue, Murdoch says, 'is a selfless attention to nature' (ibid., p. 41), more like obedience than like a resolution of the will. But the obedience is not to some authoritarian rule. It is an obedience of patient and loving regard to the real nature of things. 'The central concept of morality', she writes, 'is "the individual" thought of as knowable by love' (ibid., p. 30).

Such patient and loving regard is not primarily an apprehension of something supernatural or strange. It is an apprehension of the natural world as it really is, freed of reductive ambitions. James Griffin's 'expansive naturalism' allows that values – most clearly but not only those of a prudential sort – are parts of the natural order. For the natural order includes human intentions and interests, and it involves attending appropriately to what those intentions and interests are. I am sympathetic to this proposal, if only because human persons are, after all, part of the natural order. They are not supernatural intrusions into an otherwise seamless web of causally connected events. This is a sort of naturalism that is very unlike reductive naturalism. Just how expansive it needs to be is a subject I will be investigating later.

For the present, it seems unavoidable that even to say what sort of thing morality is requires metaphysical argument. Autonomy, in the sense of independence from metaphysical reflection about the nature of human persons, is not self-evident. It is one possible view of the nature of morality among others. Thus, I think that morality is autonomous, in that there is a distinctive and irreducible moral or evaluative and potentially moral element in human cognition. However, it is not autonomous, in that discerning this element is not independent of all ontological commitment.

2

REASON AND SENTIMENT:
A PHANTOM BATTLE?

REASON AND DESIRE

I have argued that one sort of moral commitment, a commitment to moral autonomy, in the sense of self-determination, presupposes an ontological commitment. The commitment may seem rather minimal, since all it says is that persons are rational free causes in community. This can be seen as a form of expansive naturalism. Nothing much may seem to follow from this about what persons actually choose to do. But there is more to be said.

The importance of freedom is not just that persons can act without being wholly determined by prior physical, psychological, or external factors. It is that persons can act for reasons that they themselves formulate. Not anything can be a reason. It would be unintelligible to say that I will help my neighbour because the moon is made of cheese. When we think of possible futures, there must be an intelligible reason why we choose one of them. As Aristotle said, one good reason for choosing a possible future is that we think it good, we think it worth choosing in preference to other alternatives. It seems plausible to say that all rational agents choose a future because they think it is good, not because they think it is bad. That is virtually a definition of a rational agent. So, the question becomes: what sorts of possible states of affairs are reasonably considered good by human agents? Trying to answer this question may take us further in considering the sense in which morality or moral agency may be autonomous.

E.O. Wilson, and Darwinian philosophers such as Michael Ruse, do (whether coherently or not) make moral recommendations about what courses of action are good and reasonable for human beings. Ruse has written that morality is 'all a collective illusion of the genes' (1995, p. 268). Some of our deepest-felt obligations are in fact the remnants of evolutionarily adaptive strategies from the far past, and are now counterproductive. Our tendency to prefer our own kin and to exterminate foreigners is a good example of this. Yet, and indeed partly because of this, Ruse recommends that we now adjust our moral beliefs so that they are more 'reasonable' and more in accordance with our partly self-interested but partly altruistic human nature.

Ruse is recommending changing some of our moral beliefs because of the fact that they are evolutionary stratagems that are now counterproductive, or no longer conducive to survival. When we think of changing our moral beliefs, he says, it is no use appealing to conscience or to intuition. Conscience is not the voice of God. Nor is it an 'autonomous', self-justifying intuition of what is morally right. It is a behavioural tendency that arose because it had a useful function that it has now lost. When we act morally for reasons, those reasons must be something other than blunt claims to hear the voice of God or of conscience. On evolutionary accounts, the chief cause of our moral beliefs having become hardwired into us is that they were adaptive. That usually means that they were effective in producing lots of offspring and eliminating possible rivals. It hardly seems likely that such reasons would be morally compelling today, and indeed, as Ruse says, they are probably now going to be counteradaptive. So what other sorts of reasons can there be?

There are some candidates that have frequently recurred throughout the history of moral philosophy. One is self-interest. Philosophers such as Thomas Hobbes have tried to argue that it is reasonable to aim at what will bring us enjoyment or pleasure or power, and that instituting and keeping moral laws is most likely to realize that basically self-interested aim. Another is sympathy. Shaftesbury argued, against Hobbes, that the one main affection that humans possess is a natural sympathy for others, and that the cultivation of this sentiment will bring satisfaction. Shaftesbury agreed with Hume, however, that morality is founded on sentiments or passions that humans happen to have, and especially, perhaps, on a desire for pleasure or happiness, whether for oneself or for others. A rather different view is that good reasons for action can exist whatever desires or passions one happens to have. There are objectively worthwhile goals, knowable either by reasoning or by intuition, which, when seen clearly, provide overwhelming reasons for striving to attain them. It could be held (and G.E. Moore and Ross did hold) that there are worthwhile goals that are distinctively and irreducibly moral. If we act to attain those goals, because we have perceived them clearly, then we could be said to have decided for distinctively moral reasons, and not for any other reason. We could be said to act for the sake of what is good or right alone, independently of any other incentives. That is indeed what Immanuel Kant meant, in part, by 'autonomy'. But only in part, for he rejected the sort of ethical intuitionism that Moore and Ross represented, and Kant's view of autonomy is peculiarly complex, and needs to be investigated further.

It could be said, then, that a person who believes in the autonomy of morals believes that there are distinctively and uniquely moral reasons for action, which are not reducible to any other sorts of reasons. These might be reasons that point to worthwhile goals of human endeavour (objective 'goods'). Or they might – and this is more like Kant's view – be reasons that are such that they could be adopted by any purely rational and dispassionate agent, and so are independent of any specific desires one happens to have.

There appears to be a fundamental dispute between those who believe in the autonomy of morals in this sense, thinking that there are irreducibly moral goals and reasons for acting, which in some way exist whatever people happen to feel, and those who think that moral reasons are founded upon human sentiments or desires, and would not exist in the absence of those desires. For the latter view, it is still possible to describe moral assertions as distinctive in some ways, perhaps in terms of the occurrence of some sort of identifiable 'moral sentiment' such as approval or extended sympathy. But moral reasons would be explained in terms of the occurrence of natural human desires and processes of reasoning. Morality, we might say, would be a purely human phenomenon, dependent upon the facts of human psychology, and in that sense 'subjective'. Morality would not be part of the objective furniture of the universe, a matter of truths that obtain whether or not humans believe them to obtain. Moral thinking would not give access to objective truths about the universe, and morality would not necessarily be autonomous in being free of determination by contingently occurring psychological states.

THE RATIONALIST CASE

This issue was the focus of much discussion among a distinguished group of British moralists in the eighteenth century. They framed the discussion in terms of an opposition between reason and sentiment. Generally speaking, those who supported reason were arguing for an 'objective truth' view of morality, while those who supported sentiment were arguing for the subjectivity of morals. This way of putting things may – and I think that in many ways it will – turn out to be misleading. John McDowell argues that it is misleading, since it is based on interpretations of 'objectivity' and 'subjectivity', which are inadequate. However, it is illuminating to ask what gave rise to this opposition, and this is a good introduction to enquiring into the place of reason in morality, and its relation to human desires and interests.

Samuel Clarke, in his Boyle lectures, published in 1706 as 'A Discourse Concerning Natural Religion' (excerpts printed in Raphael, 1969, vol. 1, pp. 191–225), provides a statement of the rationalist case that was to prove influential, sufficiently so to be duly castigated by David Hume.

Clarke uses the notion of 'fitness', which is not a very familiar one these days. If you understand the natures of things, he says, reason will perceive self-evident truths about how it is fitting to behave in relation to them, or to use them. For instance, if you see what a knife is, you will immediately see that it is fitting to use it for cutting things, and not very fitting to use it for digging the garden. If you understand what God is – a wholly perfect creator of nature – you will at once understand that it is fitting for created intelligent beings to revere and honour God. It is similarly fitting to admire great works of art, or to applaud human acts of heroism.

This fittingness is not merely a subjective reaction to what things are. It arises from the nature of things themselves. It belongs to them whether we, or even God, happen to like them, approve of them, or not. God, of course, being omniscient, will know what is fitting, and so will approve of it. Creatures, however, may not, for they may not understand the true natures of things very well, or they may be distracted by strong passions and desires that lead them to ignore what is nevertheless the reasonable attitude to take to things.

Clarke provides some examples of what he means. If you see what your own nature is, you will see that it is fitting to seek to preserve your own life and aim at your own happiness. It would be unreasonable to aim at misery, when what you want is happiness. And, given that you want happiness, that provides a good reason for seeking it, other things being equal. Knowledge of the facts – including facts about your desires and inclinations – provides a reason for acting in a specific way. As Clarke would put it, there is an objective fitness, an appropriateness, between the nature of humans as happiness-desiring beings and actions that procure such happiness.

The function of reason in such perceptions of fitness is not negligible. It is not easy to discern what we really desire, or to see what acts will lead to realizing our desires, or to adjust our actions to what is reasonably efficient in realizing our desires, or to decide to do what is reasonable in very complicated and highly emotional human situations. Reasoning is needed at every stage. It is not just a question of thinking of some act and being moved by an immediate feeling about it; that would be almost a definition of irrational action.

Naturally, if I desire happiness, I will tend to seek it anyway. That is part of what desire is. But it is also *reasonable* to seek happiness, and the understanding can make that judgement even when something prevents me from seeking happiness. I can say that it would be reasonable to do something, in view of human nature, even when I cannot do it. Thus, the natural desire or inclination to do X can be logically distinguished from the judgement that it would be reasonable for me to do X, and unreasonable for me not to do X if I could. Clarke insists that this judgement is made by the understanding, and that reasons are intrinsically motivating, in the sense that seeing that something is a reason for acting will – if all else is equal – move me to act. Thus, there are objective reasons for acting morally. They are discernible by reason, and are founded ultimately in the fact that the universe itself is rational, because it is created by a rational, wise God, and it is founded on the eternal natures of things which are present, in quasi-Platonic fashion, in the mind of God.

HUME ON VIRTUE

David Hume objected to Samuel Clarke's assertion that statements about the objective natures of things could imply statements about what a rational being ought to do – namely, that one ought to do what is fitting in a specific type of situation. Hume notoriously held that statements of reason only tell us about the agreement or disagreement of ideas, or about the relation of ideas and facts. On this extremely narrow definition, reason cannot tell us about what we are inclined to do, or what we ought to do. We have specific passions and desires, not because reason tells us to, but purely contingently, without reason. These passions include feelings of approval that we have towards specific types of acts.

'Virtue', Hume says, 'is distinguished by the pleasure . . . that any action . . . gives us by the mere view and contemplation' (1739, Book 3,

Part 1, Section 2, final paragraph). Hume roots moral beliefs firmly in human feelings of pleasure. But this is not just any sort of pleasure. It is a very particular and distinctive sort of pleasure. 'The hypothesis which we embrace . . . defines virtue to be whatever mental action or quality gives to a spectator the pleasing sentiment of approbation' (Hume, 1751, appendix 1). Approbation, or approval, is a distinctive 'moral sense' or feeling. Moral sense, however, in Hume, is not the perception of any objective property. It is simply a subjective feeling in the mind. 'When you pronounce any action . . . to be vicious, you mean *nothing but* that from the constitution of your nature you have a feeling or sentiment of blame from the contemplation of it' (ibid., Part 1, Section 1; my italics). That feeling does not reflect some real property, but it is aroused by the perception or contemplation of some objective property, as a subjective response that is naturally aroused by that property.

Hume has been widely supposed to have argued that an 'ought' cannot be derived from an 'is', or that a statement of fact could not logically imply a statement about what one 'ought' to do. Yet, in the statement just quoted, he himself derives an 'ought' from an 'is', a moral statement from a factual statement. A vicious action is one that ought not to be done, or approved of. But, says Hume, that just means (as a matter of fact) that someone has a particular feeling or sentiment about that action. Not only does he derive an 'ought' (you ought not to approve of this act) from an 'is' (I have a feeling of disapproval). He actually says that they mean the same thing – which is an instance of what G.E. Moore called the naturalistic fallacy, identifying goodness with some other property. Hume in fact appears at this point to be a subjective naturalist, identifying rightness or oughtness with a natural, if subjective, property of the mind.

So what is Hume complaining about, when he says,

> In every system of morality which I have hitherto met with . . . the author
> establishes the being of a God, or makes observations concerning human
> affairs; when of a sudden I am surprised to find that instead of the usual
> copulations of propositions, *is*, and *is not*, I meet with no proposition that
> is not connected with an *ought* or an *ought not* . . . a reason should be given
> for what seems altogether inconceivable, how this new relation can be a
> deduction from others, which are entirely different from it.
>
> (1739, Book 3, Part 1, Section 1, final paragraph)

He was, I think, opposing views such as Clarke's that there are objective principles of morality, knowable by reason, which all rational persons must accept. Morality, Hume wants to say, is founded on feeling, and feelings may differ from one person to another. Feelings are purely subjective, and it is feelings that move one to act, while 'reason itself is utterly impotent'. But the sort of reason Clarke is thinking of is precisely reasoning about human feelings and dispositions. He is proposing that specific feelings and actions are fit, or appropriate, to the nature of things. For instance, a feeling of sadness is appropriate to the death of a great friend, and a feeling of regret is fitting to an intellectual belief that one has caused harm unjustly to someone. In morality, there are good reasons why we should approve of some actions and disapprove of others, and Hume himself provides such reasons. We live in a society of other persons who are like us in many basic ways, upon many of whom we depend for our happiness, and in relation to at least some of whom our highest happiness is to be found. It is obvious, Clarke holds, that we should live appropriately to these facts, which means that it is reasonable to cultivate feelings of (at least limited) sympathy and benevolence. Rational thought can tell us what the basic facts about human nature and desires are, and thus suggest the sort of feelings that, if we are reasonable, we ought to cultivate. An 'ought' can be derived from an 'is', provided only that the 'is' includes facts about human desires and inclinations. Hume's famous and much misused argument is only that obligations cannot be derived from statements of objective fact, which exclude facts about human (or possibly divine) states of mind, especially desires and intentions.

Clarke would agree that, generally speaking, we do feel pleasure of a certain sort – approval – when we contemplate a virtuous act. Clarke's point is that such pleasure is an accompaniment to a judgement, made by the understanding, that the act is objectively right. The judgement is about objective reality; the feeling is a quality of a human mind. Such feelings may indeed vary from person to person, so they hardly seem enough on their own to give rise to a strong sense of obligation. Of course, we will want to seek what is pleasant, but it may seem rather odd to speak of seeking virtue because it gives us pleasure, when it so often brings suffering in its train.

We need an account of virtue that explains why we approve of it even more, perhaps, when it brings suffering on the virtuous agent than when it brings pleasure. Is it only a sort of *schadenfreude*, pleasure in another's suffering? For Clarke, we must separate the judgement that an act is virtuous from any feelings of pleasure that may normally occur to us. We can admit an act to be virtuous even though we find no pleasure in it, perhaps because it affects us in a negative way – as when someone tells us, with a certain degree of courage, an unpleasant truth about ourselves.

DOING THE REASONABLE THING

It is a fact that people tend to seek their own happiness. This is a conclusion of reason, for it derives from a study of human behaviour, and issues in a generalization about what humans tend to do. Not only do they actually seek happiness, but also it is reasonable for them to do so, and stating what makes a person happy will give a reason why they should seek that state. If I am wondering what to do, I may envisage a number of possible states at which I may aim. This requires imagination, foresight, and the capacity for abstract thought about possible futures. It is not mere sensation, or passive reception of sensory information.

Then I need to evaluate those possible futures, and think which I desire. In general, states of happiness and pleasure are more desirable than states of misery and pain. I now need to think of what states I have enjoyed in the past, and what sorts of things attract me. I need a certain amount of self-knowledge, and this again is an active intellectual operation, not just the automatic operation of my strongest impulse at the time.

Finally, I need to select a course of action that will most effectively lead to one of the desired future states. For instance, if I decide that I really want a long and healthy life, I will know that I should do daily exercise. This is an effective means to a state that I desire, if I think about it. A natural way to put this is to say that I ought to exercise, given my desires.

This 'ought' most obviously becomes an obligation if there are other competing desires that may make it difficult for me to exercise – for instance, sheer laziness, or desire for the short-term pleasure of having a drink. I may then feel the 'ought' as a duty, which may be difficult and unpleasant in the short term, though it is meant for my long-term good. This is, it could be said, part of the obligation of prudence, one of the traditional cardinal virtues.

Have I now derived an 'ought' from an 'is'? I have considered facts about me and my desires, about the relation of means to ends, and about the existence of competing desires. This consideration has involved reflection, intellectual thought, and decision, but then all understanding of the facts does so. The obligation is a hypothetical one – if I want X, then I ought to do Y. But I do want X, and this implies that I should, that I ought to, do Y. In strict formal logic, this requires the insertion of the premiss that 'I ought to do what is a reasonable means to get what I desire'. But this premiss is, as Clarke would say, virtually self-evident, or so obvious that no sensible person would deny it. In short, it would be silly not to derive obligations from facts about human desires and inclinations.

One of the most obvious obligations is the obligation to be prudent, which is founded on the fact of self-love. Lest this should be thought too glaringly obvious to be denied, we need to remember the thousands or millions of human lives that come to ruin through the misuse of drugs and through neglect of the basics of personal well-being in eating and exercising sensibly. Many people choose ways of life that are imprudent, dangerous or harmful to themselves. They may choose not to have long and healthy lives, but short and exciting lives, or lives of rebellion against life itself, which they may see as cruel and pointless.

This, perhaps, is Hume's point, that human desires are almost infinitely various. We are not calm dispassionate intellects, but animals at the mercy of passions beyond rational control, driven by forces deeper and darker than reason. A view of human nature, and of the worth of human existence, lies under the surface of this eighteenth-century British dispute between those who are sometimes called moral rationalists (such as Samuel Clarke) and moral sentimentalists (such as David Hume).

Clarke is not unaware of this, and he is under no illusion that humans are all fully rational intelligences, who can dispassionately work out all their duties, and see that it is wholly reasonable to fulfil them. His case is that people do have an immediate sense of right and wrong. That is because our duties are indeed fully and self-evidently rational, and we all know this at the level of intellectual understanding.

However, the understanding of the mind is not the assent of the will. While Clarke said that reason is the natural and authoritative guide of a rational being, we are not wholly rational beings, and this is not a rational world. Reason is perhaps a reliable guide only for passionless beings in a world of similarly passionless beings. For the rest of us, members of a violent species in a nature 'red in tooth and claw', it would be the height of foolishness to pretend to be reasonable in the midst of universal terror. Our business is survival and dominance. To appeal to 'eternal and immutable laws of reason' if we find ourselves trapped in a violent and radically unjust world will be both ineffective and, paradoxically, irrational.

Thus it is that Clarke admits the need of stronger sanctions than an appeal to reason, and brings in God as a moral law-giver whose sanctions of punishment for wrongdoing and reward for virtue are necessary to maintain virtue in the world. It is important to see that, for these 'rationalist' philosophers, God himself is subject to the eternal laws of moral reason. Or rather, those necessary laws and that rationality are essential parts of the being of God. The laws of nature can be known without appeal to God. Yet, if we do not think that nature is rational, or that moral laws have objective reality and force, we are liable to discard the laws as ineffective and irrelevant to the human situation. 'Yes', we might say, 'that is what reason would counsel, and what we ought to do were reason authoritative in reality. But it is absurd to follow the rules of an abstract and purely hypothetical reason in a world of struggle for survival and power.'

Belief in the objectivity of reason does make a difference to our perception of what morality is. If there is a supremely rational creator of the universe, who embodies in himself all the perfections of truth, beauty, and goodness, and invites us to share in these perfections to the extent that we can, then – even without consideration of rewards and punishments hereafter – we shall have the strongest motivation for committing ourselves to the rule of reason, which will be the rule of God, in our lives. Reason will not be the stern voice of duty, though it may seem to be partly that to our disordered perception. Reason will be the invitation to revere and honour the wisdom and love that moves the stars and the hearts of human beings, and, as the Cambridge Platonist Ralph Cudworth said, to love the good for its own sake alone.

In this sense, commitment to the rationality of morals and commitment to the rationality of being are connected. This was more obviously so to most eighteenth-century British moralists (apart from Hume, of course) than it is to us. We may have theoretical doubts about the existence of God, which might seem to make any appeal to God as the foundation of morality ineffective. In that case, we will have to make do, and we may well think it is sufficient to make do, with a sense of what reason itself requires. Then, we may say, when we see what a reasonable act is, what reason requires, we obviously have good reason to perform it. If a free act is an act performed for reasons, then in seeing what reason requires we have all that we need for morality without God. But perhaps we can see how it could be that commitment to the existence of God could be partly motivated by commitment to the objectivity of reason, insofar as that might suggest that the cosmos itself embodies a rational and intelligible structure.

Samuel Clarke sees God as the objective Reason of things, and I regard this suggestion as having some force. Nevertheless, we may see what is reasonable without belief in God, and I agree with Clarke that to see reason as authoritative for how we live is already to have moved beyond empiricism and materialism to a worldview that takes the place of reason in reality to be an ineliminable and important one.

BEING REASONABLE ABOUT FEELINGS

Clarke's defence of the rationality of morality has little trouble in coping with duties of self-love, with the virtues of prudence and temperance. It is a little less obvious when he goes on to say that it is obviously fitting that not only personal happiness, but also universal happiness should be aimed at (even given that all people do desire happiness), rather than universal misery or indifference to the happiness of others. What he has in mind is that any impartial reason would see that there is no reason for preferring the happiness of one person to all others of the same general kind, so, if it is good for one person's happiness to be increased, it is immeasurably better for the happiness of all to be increased. This, says Clarke, is obviously so if the choice of universal happiness does not cost anything. It is just better that universal happiness should exist than that a lesser degree of happiness, especially if unequally distributed, should exist. This, he says, shows a fitness (or appropriateness) in relation to the eternal and immutable natures of things. It is an evident rule of reason with which all rational beings must, when they are purely rational, agree.

David Hume disagrees, issuing one of his most extreme counter-intuitive utterances: 'It is not contrary to reason to prefer the destruction of the whole world to the scratching of my finger' (1739, Book 2, Part 3, Section 3). That is because of Hume's restriction of reason to considering the relation of ideas, or the correspondence between ideas and facts. Preference, on this view, cannot be a matter of reason. That I prefer one thing to another is a matter of passion, liking, or sentiment, which reason has nothing to do with.

Hume's point is extremely paradoxical – I would put it more strongly, and say totally unconvincing. It may be true that a purely rational being would have no feelings, but a rational being would know that humans have feelings, and would take those into account. They are among the facts that reason has to take notice of. Reason would note that all humans have feelings, and that they prefer pleasure to pain, and pleasant existence to non-existence. Reason, which is a principle of impartiality and generality, would note that the happiness of many people is worth more than the happiness of one, or than the slight pain of one. On any impartial view, given that beings like pleasure and dislike pain, one slight pain is obviously preferable to the destruction of the pleasures of millions. There is to some extent a rational calculus of pains and pleasure – Utilitarianism is founded on that fact, though it perhaps sometimes tries to make the calculus too precise, and in its hedonistic forms ignores other goods than pleasure. So, given only the facts of human desires, reason would know that all rational and sentient beings would prefer a scratch on a finger to the destruction of the world. Since I am a rational and sentient being, I too would prefer that, and it would be unreasonable to prefer the opposite.

How could Hume fail to see this? He is pretending that rational beings have, as such, no preferences. He is saying that feelings do not have a basis in reason. But when Hume says, 'Reason is and ought only to be the slave of the passions' (1739, Book 2, Part 3, Section 3), he does not mean that reason must serve whatever passion we happen to feel in the heat of the moment. He is at pains to relate moral beliefs to 'calm passions', which consider things without reference to our particular interests. He further notes that we assess men's motives, not their accomplishments, so morality is concerned with the efforts that people make rather than with their actual achievements. He stresses that the feelings of approval that I have for actions that are useful or agreeable either to the agent or to people in general are feelings that are shared by all people ('The notion of morals implies some sentiment common to all mankind': Hume, 1751, Section 9). He notes that these feelings will apply to members of society as a whole, not just to my friends ('It also implies some sentiment so universal and comprehensive as to extend to all mankind'). And he accepts that, insofar as moral action aims at general utility (social peace and happiness), reason must carefully work out what act will have the greatest utility.

We may well feel that it is, after all, the office of reason to distinguish calm from violent passions, to judge whether our feelings are appropriate to their objects, to distinguish motives from accomplishments, to pick out the feelings that are common to all humans, and that apply in principle to all humans, and to work out which motives will have the greatest utility.

How does all this really differ from Clarke's view that reason can tell which feelings are appropriate or fitting to their situation?

It turns out that, for Hume, only feelings of a very particular kind – calm, dispassionate, sympathetic, socially useful, widely shared feelings – will qualify as moral feelings. Moreover, it is likely that feelings of approval can only be identified as such when they are associated with judgements of the understanding. Just as 'hope' is a feeling of an expectation of good in the future, and 'regret' is a feeling of contrition for a wrong done in the past, so 'approval' is a feeling of admiration for a virtuous act. If this is so, I must be able to identify what a virtuous act is before I can identify a feeling as one of approval. Hume says that virtuous acts are those that are either agreeable or useful to oneself or to society (acts of prudence and benevolence) ('The distinction of vice and virtue arises from the four principles of the advantage and of the pleasure of the person himself and of others': Hume, 1739, Book 2, Part 3, Section 2). Only if our natural affections, long-term prudential self-interest, and an extended sympathy with others are engaged will we reasonably approve of an act.

What Hume is asking us to do is to adopt the view of an impartial spectator (Adam Smith's phrase for one whose interests are not directly involved in a situation) who adopts a hypothetical view of the sort of character that would, if it were immediately known to us (which it is not) and was causally effective (which it may not be), be either agreeable or useful to social cohesion. We are then asked to think of certain feelings that would be aroused by that view. These are not actual feelings that occur when we actually encounter a particular situation. They are hypothetical feelings that would occur if we were not directly involved, but pretended that we were (that is sympathy, or what we would feel if we were in another's place, yet without their self-interested view of things).

How can such hypothetical feelings move me to act? Actual feelings may move me, because feelings of pleasure are closely associated with tendencies to seek out objects of pleasure. It may be said that sympathy is not such a sophisticated thing. It is just an immediate feeling of pleasure in another's pleasure. But Hume says, 'There is no such passion in human minds as the love of mankind' (1751, Section 2, Part 1). Humans do have limited natural benevolence, but that is all. How, then, can he say that the fundamental sentiment of morality is 'a feeling for the happiness of mankind' (1751, appendix 1)? Only if such benevolence is not a directly felt passion. It is a hypothetical supposition that thinking of a happy person would be more pleasurable (if my sentiments were rightly ordered) than thinking of a miserable person. But that is precisely what Clarke proposes as the office of reason.

The conclusion is that to say 'X is right' cannot, as Hume says, mean 'I approve of X' (i.e. I actually have an identifiable feeling about X). I may approve of the benevolence of an unknown stranger on the other side of the world, without having any actual feeling about it at all. My approval is a judgement consequent on the reflection that, if I were the recipient of this benevolence, I would be pleased by it. Approval, then, does not consist in just having an actual feeling. It involves a judgement about what we would feel if we took a disinterested and sympathetic view.

AN UNEASY TRUCE

Clarke and Hume, strange as it may seem, broadly agree about the use of reason and the importance of feelings in morality. They agree, too, about the most general principles of morality. Clarke cites two main moral principles with regard to others – equity (the Golden Rule) and benevolence. We should treat others as we would like them to treat us in similar situations, and we should care for universal well-being. We should do so because that is what dispassionate reason would legislate for a society of rational sentient beings who have a natural need and affection for society. Certainly, it seems true that a society of mutually helpful happy beings is one that any rational being with no special interest in the case would prefer to a society of warlike miserable idiots. If there were a benevolent and rational God, this is what God would prefer and therefore command. Hume agrees with this (though he is not very concerned about what God might prefer), and it is consistent with his four principles of morality – the advantage of the agent, the advantage of society, the pleasure of the agent, and the pleasure of society.

What Hume stresses is that our natural affections are subjective properties that we just happen to have, and that reason seeks to invent principles of morality that will extend our sentiments of benevolence and long-term self-interest so as to establish conventions of social justice. By contrast, Clarke wants to root morality in eternal and immutable principles of reason, and connect rationality to the nature of things as eternally conceived in the mind of God. He and the rationalists in general are strongly opposed to 'divine command' theories such as those of Hobbes and – perhaps surprisingly – Locke. But the rationalists do want to say that morality is a matter of truths to be discovered, and that the nature of those truths – as necessary and eternal – points to some reality beyond the contingent and physically caused sentiments of human minds.

Suppose reason commanded that you love your neighbour, whereas your natural affections led you to despise your neighbour. Then you might say that you should follow reason even when it contradicts your natural affections. But, of course, Hume's case is that your natural affections do not lead you to despise your neighbour. As social animals, we are inclined to find our highest fulfilment in benevolence and kindness. In short, 'natural' inclinations are those that are appropriately adjusted to their object – people with whom we need and desire to be in close relationship – and that is exactly the sort of 'fitness' with which Clarke is concerned.

What is reasonable largely depends on the sorts of desires and inclinations we have. What we want to do may be more or less reasonable, depending, for instance, on whether it is possible for us, whether it will really be satisfying, and whether it will help or harm us. It is possible to modify our passions by discipline and habitual training, yet it is still true that what it is reasonable for us to do will depend upon our abilities and natural dispositions.

What Hume and moral-sense theorists such as Shaftesbury and Hutcheson show is the importance of the social affections, of sympathy and compassion, in human life. Their account of human nature provides a much more acceptable view of moral sanctions, of moral punishments and rewards, than that they are arbitrary consequences determined by the sheer will of an omnipotent God or a Hobbesian absolute monarch. The quality and amount of human happiness or misery correlates with the extent to which we relate positively, creatively, and lovingly to others. The reward of virtue is not any sort of happiness, but a kind of happiness that can be experienced only by those who love and rejoice in the company of others. The punishment of vice is not just some degree of pain (the infliction of pain without any remedial intent being arguably as vicious as the offence for which it is inflicted), but the kind of self-inflicted misery of those who hate, fear, or despise – and are in turn hated, feared, and despised by – others.

Given enough time and a constitution of nature such that the natural consequences of actions work out to their full extent, we might be persuaded that such happiness and misery are indeed the natural consequences of human actions, and that virtue is indeed the only true happiness, and vice the only true misery, of human lives. It is not so clear, however, that human life in this world is like that. All too often, virtue leads to suffering and death. In this sense, a belief in life after death seems essential to the view that virtue is true happiness. And that is enough to rule it out as a realistic moral motivation for many people.

Hume thinks that we have a moral sensibility that leads us to approve of virtue, to have social affections of sympathy and a sense of fair play, and to love and esteem those who are virtuous. The rationalists think that this is too rosy a view of human nature, which may be more given to selfish egoism, hatred, and the lust for power than the sentimentalists suppose. There is a pleasing irony in the fact that the 'sentimentalists' tend to think that humans are more reasonable than do the 'rationalists'.

If, as Hume supposes, our passions are the masters, not the servants, of reason, and if our passions are selfish as well as sociable, there is not much reason to trust our sentiments and take them as authoritative in morality. Samuel Clarke does not wish to ignore sentiment, but he wishes to distinguish the morally acceptable sentiments from the brutal and violent passions described by Hobbes. The irony is that I suspect Hume would agree, and it is only his general scepticism about reason (which is bound up with his rejection of a universe ordered by a rational God) that forces him to ground morality on the passions alone. It seems clear that these differing approaches to morality rest upon deeper differences about the nature of human beings, and about what we may more grandly call metaphysical foundations.

People do not have to be moral or reasonable in their actions. I can justify moral principles as principles calculated to sustain a safe and healthy human society, and to support individual well-being on the whole. I can see that these are wholly reasonable foundations for morality. But, at the same time, I can opt to be a 'freeloader', who takes advantage of the morality of others to procure my own interests. This is a risky gamble, which social sanctions will seek to bring to ruin. But in many societies and for many people it may succeed. Moral principles, principles rationally calculated for the public good and for the personal good of many, may carry little sway with me, especially if I am beyond their reach.

The 'rationalists' (such as Samuel Clarke, and others such as Richard Price and Thomas Reid) object that our feelings could easily have been different, and on a Humean account are only contingently connected to their objects. However, the sentimentalists can respond by saying that there are good explanations for why our feelings are as they are. Evolutionary theory has now provided better explanations than were available to them, and it gives a good explanation for showing that our basic feelings must be as they are.

Both rationalists and sentimentalists agree that our natural feelings often need to be modified by reason. So, the obvious resolution of this eighteenth-century dispute is to say that morality consists in discerning what actions are reasonable for an intelligent being with passions and emotions. The rationalists are right in saying that morality is a matter of judgement about human desires and inclinations, and that they can and must be shown to be reasonable. The sentimentalists are right in saying that moral commitment must be founded on passion and affection, and that there is a distinctive moral sensibility that cannot be reduced to abstract deliberations of reason. The justification of morality, for both, seems to consist in showing that, for beings constituted like us, some ends are reasonable (if they are fulfilling for humans as such), and some means are reasonable (if they are well adapted to achieve those ends). Morality seems to be a matter of states reasonably choosable by beings with more or less strong passions of both a social and a self-interested character. A truce can be achieved. But it is an uneasy one, and it conceals a deeper level of disagreement.

3

HYPOTHETICAL AND CATEGORICAL MORALITY

It may seem that, on the account of morality just given, there is autonomy, in that human agents are asked to use their reason to discern how the passions should be directed, and not depend merely upon alleged religious revelations or social conventions and traditions. Yet, according to this account, morality as a form of discourse is not autonomous in the sense of being a totally distinctive and self-contained area of human thought. Reasonable moral beliefs depend upon the existence of specific interests and desires, which need to be identified and analysed, with the help of psychologists and biologists. And such beliefs will be formed by the use not of any special moral intuition or faculty, but of ordinary human reasoning powers. Morality can be seen as naturalistic, inasmuch as it derives from natural human passions and reasoning powers. This will be a very expansive naturalism, at least in the hands of someone such as Samuel Clarke, since it may appeal to 'eternal truths of reason' and may imply a wider metaphysical belief in the intelligibility of being. Nevertheless, it may look as if, while Samuel Clarke may have established, against Hume, that reason plays a much greater part in moral thinking than Hume's official account seems to allow, a generally Humean approach to ethics, based primarily on the existence of human desires and sentiments, has won the day.

I do not think that this is so, and I will try to show why I think that by considering 'Morality as a System of Hypothetical Imperatives', a paper by Philippa Foot (reprinted in Foot, 1978). Her paper, as its title implies, is an attempted rebuttal of Kant's claim that morality is concerned with categorical, not hypothetical imperatives. That is, Kant claims that morality is not a matter of saying that you should do X if you want Y (that is the hypothetical). It is a matter of doing X just because X is right, or for its own sake alone.

There are complications about Kant's views that I do not want to consider, so I will take a lapidary statement of her case from Foot: 'Moral judgments are, I say, hypothetical imperatives in the sense that they give reasons for acting only in conjunction with interests and desires' (1978, p. 177). Her main argument is that moral beliefs are founded on the existence of desires of a certain sort. In an earlier paper, 'Moral Beliefs', she had said that those desires must in some way be for the benefit of the agent, but in this paper the relevant desires can be for such things as the good of others, or for justice or liberty. Still, they must be desires that agents may or may not possess. Moral considerations, she holds, will only apply to those who possess certain sorts of desires, and such a statement as 'You ought to be moral' makes no sense (ibid., p. 169). Thus, moral agents are like 'volunteers in the army of duty', and, if you do not share the appropriate concerns, no argument of reason will ever convince you or even apply to you.

I think it is true that moral judgements give reasons for acting only in conjunction with desires. There would be no reasons for acting if there were no desires. If no being ever wanted or feared anything, never enjoyed or suffered from anything, it would be hard to think of a reason for choosing one state rather than any other. On the other hand, I think that moral judgements give reasons for acting whether or not a particular person P has, or even whether whole groups of persons have, specific desires. This is one of Samuel Clarke's main points, and it is made in defence of the claim that moral reasons have peculiar, often overriding force and authority for all human agents, whatever actual desires particular individuals have. That, I think, is the force of saying that they are categorical.

Foot touches on a crucial point when, comparing rules of etiquette with moral rules, she says that, unlike rules about how to hold your fork, values like compassion, liberty, and justice 'arouse devotion' (1978, p. 166). They are regarded as of great intrinsic worth. They have what is often called normative force, and seem to compel our admiration, whether or not we do anything about them. Because of this admiration, they provide compelling reasons for action. Compassion, for instance, is not just an attitude you may happen to have or not have on seeing suffering. It is an appropriate attitude to have. To use Clarke's term, there is a 'fitness' between perceiving the suffering of another and compassion. The argument to back this is very short. Any rational person can see that their own suffering is to be avoided. They can see that the suffering of others is relevantly like their own. So, they can see, with just a little impartiality and emotional involvement, that the suffering of others is to be avoided. That something is to be avoided, and that it exists, gives a reason for action. That reason may not move someone to act; we can turn aside. But it is still a reason, and it is a reason for all rational agents, whether or not they care about it. I cannot reasonably say, 'I do not care about P, therefore there is no reason for me to help P in distress'. From my lack of feeling, nothing follows about the reasonableness of actions. There is a reason to help P – P's suffering – and that reason is independent of the feelings of the person who does not care about P.

Does that mean the uncaring person has no reasons to ignore P? No, there are many reasons to ignore P – it is too difficult for me, there is little I can do, I cannot help everyone, I have a reason for pursuing my own pleasure, and to look after my family. There are lots of reasons. It is false that P's suffering has 'no automatic reason-giving force independent of the agent's desires' (Foot, 1978, p. 176). But that reason may not weigh with me, because I also have reason to be selfish.

This is why, in a sense, I am indeed a volunteer in the army of duty. I need to decide between reasons that lie before me. It is not, however, an army of those who happen to care about certain things (like a tennis club, perhaps). It is an army of those who freely choose the good, because it is good. They do not happen to have desires they cannot help. They choose to cultivate other-regarding desires, even though that often takes 'reso- lution and self-discipline' (ibid., p. 170). This sort of choice, between self- regarding and other-regarding desires, suggests another sense of personal autonomy, as the freedom to choose between good and evil. It is another sort of self-determination, but one that draws attention to an irreducibly moral or normative element in free choice. Basic self-regarding desires, like the desire for physical pleasure, do not require resolution and self- discipline. Discipline is required only if the desired goal is difficult to achieve but nevertheless considered to be truly worthwhile, to be an appropriate object of devotion.

If the value of compassion, and the thought of a truly compassionate person arouses devotion, that implies admiration, emulation, and an attempt at a sort of ontological closeness. When I am truly devoted to something, I will not only admire it, but I will also seek to be like it, or to model myself upon it. I will seek some personal bond with it, in whatever way is appropriate. If it is a club, I will want to join it. If it is a person, I will want to be with that person. If it is an abstract idea, I will seek to be close to those who express it in their own lives. To accomplish these things in the face of obstacles and difficulties, I need discipline. So the apprehension that evokes devotion also evokes commitment to self-shaping activities that enable one to apprehend and understand, to feel and appreciate, and to embody in oneself an image of the object of devotion.

Partly for this reason, one can always sensibly ask, 'Why should I cultivate other-regarding desires?' or 'Why ought I to be moral?' A sensible answer would not be just to reiterate a blunt command, 'Be good'. It would be to try to get someone to see what values, and what exemplary instances of those values, appropriately arouse devotion, and therefore provide a compelling reason for action and make a commitment to self-discipline appropriate.

I will just comment, as it were in passing, that, if there were a God who was the exemplary instantiation of all compossible goods, this God would properly evoke devotion – admiration, and the desire to imitate and be as closely associated with this object of devotion as possible. The appropriate intellectual understanding of God would thus of itself evoke appropriate feelings of reverence and a commitment to disciplined-response action. In this way, a belief in God might underwrite the normative character of moral assertions in an intelligible way. But I do not wish to presuppose the existence of God. My concern at present is to explore the possibility – a possibility Philippa Foot denies – of meaningfully answering a question like, 'Why should I do what is right?'

Foot writes that someone who says, 'You ought to care about liberty' is just using the word 'ought' as a sort of magical incantation. But actually they might be trying to draw your attention to what freedom is, and what the lack of it is, and to see that it is something that is worthwhile for its own sake. If you take freedom in a broad positive sense, as a power of creativity exercised fully, then you may come to see it as intrinsically worthwhile. It is not that you give it value because you happen to have a subjective feeling about it, but that you come to see it as valuable and in consequence you seek to cultivate feelings which will bring it about more effectively.

Morality is not based on the occurrence of actual sentiments, which are non-rational feelings we may or may not have. It is matter of seeing, a sort of seeing that is a combination of intellectual understanding, appropriate feeling, and responsive action, a sort of affective and responsive knowing. To learn to see justly and respond appropriately is itself a training in morality. The reasons for moral action do not, from this point of view, lie in sentiments people happen to have. They lie in forms of apprehension and attitude, in seeing what is really there and, arising out of that apprehension, in undertaking a commitment in appropriate response to what is seen.

VIRTUE AND HUMAN FLOURISHING

Philippa Foot takes a slightly different approach when she argues, against prescriptivism, that factual premises can entail moral conclusions. The argument goes like this, in her paper 'Virtues and Vices': 'virtues are in general beneficial characteristics, and indeed ones that a human being needs to have, for his own sake and that of his fellows' (1978, p. 3). It is not the case that reasons for being courageous, temperate, or wise are only reasons for people who happen to have specific interests or desires. They are reasons for everyone. For virtues are connected with human good and harm. It is impossible to call anything you like good or harm. In 'Moral Beliefs', Foot argues that all human beings need to be prudent if they are to flourish as human beings, just as they need the use of their hands, eyes or limbs. 'The proper use of his limbs is something a man has reason to want if he wants anything' (1978, p. 122). So from a factual premiss – 'All humans need prudence' – one can infer a moral conclusion – 'Prudence is a moral virtue'.

Virtues are excellences of character. They describe an important part of what it is to function well as a human being. To possess the virtues of courage, prudence, and temperance is, in general, a necessary condition of functioning well as a human being. Therefore, if a human agent wants anything, they necessarily want to be able to exercise the capacities that will enable them to get that thing. To exercise those capacities well improves the possibilities of getting whatever one wants. So everyone has a reason to want the virtues, if they want anything at all.

It is fairly easy to see how courage, prudence, and temperance are needed to give a person a good chance of getting what they want and need. There are, however, problems with the fourth traditional virtue – justice, and also with charity, regarded as genuine feeling for others. It may seem that not everyone needs to pursue justice or charity, as a condition of being able to get whatever they might want. Yet it may not be so difficult to argue for the virtues of justice and charity along the lines of asking what makes for human flourishing, and what virtues are necessary as conditions of human flourishing. Humans are not, after all, isolated individuals, caring only for their own personal welfare. They are essentially social animals, with a very long period of dependence upon others in infancy, and a reliance upon others for most of the necessities of life – food has to be procured, houses built, health services provided, and society protected from enemies. Humans have a reason to support a society that provides these things, if they want anything at all. Some sense of fairness or of a social structure that is generally acceptable to most of its members is needed. And dependence upon others requires at least a limited concern for their well-being, and a recognition that their welfare is of concern to all of us.

In this way, recognition of what is good for human living, founded on a basic knowledge of human nature, provides us with a basic recognition of what is good and harmful for sentient, rational, and free agents, and that is moral knowledge.

If there are basic facts about human beings that are virtually universal – if all humans desire physical pleasure, or to avoid physical pain – then some goods can be inferred non-deductively but reasonably from facts. Pleasure will necessarily be good, not in the absence of any affective agent, but given the basic nature of affective agents. This seems to be an entirely naturalistic morality. One would need no reference to non-natural or irreducibly moral facts. As Philippa Foot said, 'I am not clear that it makes sense to speak of 'a moral use of "good"' (1978, p. 119). Though 'good' would not *mean* 'pleasant', it could mean something like 'reasonably choosable by an affective intelligent agent'. Morality will not be autonomous, in the sense of having an irreducible and distinctive content. It follows from reasonable reflection on facts of human nature.

DISTINCTIVE HUMAN GOODS

The argument from qualities that are conditions of human flourishing, and from virtues that all have a reason to want if they want anything at all, is a powerful one. It is distinctive of human persons to be free reasoning agents, and there are some capacities that are presupposed to the exercise of free and rational agency. These facts give rise to a sort of presuppositional argument for a set of basic human virtues, an argument for the excellences that humans need to pursue if they are to exercise their distinctive natures adequately.

Free agents will need knowledge, and not just any sort of knowledge, but knowledge of possibilities, between which choices can be reasonably made. They will need some criteria for judging between various possibilities, and preferring some to others. That will require something like feeling or appreciation, a more than merely cognitive responsiveness to the nature of things. They will need power to act on the basis of reasons. And they will need a structure of social relationships that enables purposes to be effectively put into practice in the face of many obstacles and difficulties.

All these factors give rise to specific virtues, which are qualities of character that humans have reason to cultivate, in order to enable them to achieve their goals most effectively. We can divide the virtues into intellectual and moral virtues, as Aristotle did – and, though the classification I am using differs in some respects from that of Aristotle, it could be seen as broadly Aristotelian.

Among what may be called the intellectual virtues, first there are intellectual capacities of understanding, wisdom, and conceptual reasoning. These are often picked out as capacities that require complex conceptual and linguistic skills. They may not be exclusively human, but they are certainly characteristic of a relatively small group of animals with large brains, and they are certainly present in humans to a uniquely high degree. We might say that it is right to cultivate the exercise of these capacities, through education, debate, and empirical observation. Obviously, a mathematician will exercise them in one way, and a manual worker in another. But both are capable of some degree of critical thought and information gathering, and so both can exercise the virtue of understanding in an appropriate way.

Second, there are affective capacities of appreciation and empathy, such as the appreciation of beauty and estimation of the intrinsic worth of various states and activities. They involve feelings and desires as well as pure intellect. It may reasonably be felt that it is good to seek to appreciate the values of our world as fully as we can, and attain as wide and deep an experience as is possible for us in our situation.

Third, there are volitional capacities of creativity, free action, and productive activity. From writing books on economics to making pieces of furniture, there are many forms of creative activity and there are many decisions we make about how we are going to live and respond to the things that happen to us. It is arguably necessary to a fulfilled human life that we should pursue some creative activities, and express our positive freedom as human agents.

Then there are what may be called the moral virtues, virtues of character, the social capacities of relating to and working with other people, sympathizing with and caring for them, or co-operatively working with them in friendship to build up a just and secure society. Such considerations will provide good reason for co-operation with others, in ways that will increase general human well-being for all.

These considerations might be summarized as follows. If 'goodness' is a sort of excellence, and if we ought to pursue excellence as a matter of obligation, then the good for human persons will consist in the realization of personal mental states of knowing, feeling, and willing, and interpersonal states of justice and friendship. What will be right is to realize such states, and to refrain from acts that impede or destroy them, either in ourselves or in others. And what is virtuous is to form a character such that we naturally incline to do what is right and to avoid what is wrong. As Aristotle put it, 'Happiness [well-being] is activity and the complete utilization of all our powers' (*Politics*, Book 7, ch. 13, para. 2). It may be an exaggeration to speak of the 'complete' utilization of 'all' our powers, but that human well-being consists in the utilization of distinctively human capacities is a plausible and attractive proposal.

In morality, we are concerned with the existence of states that are good (worthwhile for their own sake). Morally right acts are those that are, in a rather general and as yet unspecific way, conducive to good for any and all rational agents. Knowing what acts are right, we can then discover what sort of character persons should have to perform right acts most efficiently and easily. In general, we may say that moral virtue consists in a reason-governed realization of distinctively human capacities in a social context that should enable such realization to be possible for all.

It is not difficult to construct, in some way such as this, a list of moral virtues, of ways in which it is good to act, for human beings as they actually are. There is no problem in knowing what sort of life is a good human life, and morality in some sense follows from a just apprehension of human nature and its distinctive capacities. There is no excuse for a rational being to say that they do not know what moral goodness is, or that they cannot tell good from bad, or that they do not know how a human being ought to live. These moral guidelines are built into human nature, in a quite natural way, and do not require any supernatural interference to provide secret moral information or otherwise unknowable moral rules for humans to follow.

LOVE OF THE GOOD

It looks as though we can have a fully humanist and naturalistic morality that can be rationally defended. We can dispense with appeals to any sort of metaphysical or religious foundation for morality. There is a rational basis for constructing a list of goods of human flourishing, based on the very idea of freely acting on the basis of consciously evaluated reasons. And yet the sort of moral outlook I have sketched leaves an uneasy feeling that the goods involved in an idea of human flourishing are not, as described, as fully normative as it might at first seem.

The idea of human flourishing, which can be established by more or less normal human observation (though we may have to learn to 'see justly' and to think impartially and sympathetically), can provide the basis for a naturalistic and humanistic morality, which could in principle be agreed by the vast majority of human agents, and against which we may profitably measure the rationality and binding force of our inherited moral principles. But it may not be fully satisfactory to found morality wholly on cultivating virtues that are seen as conditions for being able to realize whatever human desires we may happen to have in a more effective way. This may seem to be, in the end, a rather instrumental view of morality – moral virtue is good as a means to some non-moral goal. What many people would feel to be lacking in such an account is the sense that some states are worth choosing for their own sake, whatever our actual desires may be.

Hume founded his system of morality upon sympathy and 'a feeling for the happiness of mankind'. Yet this view seems to founder on the fact that our basic passions might be very different from this. Hume himself pours scorn on the idea that there might be a feeling for mankind as a whole, and states that such a feeling needs to be manufactured artificially. Evolutionary psychology suggests that human benevolence will be limited. In fact, it is so limited that hatred for almost everyone outside one's own favoured groups is more characteristic of humanity than universal benevolence. Eighteenth-century British moralists such as Shaftesbury, Hutcheson, and Hume were all estimable, sociable, and agreeable fellows. But what if their view that morality is founded on our natural sentiments is adopted by a society of racist and elitist thugs, whose natural sentiments are of hatred for foreigners and contempt for the weak? What right will we have to condemn them, except that we have different feelings, a fact that, used as an argument, seems lamentably weak and pitifully arbitrary?

Is there not something more than all this that is needed to inspire humans to the passionate pursuit of virtue for its own sake? There may be a sense of encounter with a morally demanding reality that cannot be reduced to reason, though it can be seen to be rational, and that cannot be reduced to natural affection, though it can be seen to engage the natural affections of those who are responsive to it.

Foot, after all, speaks of 'devotion' and 'discipline' as characteristic of the life of virtue. But what sort of things can inspire devotion and resolute effort in the face of obstacles and difficulties? Consider the possibility of love of the good for its own sake, not as an actual desire that one may or may not have, but as a desire that it would be good to have as a human being. There are things that many people think are more worthwhile than the continuation of their own existence or than their own flourishing. Indeed, it is almost necessary for achieving happiness in a human life to believe that is the case. The most obvious example is passionate love for another human being. Such love is capable of bringing the highest happiness, though it may not, but that is not its point. Love is centred on the object. It cares passionately about it, finds joy in it, admires it, cares for it, and, if necessary, is prepared to die for it. In love, the self is centred on another, and thoughts of personal happiness recede into relative unimportance. It would be silly to ask why I should do what a loved one wants. If I understand what love is, I will see that serving another has become my goal, and if my love is deep, even at any cost. Here, knowledge of the other – the sort of knowledge that involves us passionately – is intrinsically motivating. To see what the loved one is to me is to see why I may give my life for the one I love.

There are many analogies in human life to this sort of love. There is loyalty to one's comrades in the army, loyalty to one's country, devotion to truth or to art. These all involve activities that subordinate the self to something beyond it, taken to be of great worth, to which a person may commit themselves, in response to something both attractive and demanding, which makes life seem worthwhile. People may make mistakes about what is really worthwhile, but, when one thinks that something is worthwhile for its own sake, it may well be because one's knowledge of it is intrinsically attractive and motivating. Such a view asserts that there is objective goodness or value in reality, to be discerned by humans. It is such discernment that evokes devotion and self-discipline, and that suggests something more to morality than cultivating capacities that make it easier to obtain things that one may desire.

There is a morality that may be founded on human sympathy together with cool self-love, and a recognition of the necessity of a cohesive society for the secure pursuit of most of our interests. Yet we may be left feeling that this rather comfortable morality lacks the resources for passionate resistance to injustice or for real self-sacrifice for the sake of others. At least for many people, including some of the great moral heroes of history, morality has an objectivity and seriousness that such a morality cannot encompass, which requires a more transcendent source if it is to be truly compelling. That is a good reason for seeking a view of morality that is more than hypothetical and naturalistic, that commands rather than serves our natural human desires, and that centres on an ideal that is worthy of human devotion and commitment.

4

NATURALISM AND ITS DISCONTENTS

ENRICHED NATURALISM

There seems to be something importantly right about connecting moral commitment to considerations of human well-being and the realization of natural human capacities. But there is also something important about giving moral values an objectivity and authority that purely naturalistic views overlook. There are forms of naturalism that try to give moral values such objectivity and authority, and to give values a place in the fabric of reality that can be apprehended and recognized without transgressing the bounds of naturalism. In this chapter, I want to explore how far those bounds must extend, if account is to be taken of the existence of objective moral values.

The philosopher John McDowell has described himself as an 'enriched naturalist', and holds that morality is indeed a matter of 'seeing' rather than of prescriptive decision. Having a moral belief is seeing things in a certain light, and within a general conception of how to live virtuously. 'A conception of how things are', he says, 'might constitute, on its own, a reason for virtuous action' (1998, p. 81), without there being any contingently occurring desire that has to be added. So, morality does not depend, as on one Humean view, on the presence of certain desires such as sympathy, which is an independent part of our mental mechanism.

This seems like a quasi-intuitionism, existing within a wider but not systematically analysable form of life. It is not further justifiable in any non-moral terms at all, not in terms of desire, not in terms of divine commands, and not in terms of universally compelling rational thought.

There is no foundation for ethics beyond the 'formed evaluative outlook of a virtuous person'.

This McDowell calls a form of naturalism – though not in the sense that it conforms to scientific facts or is reducible to statements of the natural sciences. It is an 'enriched naturalism', according to which values are parts of the natural world, disclosed by forms of vision that are not universally shared. There is 'a natural way of being in the world, for which ethical reasons are sufficient, needing no grounding in some mysteriously extra-natural power'.

It is clear that McDowell is not a subjectivist, founding morality on feelings or sentiments of humanity. He says, 'Occasion by occasion, one knows what to do, by being a certain kind of person . . . one who sees situations in a certain distinctive way' (1998, p. 73). But if one asks what kind of person that is, the answer is that it is a 'virtuous person'. If one asks what virtue is, the answer is that having a virtue is 'seeing in a certain light'. However, if you see things in a certain light, and if there is no external reason for seeing things in that way, the lack of rational grounding for this view does seem to me to be a major problem. It seems as though possessing the ability to see things in the required light is as contingently occurring as the possession of a sentiment such as that of sympathy. And it seems as though the occurrence of such a 'seeing' is more or less exactly what G.E. Moore meant by 'intuition' – namely, having no further argument to justify one's apprehension. The only difference is that these intuitions are not universally shared – which seems to me to make the claim that one really sees them weaker rather than stronger.

The natural inclination is to say that, when one sees that certain things are good for their own sakes, one claims that one's view is correct, and that means, in part, that it is rationally grounded. There must be some reason for thinking that it is correct to see things in that way, and the reason one really wants, however hard it may be to get it, is just that wider views of reality that one also holds, and that are rationally defensible, corroborate the claim that this is how things are. The combination of saying that there is no external reason for the goodness of things, and that people reasonably see things in different ways, is an unstable one.

McDowell is influenced by the view that it is not possible to stand outside one's own conception of how things are, and attain a truly 'object-ive' view. So, there is no alternative to seeing things as one sees them, either in philosophy or in ethics. One can still claim that one sees things as they are, and in that sense objectively. But 'it is a mistake to con-ceive objectivity in terms of complete independence from subjectivity'

(McDowell, 1998, p. 180). We see the good (that is, we see that many things are good for their own sakes), but we do not deny that others see things differently. 'A manifestation of reason might be recognizable as such only from within the practice' (ibid., p. 70). We can make no claim to a 'view from nowhere', and that is taken to mean that there are no reasons 'that could enforce the claims of virtue on the rational will of everyone' (ibid., p. 193).

We see the world as containing values, which we do not see ourselves as simply projecting onto an otherwise neutral and value-free reality. McDowell rejects Simon Blackburn's view that 'we profit . . . by realising that a training of the feelings rather than a cultivation of a mysterious ability to spot the immutable fitness of things is the foundation of how to live' (1981, p. 186). It is not that Blackburn is wholly mistaken. But he fails to see that a training of the feelings is precisely what makes one able to spot the presence of values in the fabric of reality. Feelings and apprehensions do not need to be split apart in this way. Apprehending value is a matter of the light in which we see things, and it needs and can have no external grounding, whether in scientific facts (trying to ground morality in a scientific worldview involves a deflated view of reality) or in 'supernaturalist rationalism' (which involves an inflated view of reality). We just need, as Iris Murdoch says, to learn to see things appropriately, as they are. We need to make our way of seeing the world 'fit' the way the world is, a rich and value-laden reality.

There is something importantly right in what McDowell says. I think it is correct that certain goals of human activity are objectively worthwhile, not just projections of sentiment. I think it is correct that they are perceived as commanding to those who are committed to virtue – right seeing requires right dispositions to see justly. It is also surely correct to say that people, however intelligent and well informed, will never wholly agree about the sorts of reasons that move them to certain views, both theoretical and ethical, and there seems no neutral way of resolving their disagreements.

However, I feel uncomfortable with the thought that there is nothing I can do but simply assert my view while admitting – indeed affirming – that it has no grounding in reality other than what can be found in the ethical assertions themselves. That seems a sort of 'ethical fundamentalism' that cuts off the possibility of further understanding. I think that at this point McDowell is influenced by Wittgenstein, who often viewed philosophy as therapeutic, as dissolving philosophical problems away and leaving ordinary forms of speech in order as they are without resting on any grand metaphysical claims. So, McDowell sees the attempt to found morality on any sort of metaphysical foundation, whether naturalistic (scientism) or supernaturalistic ('rampant Platonism'), as a mistake. Moral language, with its claims to objectivity, is in order as it is.

Such a view can, however, lead to a passive acceptance of the status quo in morality. Moral philosophers may say that they have no special insight into first-order moral questions, and that their job is just to report on the informal logic of what is thought and said in their society. They may report the outlook of a virtuous person in a specific society, an outlook which enables such persons to see things in a certain light. But they will be bound basically to accept the general norms of their own society. And that seems a very conservative and passive situation for a philosopher to be in.

The fact is, though, that in modern societies there is not just one tradition of linguistic practice. Different forms of life overlap and jostle one another. For instance, there are forms of religious life that interweave with forms of moral life, and with specific views of human nature. Forms of life have their own developing histories, interacting in various ways with other forms, both secular and religious. These forms are not impervious, but are interconnected. There is not just one self-enclosed moral tradition, but a tapestry of many interwoven strands. Each embraces, rejects, or seeks to cohere with others, and most attempt a more comprehensive view within which their moral viewpoint and its conceptions of virtue can stand. Morality is not self-contained, but part of a wider conceptual system, one of many in historical interplay.

Wittgenstein said that 'Our knowledge forms an enormous system. And only within this system has a particular bit the value we give it' (ibid., 1979, para. 410). The various language-games of which he often writes must be seen, not as isolated and unchanging sorts of discourse, but as potentially interacting parts of a wider whole – 'what we believe . . . is a whole system of propositions' (ibid., para. 141). That, put in different terms, is very like saying that moral views ought to fit into a wider system, including views of human and cosmic nature – what traditionally was called metaphysics.

Moreover, our knowledge system of course relates to what is the case – 'doesn't it seem obvious that the possibility of a language-game is conditioned by certain facts?' (ibid., para. 617). Wittgenstein's point is that language-games do not just simply show or picture the facts, and have their proper contexts of use within particular forms of life, which may indeed differ between different social groups. Nevertheless, it seems clear that the different parts of our system of knowledge can, and sometimes should, interact and function within a general grasp of what is the case. Even though we have no independent and infallible access to the 'facts' apart from the concepts we have, those concepts must 'work'; they must mesh with reality in some way, and are not simply made up as free-wheeling imaginative creations.

Bearing these points in mind, I think it is right to measure the 'fit' of our moral concepts to both the scientific and the general worldview concepts that form part of our system of knowledge, and to assess the adequacy of our whole system to enable our forms of life to function well. When we do this, we may find an argument that begins from the consideration of distinctive human capacities and predispositions and moves reasonably to an awareness of what, in general, makes for a good human life. It may provide the conclusion that, if there is such a good, it is not too difficult to know, at least in general, what sort of thing it is. It consists, among other things, in understanding, sensitivity, appreciation, and creativity, and not in ignorance, callousness, hatred, and enslavement. Such reasons are knowable as such by every human agent, not only by those of virtuous perception. In other words, our moral views are affected by our views about human nature and by our more general view of the world at large. Such wider views can form a foundational context for how we see morality, and philosophers (though not only they) may play a revisionist role in seeking greater coherence, comprehensiveness, and integration among the common-sense moral beliefs of our society.

When we move to more specific conclusions, however, it is clear that there is not just one view in our society of what human nature is, and of how seriously we should take our pursuit of the human good. The language-games of morality are affected by wider scientific and philosophical commitments, and by possibly creative interaction with alternative understandings of human nature, different forms of the moral life. One should not assume, therefore, that an account of morality is bound to be naturalistic, even in an enriched sense. Perhaps theistic moralities have a distinctive way of speaking of human nature and destiny. That way need not be a form of what McDowell calls 'rampant Platonism', which he defines as a theory 'constituted independently of anything specifically human' (1994, p. 77). On the contrary, a Platonic view will almost certainly embody a distinctive view (a 'Form') of what it is to be specifically and distinctively human.

McDowell is, I think, correct in defending the view that moral reasons and values are parts of the fabric of reality, and can be discerned by virtuous persons. It is not so clear that this leads to a purely naturalistic, 'stand-alone' account of moral values, which seems only to be expressive of one of our historical culture's viable forms of life. If moral reasons are objective, they should in principle be accessible, at least in general, to all agents who are seriously concerned with what is objectively good and right. Yet it is still the case that many different interpretations are taken of what exactly these reasons imply for human conduct in specific situations, or of what practical force they have in human, not wholly reasonable, lives.

There is much more to be said, in other words, about whether all moral forms of life can be fitted easily into a naturalist mould, however enriched. Yet it seems to me that McDowell makes a strong case for saying that free rational agents will necessarily choose what seems to them to be good, and that there are some things that are objectively good – they are worth choosing for their own sake, whether anyone actually chooses them or not. We can know, by reflection and empathy, not by some sort of super-natural intuition, what these things are, at least in general. They are not adequately construed just as hypotheticals – things that would reason-ably appeal to us if we had specific feelings. They are categoricals – things that ought to appeal to us, whatever feelings we have. They have an ontological foundation. They are founded on a rational consideration of human nature, which reveals the nature of moral values. Thus, there is good reason to speak of moral values as objectively rooted in the fabric of the world.

BASIC GOODS AND HUMAN FLOURISHING

John McDowell describes his view as 'naturalistic', and opposed to any supernatural, mysterious, or spooky forces in the world. I wonder, however, what the force of 'naturalistic' really is, when it no longer has the fairly definite meaning of being confined to objects properly investigated by the natural sciences.

Perhaps part of what he means is that the nature of morality can best be seen by studying human nature. It is a sufficient basis for morality, it may be said, to ask what makes for human flourishing or well-being. There is no need to appeal to any extra-human factors as a grounding for morality. It may occur to someone that, if you place values in 'the world', you are not necessarily locating them just in human nature, but I will overlook this point for the moment. Suppose we concentrate on human flourishing, and ask whether it is a sufficient grounding for morality. I have already suggested that it is a grounding, and that it is legitimate to ask for such a grounding. So, is this it, and all there is to it? I suggest that it is not.

When John McDowell is discussing what it is that makes for human flourishing, or what is needed for humans to live well, he remarks that the list of things you might come up with are what have been called 'Aristotelian categoricals'. It might be true that it is good for humans to have knowledge, power, and friendship. These qualities may be needed for a good human life. But this fact would not entail that it is good for every individual human to have such qualities, much less to have them in a maximal, or in any specific way ('Two Sorts of Naturalism', in McDowell, 1998, p. 171). If you say to me that it is in general good for the human species that people should sacrifice their lives for their friends, that is a reasonable consideration. But there is no particular reason why it should have great weight with me, when there are plenty of others ready to act in the required way. There is nothing irrational about refusing to follow a rational principle, when it only holds anyway for most people, for the most part, and for much of the time.

It is good for humans to have knowledge, since it is a distinctive human quality and knowledge is needed to accomplish many desirable purposes. Yet it could not be reasonably argued that all sorts of knowledge are, or as much knowledge as possible is, good for everyone to pursue. People only need the sorts of knowledge that will help them to achieve their goals. Perhaps there could be a sort of division of labour, some people specializing in one sort of knowledge, and others in other sorts. Some people would hardly need more than a bare minimum of knowledge, receiving what they need to know from others who like learning and studying.

I doubt whether one could get as far by this method as arguing that it is good to seek truth and understanding just as such, and for its own sake, and for everyone. It is even more unlikely that we could infer that it is a duty to pursue these virtues to the greatest possible extent. Some people would enjoy increased understanding. It may even be the case that most people would be happier in learning new and interesting facts. But not all would, and not all would need to.

Would it be morally reprehensible to fail to know or understand? Well, it might, if such knowledge was important for human welfare. For instance, if a doctor did not know how to cure some disease, this might be considered reprehensible, because it would undermine the possibility of achieving other goods. Moral duties would inevitably arise as complex societies bound people with various desires and needs together, and individuals were allocated social roles that became important for maintaining such societies. Moral duties would be largely functions of social differentiation, and would be relative to one's social role.

Similarly with power, a soldier who has the duty of defending a state against its enemies would fail in that duty if they lacked the power to fight. But scholars would not need to have such power – though they might require the power to read and argue well. Thus, we could establish a list of basic goods, but they would need to be more closely specified in terms of the duties and benefits of specific social roles. This would not imply that absolutely everyone had some duty actively to pursue understanding and creativity. It does not follow from the fact that humans have distinctive powers that all of them ought to exercise those powers in a particularly positive way. We all have powers we do not exercise – I could have been a much better pianist than I am, and I could have learned the violin – and that is not immoral. We need something more than the fact that we have distinctive powers, and that it is good for (some) people to exercise them (to varying degrees), if we are to make human flourishing a basis for moral affirmations.

We could view basic goods more minimally, just as what all humans need, whatever their commitments to virtue. Naturally, humans want food, sex, health, security, and some degree of social bonding, if they want to flourish at all. Such considerations are not negligible, and do give a basic idea of what is good for humans. But it is a very basic idea. Is it enough to be well fed, healthy, secure, and enjoy some degree of social recognition? Is that all there is? Or are these just the basic preconditions of a good human life? After all, one could have all these things, and be totally malevolent, a liar and a thief (a successful and undiscovered one, of course).

THE PURSUIT OF HAPPINESS

Perhaps we could try saying (as Aristotle did) that all rational sentient beings aim at *eudaimonia* – construed variously as happiness, well-being, or fulfilment. Aristotle thought that human flourishing consists in cultivating moral and intellectual excellences in an appropriate way. But isn't that just an option for some (in his case, for the leisured elite, and then rarely, not for long, and usually ending in disappointment)? And, as a psychological remark ('if you cultivate the virtues, you will be happy'), isn't it just false? Those who strive for understanding and creativity often fail, fall into depression, and wither away.

As for happiness, the difficulties with the Utilitarian proposal of seeking the greatest happiness (or pleasure) of the greatest number are well known. Leslie Stephen put it well when he said, 'If I wanted to make you happy, which I do not, I should do so by pampering your vices, which I will not.' Even if we make happiness our aim, it is not necessary to aim at the happiness of 'the greatest number'. That seems to many philosophers both unrealistic and impossible to quantify, anyway. If we contemplate what most people think makes them happy (and perhaps it really does), we might find it totally unacceptable or unworthy. We really, whatever we sometimes say, want more for people than that they should just be happy, in any way they choose. We want them to accomplish worthwhile things, make the most of their talents, and feel proud of themselves. But they are not likely to do that if all they want is to get as much pleasure as possible. While, if they want to make as many people as possible feel pleasure, they are likely to be permanently harassed and depressed.

Appeal to human flourishing as a basis for morality needs rational grounding to become plausible. The rational grounding it needs is a conception of human flourishing that already carries an objective moral loading, a sense of what it is for a human to live well that is more than a brute description of what human nature is like. It is a description of what human nature is like, but it is a description that already incorporates a moral view as to what it should be like. And the 'should' is ineliminable. It is what McDowell calls a conception of what a human life ought to be, when seen in a certain light.

It is all very well to say (although it is almost certainly false) that everyone aims at happiness. One needs to ask in what happiness consists, and whether it is the one and only, or even the most important, aim in a human life. There are many different sorts of happiness, and I doubt that happiness, taken purely in itself and without regard to what makes one happy, is a worthy goal of human life at all – though I would hardly deny that everyone would like to be happy. That, however, is far from making happiness the one major goal of a human life. Everyone would also like to be healthy. But for many people health is an instrumental good, a condition of doing worthwhile things, not an end-in-itself.

Happiness is not quite an instrumental goal – we do not want to be happy in order to achieve some other state. It is what could be called a concomitant state – one that properly follows from doing something worthwhile reasonably well. Different sorts of happiness differ in accordance with the sort of worthwhile thing one is doing. Moral happiness is the sort of contentment and sense of well-being that properly follows from moral activity. It is a distinctive sort of affective state, a state that has a cognitive content and is not just a non-conceptual passion (it involves believing that what one did was good, and that one did it responsibly), and unfortunately it does not necessarily follow from doing that activity (at least if one rejects the heroic Stoic view that one can be happy on the rack).

To be happy, in whatever manner and by whatever means, cannot be a direct goal of moral action. The goal must be the worthwhile state, responsibly achieved, and the hope must be that the appropriate and distinctive sort of happiness will follow. In this sense, all moral activity involves a hope for an appropriate form of happiness. But hope may be disappointed, and that should not prevent one from undertaking moral action. There must be some connection between morality and happiness, but it cannot be the direct connection of doing something simply in order to make oneself (or even other people) happy.

IDEALS OF UNIVERSAL FULFILMENT

It may therefore be felt that those who try to construe morality solely in terms of a morally neutral idea of human flourishing have lost something that can only be captured by speaking of aiming at good for its own sake. One thing that has been lost is the sense that aiming at goodness is a battle against temptation and evil. On the account I have given so far, it may seem that evil is just irrational, and consists in aiming at things that no intelligent agents would reasonably choose, because they do not contribute to human flourishing. But, of course, intelligent agents do often choose things that others would call evil. An evil choice would be one that causes pain to others, or oppresses them, or causes them harm. We know what good and harm are, and, if we have an idea of basic goods, then we necessarily also have an idea of basic evils. Basic evils will be the contradictories of basic goods – things such as physical pain, ignorance, weakness, and hatred. These are not reasonably choosable for oneself. But they can be freely inflicted upon others.

One might try arguing (as R.M. Hare did) that, if we were truly reasonable, we would say that, if something is good for us, then it is good for anyone like us. Other humans are relevantly like us, and so we know that it is good for them to be happy, knowledgeable, and capable of exercising their powers freely. Other things being equal, then, it will be reasonable to aim at anyone's happiness, knowledge, and freedom, just as much as it is to aim at our own. Making an exception in your own case is just irrational.

This argument, however, fails to understand what human desires and preferences are. Psychologists and novelists can tell us, with a great deal of plausibility, that most of us desire to cause pain and discomfort to others, to subdue them to our own power, and to enslave them as far as we can. If this is so, then it may well seem reasonable for each of us to choose things that fulfil our deepest desires. So, torture, subjugation and enslavement are reasonably choosable by each of us. We can see that it would be quite reasonable for others to feel the same way. The consequence will be that human life will be one of continual competition and warfare, and, odd as it may seem, reasonably so.

That is the problem with human desires. They are concerned with basic goods, but they are just as much concerned with destroying and subjugating others (while, of course, if we must at least pay lip service to what is rational, allowing that it is reasonable for them to try to do the same to us). If this is the case, morality cannot, after all, simply be a matter of rational choice, and we cannot define goodness simply in terms of what individuals think is needed for their flourishing. If we truly desired the good of others, then, of course, it would be reasonable to try to treat them as we treat ourselves, and aim at some sort of universal goods. We even know what these goods would be. We do not have to learn them from some supernatural revelation or other authority.

It may be felt, however, that such goods belong only to an impossibly ideal world, in which each desired the good of all and was content to take that as an aim. However, the real world is not like that. We can reasonably desire what is creative. But we may equally well desire to conform and obey, and let others take responsibility and initiative. Or we may desire to compete with and dominate others, to destroy their plans so that our own power may triumph.

It may be reasonable to desire greater understanding and sensitivity. But we may desire, instead, to enjoy things as they come without enquiring too closely into their nature. Or we may actually dislike, even hate, others, and enjoy seeing them come to grief. Our desires may be for the compassionate love of others. But more often they are likely to be indifferent to others. Sometimes, we may find ourselves enjoying being cruel to others and causing them pain. Human desires are so various and complex that they are an unstable and shifting basis for any moral system.

What is needed is to train our desires so that they are desires for universal good, rather than for self-interested good. And we also need to see the good as including a set of ideals for which we should strive in a positive sense. The moral good of knowledge does not just consist in knowing some relevant information. It is being committed to seeking fuller understanding of truth for its own sake. The moral good of compassion does not just consist in trying to eliminate pain, good though that is. It also seeks to aim at a fuller appreciation of and sensitivity to beauty and a fuller empathy with the inner lives of other persons. The moral good of freedom does not merely consist in seeking relief from oppression. It also seeks creativity and the creation of new forms of beauty. The moral good of co-operation is not limited to co-operation with our friends. It seeks to extend our feelings towards universal compassion for all sentient beings.

We can see that these are estimable goals of human activity. But a perception that they are goals that evoke moral discipline and effort, that will realize true personal fulfilment, does not arise simply from inclinations that we happen to have, or from the fact that we see them to be necessary for some morally neutral conception of human well-being. It arises from an irreducible and distinctive moral perception. We do not just rationally agree with what would be good in general for human agents. We are commanded by the thought of what is intrinsically worthwhile (that is, by the thought of the Good) to pursue moral ideals as a condition of realizing our humanity.

I agree with the point made by Angus Ritchie (in *From Morality to Metaphysics*, 2013) when he argues that there is what he calls an 'explanatory gap' between a purely naturalistic account of morality, perhaps based on evolutionary psychology, and the moral belief that we are bound by categorical and universal moral obligations. How, he asks, do humans in a naturalistic cosmos come to have the capacity to see objective moral norms? They might come to see what is good for humans or what makes for human well-being in general. But that is a long way from believing that we are confronted with a moral demand to pursue an objective human ideal even at great cost to ourselves.

Ritchie considers the views of a number of contemporary writers on ethics, including Foot and McDowell, who give constructivist or naturalist accounts of morality. He argues that no such account can bridge the gap between knowing in a general way what is good or harmful to human lives, and believing that there are objectively demanding moral truths to be acknowledged. I myself believe that a naturalistic account can be given of how we are able to arrive at knowledge of moral truths. The use of reason and sympathy can lead to the postulation that there are objective and basic human goods. After all, even a naturalist need not hold the reductive view that all our beliefs are solely due to selectively advantageous considerations. Some beliefs may arise because of perception and intelligent reasoning, and many moral beliefs surely do.

What is more difficult for a naturalist, even an enriched one, to explain is the categorical force and universal range of some of our moral beliefs. McDowell thinks no such explanation is needed, or can be given. Maybe so. But many people believe that there is an existent supreme value, God, that can be known, and with which union or fulfilling relationship can be attained. If reality is directed to this goal and structured so that the goal is achievable, then we can see that moral values – values that lead to and constitute this goal – will be objective, authoritative, and causally effective. As Ritchie says, such a purposive view of reality would explain the categorical force of morality in an intelligible way. We would have a metaphysical view that makes good sense of a categorical morality.

Whether that metaphysical view is itself justifiable is a different matter. It raises a question about whether such an account would be truly naturalistic any more, and about what the boundaries of naturalism are. And, of course, it raises a question about whether we really want to accept that there are objective and categorical moral demands. If we do, and we aim at goodness for its own sake, then we aim to do what makes for personal flourishing and fulfilment, and we aim at this for all, and not at what is good only for ourselves, or perhaps for ourselves and our families or friends. We know what acting in such a way would be. But, given our actual desires, is it reasonable for us to act in that way? We only need to look at international relations to see that most people do not think so. They think it would be wrong not to put the interests of their own country first. It would be ridiculous to aim at good equally for everyone in the world (even though it may be good to help those in desperate need if it is not too expensive to do so). Perhaps none of us really has such a desire. Perhaps few of us think it would even be reasonable to have such a desire, in an essentially competitive and rather cruel world.

THE IDEA OF THE GOOD

The morality of personal flourishing only really seems to work for ideal persons who exist in an ideal state. When Plato sketched out his idea of what this might be in his Dialogue *The Republic*, he saw that human beings would not be able to sustain such an ideal morality. He had two different responses to this. One, outlined in his last Dialogue, the *Laws*, recommended a virtually totalitarian society in which moral order would be imposed by force, and free thought would be banned and even punished by death. For this reason, commentators such as Karl Popper have condemned Plato as an enemy of an open and free society. That would be just, if such social repression was the logical outcome of Plato's general ideas on justice and the Good. But, of course, it is not. In *The Republic* itself, Plato mentions another, more acceptable but perhaps more tragic, possibility. 'Perhaps it [the ideal commonwealth] is laid up as a pattern in heaven, where he who wishes can see it and found it in his own heart', he writes, 'But it doesn't matter whether it exists or ever will exist' (Plato, 1986, IX, 592, p. 420). Justice is something one can only hope to establish in one's own life, in 'the Republic of the heart'; and even then it is unlikely ever to exist in any fully actualized way.

That is why the Good, for Plato, remains transcendent. It is not, and perhaps never will be, fully realized on this earth. Yet to say that it exists is a way of saying that there is something that exerts moral pressure on those human beings who are open to it. And they, foolish though they are, are perhaps the wisest and best of the human race.

If we humans are to be moved by such considerations, we need something that will engage our deepest passions and overcome our natural partiality. We need, perhaps, some sort of devotion to a higher cause that takes us beyond ourselves, and to which we can be passionately committed. Yet even here there are moral temptations and dangers. Few things are as harmful to human life as the passionate commitment to a higher cause that propagates one commanding ideology, and subjugates all else to its demands. Fervent loyalty can be evoked by such causes, but they can subordinate others in ruthless ways – as we see in some of the excesses of the Spanish Inquisition and in the Marxist-Leninist ideologies of the twentieth century, the real enemies of an open society.

If our passions are to be engaged by a higher power or cause, it is important that the cause should not reinforce ethnic hatreds and repressive intolerance. The cause must deepen and extend moral insight. While there is a proper place for personal loyalties and responsibilities, there needs to be a cause that is not limited to one group or creed, but that is truly universal in its extent. Perhaps only in that way could human desires be trained to aim at a universal good. But what could that cause be?

At this point, there is available a short route to God. God could be the supreme impartial spectator of the human scene, and God might command us to do what God knows to be truly for universal good. God might reinforce those commands with inescapable sanctions of reward and punishment. Then we would have very strong reason for doing what is objectively (impartially) good. This might sound like the case that I myself would make. But the route is too short, and it seems to lead back to self-interest, even if that interest is very long term. It would destroy any concept of the autonomy of morals by making morality depend in a direct way upon divine commands and prudential self-interest, and that may seem a very paradoxical view of God, who is supposed to ask humans to be selfless and genuinely altruistic, not reasonably selfish. There is something wrong with many versions of what is often called 'divine command' theory. They seem to deprive morality of its dignity and intrinsic authority, and also to turn God into a ruthless dictator who imposes morality upon humans by sheer power. Even an impartial spectator God seems rather too uninvolved and disengaged to evoke total reverence and loyalty. Perhaps we must do without such a God, and see what reason on its own can offer.

One might return to Plato's proposal of 'the Good' as that objective reality that is most worthy of human attention. As Iris Murdoch put it, 'Loving attention' is the purified state of mind that is capable of seeing the reality of things. Attention to the independent existence of what is excellent, an attention that overcomes selfish passions, can be the centre of a moral viewpoint. It is not then the fact that I desire something that makes it good. It is rather the fact that it is good and beautiful that makes the person who sees justly desire it.

The question arises whether there is anything that is supremely good and beautiful, or whether this is a mythological projection of human dreams of perfection, which does not correspond to anything in reality. Might the sort of 'just attention' to reality that Murdoch recommends not lead to despair rather than reverence for a good which is so transient, flawed, and doomed to extinction?

She admits, indeed stresses, that human life is bedevilled by the 'fat, relentless ego', and that evil is so apparent and prevalent that it rules out the existence of any sort of 'finality' or objective purpose in reality – which rules out God. Yet there does seem to be something about achieved excellence in both art and in human living (and in scientific understanding too) that strikes us with admiration and awe. She writes, 'There is . . . something in the serious attempt to look compassionately at human things which automatically suggests that "there is more than this"' (1970, p. 73). Hovering between compassion and despair, she finds herself strangely compelled to opt, as Existentialists such as Camus and Sartre did, for 'the higher ground', absurd though it may be.

PERCEIVING VALUE

If we believed in the objective existence of goodness, would that provide the emotional purchase we need to transform our self-centred passions into a passionate love of what is truly worthwhile? There is a surprising sort of convergence between the thought of Iris Murdoch and James Griffin, who has provided a subtle and compelling analysis of value, both moral and prudential, from a naturalistic viewpoint, though they see things very differently. The convergence is that there is a just and normative way of seeing reality, and that the natural world is expansive, including values in its ontology.

Professor Griffin, like McDowell, objects to drawing a sharp distinction between 'objective' and 'subjective' moral values. Values are not objective in the sense that they are actual and existent independently of whether anyone would or should desire them. They are not subjective in the sense that they depend wholly on the existence of actual desires that add value to wholly neutral acts. The former view would suggest a 'perception' model of value, that we simply perceive existent values, independently of our desires, and perhaps add a subjective desire or reaction later. The latter view would suggest a 'taste' (one sort of Humean) model of value, that some thing or state is valuable only if we actually desire it. Griffin rejects both views, and wants to give values 'a kind of realist status' (2000, p. 293), but one which is apprehended in a way that blends perception and reaction in an inseparable unity. As we only understand another person if we are empathetic with them, so we apprehend certain basic values only if we perceive justly and rationally.

This account seems to me to be correct and illuminating. Values only become actual when perceived in a reactive way, but they are characteristics of reality, to be included in our list of what exists and is not wholly invented by humans. The sense in which values exist remains to be investigated.

But that values are parts of the fabric of reality, and that they are apprehended by a form of perception that is both cognitive and affective in an inseparable way, is agreed by McDowell and Griffin.

Griffin ties values closely to actual human capacities and interests, and to the sort of flourishing and well-being humans are actually capable of. He views such injunctions as the biblical statement 'Be perfect' as an unrealistic and unhelpful attempt to transgress the limits of what is humanly possible. He says that secular ethics is basically about '*human* capacities and incapacities and what it is for *human* life to flourish in a *modern* society' (1998, p. 13). The italics (his) show the importance he places upon seeing the limited nature of human capacities, and the importance of seeing how they can be deployed in diverse social conditions. There is no doubt that this can be a basis for secular ethics, and it seems adequate for societies of good-hearted and well-intentioned beings in a liberal society where all are concerned for the common good. But are humans good-hearted and well intentioned? And is modern society devoted to the good of all? If we take a look at the modern world, one of the most obvious facts about it is that it is replete with corruption, violence, torture, tyranny, and war. If we take a look at human capacities and incapacities, they seem most obviously to be capacities for domination and destruction, and failures even to meet minimum standards of politeness and tolerance. This is far from the dreams of universal compassion and passion for justice that are to be found in the works of liberal and humane philosophers.

Humans have limited capacities and interests, as Professor Griffin points out. He seeks to use this fact in a positive way, to recommend that we do not ask too much of humans, and that we relate our moral requirements to ones that will meet the reasonable interests of most people. He is not impressed by what he calls 'capacity-blind morals', which place absolute moral demands upon people without taking account of the very real limits of people's capacities. But I suspect that, in speaking of 'human capacities and interests', he is already exercising a form of moral censorship, so that he only thinks of capacities for good and interests that give reasons for respecting the interests of others as well as those of oneself and one's kinship group. This is what he means, I think, by speaking not just of actual human desires, but of 'informed desires'. Those are desires that would be reasonable from an impartial and fully considered viewpoint. The problem is that most people's desires are neither informed nor impartial. Dramatists such as Sartre and Ibsen, and aphorists such as Nietzsche, provide a different account of human desires. Humans are predators struggling to survive and dominate in a harsh world, 'red in tooth and claw'. The will to power is the major human interest, often disguised in the words of moralism, and the prevailing capacities of humans, as evolution requires, are the capacities to procreate and eliminate rivals, and to attain power, status, and pleasure while one can, before death reduces all human effort to failure and pointlessness.

If one took a more pessimistic view of actual human nature, one might rephrase Griffin's recommendation thus (I in no way imply that he would agree with this): that a rational recommendation for human behaviour might be not so much about 'what it is for a human life to flourish in a modern society', as about 'what it is for the will to power to flourish for a short time in a violent and unjust world'. But that is hardly what ethics is about. Ethics, for most people, is about countering the will to power (countering many natural human capacities) and countering the violence of the world (a world in which the violent and deceitful flourish). Griffin's perspective is that humans are members of a society of reasoning and causally free agents who will do what seems to them good. I have agreed that this is indeed a presupposition of any adequate morality. The problem is that humans do not reason very much or very well, and that they are often influenced more by social pressures, genetic predispositions, and passionate desires than by autonomously chosen goals. The minority who do believe that they can freely choose goals for themselves, and ask what these goals should be, can see that in this world the strong flourish and the weak perish. So, in making reasonable choices, they are liable to distinguish between the 'moral' rules they will lay down for society, and the very different and largely self-serving principles by which they actually live. The 'natural' world is a darker place than humanist and liberal morality pretends.

It is this fact that makes morality not a matter of the humane and dispassionate calculation of maximization of compatible interests, but a matter of a relentless and passionate battle of the moral will against the insistent pressures of lust, hatred, aggression, and arrogance that dominate human lives. It is not, after all, that humans actually are reasoning free agents, but that they *should* be reasonable, free, and devoted to what is truly and objectively good. Of course, what is good must relate to human interests and to human flourishing. But that presupposes that human interests tend to what is truly good, and that human flourishing is a flourishing in goodness, not in the fulfilment of whatever desires individuals happen – or are determined by evolutionary mechanisms – to possess, or even what desires they would possess if those desires were fully informed by attending seriously to the natures of human beings and the things they value.

I have argued that humans are rational and free agents living in community, and there is among them a widespread and rationally defensible notion that they should be devoted to the pursuit of goodness for its own sake, even at the cost of a sacrifice of self-interest. I have also argued that one reasonable grounding for human knowledge of right and wrong is not supernatural intuition, but reasonable reflection on the distinctive capacities of human beings, and on what makes for human flourishing. But I have insisted that the notion of human flourishing has what might be called an irreducibly gerundive moral quality. It is not just that humans will, as a matter of psychological fact, flourish if they behave morally. Rather, personal flourishing is to be defined in terms of capacities that they ought to exercise, and that will, if fully exercised, constitute human flourishing. That ineliminable 'ought' gives values a place in the fabric of reality.

5

NATURAL LAW

NATURAL LAW AND DIVINE LAW

Traditional Christian morality is very close (for some, surprisingly close) to a morality of human flourishing. For instance, when Thomas Aquinas treats of 'natural [moral] law' in the *Summa Theologiae*, he recommends that the enquirer begins by looking at human nature to see what its 'natural tendencies' (*naturalem inclinationem*) are. They fall, says Thomas, into three main groups. First there is a tendency, shared with all things, to self-preservation. Second, there is a tendency, shared with all animals, to mate, and produce and rear offspring. Third, there is a tendency, unique to humans, to sustain one's rational nature, to seek truth, and to devise rules for living sociably with others.

Particular moral rules derive from one basic rule of natural law, which is 'that good is to be sought and done, evil to be avoided' (Aquinas, *Summa Theologiae*, 1a2ae, 94, 2) – a simple deduction from Aristotle's definition of 'good' as what all things seek, or, if they are fully rational, what they ought to seek. Armed with this basic moral precept, and a list of natural inclinations, we can say that what is good is what is natural, or what we have a natural inclination towards – such things as food, drink, health (the first group of precepts), sex, procreation (the second group), friendship, truth, and understanding (the third group), for example. Later natural-law theorists (Grisez and Finnis, for example) propose slightly different, but similar, lists of human goods. The primary precepts of natural law aim at the rational fulfilment of such tendencies of human nature.

Moral reasoning will not be a matter of just intuiting some moral truth. It will be a matter of reasonable decision. It is foreign to the idea of natural law that duty should be in fundamental opposition to the fulfilment of our natural inclinations. Such fulfilment is precisely what inclinations tend towards, at least when they are ordered by reason. There is no direct appeal to religious revelation or to divine commands here. The moral view could well be seen as hypothetical (founded on the natural inclinations humans happen to have) and naturalistic (knowable by reason, not revelation, by a study of human nature).

There is another sense, however, in which natural-law morality must be seen as categorical and non-naturalistic. In natural-law thinking, there is, as in Aristotle, an appeal not just to a contingent but also to an essential human nature and its proper purpose. Thomas says that the natural law is 'a sharing in the Eternal Law by intelligent creatures' (Aquinas, *Summa Theologiae*, 1a2ae, 91, 2). And the Eternal Law is the idea of the essential natures of things, which defines their goal and purpose, in the mind of God.

Natural law is not, therefore, a matter of just following your natural inclinations whatever they may happen to be. It is a matter of following the inclinations that have been set into your nature by God, who has in the divine mind an ideal goal for human life. There is a reference to God, as the source of objective moral truths, hidden in what seems to be a purely 'natural' law. If God is non-natural, and if God's ordinances are absolutely binding, this will give a non-natural and categorical character to moral laws. But it must be noted that the existence of goals for human life in God is aimed at a fulfilment of human nature, and not its suppression, so that this is as far as possible from being a tyrannical insistence upon blind obedience to God.

It is possible to have a morality that is based on a study of human desires and inclinations, and advocates human flourishing as a key moral principle. But I have argued that such a morality may only be justified in speaking of some very basic human conditions of well-being, which will hold for many people and to some extent. It would have great difficulty in holding that there is an absolute obligation to promote a wide range of human capacities for their own sake, to the fullest extent, or never to frustrate them (except, possibly, when they unavoidably conflict), or to promote them not just for oneself and one's friends, but for everyone.

The standard Christian account of natural-law theory, as provided by John Finnis (1980), for example, is very different. It assumes an essentialist view of human nature (that there are certain distinctive inclinations that are to be promoted for their own sakes). It has a teleological understanding of human nature (there are objective purposes of nature to 'perfect' these inclinations). It assumes that these goods are to be promoted universally, for all. And, at least in its Roman Catholic form (for instance, in the Encyclical *Veritatis Splendor*, 1993), it assumes that the goods somehow give rise to absolute obligations (the purposes of nature are never to be frustrated).

Reasonable atheists would be justified in promoting goods as merely instrumental conditions of things they happen to want. They may well reject ideas of perfectionism, or of an 'ideal goal' for human lives, as impossible to attain and psychologically harmful. They may feel obliged to aim at universality only as far as social stability requires. And they will almost certainly deny that there are any purposes of nature, or that it is 'nature's purpose' that we should perfect our natures.

A moral realist may hold that there are objective goods and ideals of human perfection that are binding on all, and that give rise of themselves to categorical obligations in appropriate conditions of moral choice. However, such a view so far lacks intelligible metaphysical foundation. It does not give a clear idea of where or how objective moral facts exist, or of how ideals of human perfection can apply in a world where they often seem impossible to achieve, both because of the evil of others and one's own weakness of will. It is hard to see why one should aim at the good of all, in a world of intense competition and violence. And it is hard to see why the obligation to aim at good should be categorical, when it may well seem enough just to do one's best insofar as it does not conflict with a moderate degree of self-love.

A theist can supply a firmer metaphysical framework for a categorical morality. Moral facts will exist in the mind of God. The perfecting of personal virtues becomes achievable with divine help. Divine concern for all creation will commend the good of all to creatures. And God's demands are as categorical as God's love is unlimited. Moral facts obligate; but God's purpose for human lives ensures that such obligations are (correctly) seen as categorical and realizable.

This helps us to see that standard (Christian) natural-law theory depends on the existence of God even if it does not explicitly say so. It is God who defines what essential human nature is; God who sets the purpose of perfecting human nature; God whose perfection and promise of fulfilment underlies the categorical obligation to pursue that purpose; and God whose universal concern for all creatures extends our own concern for fulfilment so that it embraces everyone. This is why humanists do not usually accept natural-law theory, even though they often base morality on considerations of human flourishing or well-being.

Mark Murphy's (2011) helpful discussion of natural-law theory complains that standard natural law theory is too independent of God, and could be accepted without any reference to God. I have suggested that this is unfair to the theory, but it may be true that theists want a more personalist element to moral law and obligation, an element capturable by the otherwise misleading phrase 'No law without a law-giver'.

Murphy holds that 'every moral fact is explained by some moral law' (2011, p. 60). I think that is the reverse of the truth. Moral facts – such as 'knowledge is good' – explain moral laws – such as 'Do not lie' – as entailments of the fact that something is good (worth choosing), where there are created moral agents in situations of moral choice who are faced with either promoting or frustrating the good. There may be an infinite, and therefore unstatable, number of moral laws that could arise from such a fact, and the fact would hold whether or not there were any created agents or moral laws. Further, there may be goods without and prior to all obligations and laws, as in the case of God, who is good but under no moral obligations. So moral facts about good are logically prior to moral laws, and laws with their concomitant obligations arise directly from moral facts without any additional element of divine command.

Nevertheless, if moral facts (values) are in the mind of God, and if God chooses to make some values actual, then God contingently chooses to make some goals incumbent upon human agents. Humans are not just faced with a passive Good, with no purposes and intentions. A personal God adds to the natural necessity of obligation an additional element, which is that God selects a purpose that God does not wish to be frustrated. In this way, God enters immediately into the explanation of obligation in the way Murphy desires. God adds (concurrently, as Murphy says) to the natural necessity of obligation, an element of divine will or command. God does not invent moral laws, as if arbitrarily. But God promulgates moral laws, and an element of personal obligation to an all-perfect creator enters the situation, which is an important part of Christian moral experience.

NATURAL AND PERSONALIST PURPOSES

A major problem for this traditional Christian view is that it seems to assume that there are purposes and goals in nature. Most modern biologists insist that there are no purposes in nature, and that modern science only got started when the influence of Aristotle was overcome, and when scientists stopped asking what 'the purpose' of natural processes was, or what the 'essential nature' of things was, and concentrated on formulating non-purposive laws of nature that obtain between events or entities that are in continuous change.

This does not mean that belief in a God who formulates goals for human life and for the cosmos has to be given up. It probably does mean renouncing Aristotle's belief that every object has an unchanging and essential nature, and aims at a state 'for the sake of which' it exists, that is, the perfecting of its essential nature. However, a more general teleology of nature may still have much to be said for it. It depends, after all, on what God's aims are, and how they are incorporated into the physical structure of nature.

God might have the aim that the cosmos should generate intelligent and morally responsible life. God's aim for human life might be that understanding, sensitivity, creativity, friendship, and justice – the personal goods implied by reflection on the distinctive capacities of humans as moral agents – should be maximized as fully as circumstances permit. These would be worthwhile goals, and they could exist objectively in the mind of God as patterns for how the universe would develop. But it would not follow that every physical object would have a final cause, an ideal pattern to which it tends. It would not follow that every physical process would have an ideal pattern of fulfilment that ought never to be frustrated. There might well be an intelligible place for both chance and free creativity in the natural world.

Not all natural processes bring health and safety, and it would be a misuse of language to confine the word 'natural' to processes that did so. In which case, it may seem that natural processes can sometimes be harmful, and that it would be right to interfere with them when we can prevent harm by doing so. Nature's processes are not sacred. They are often arbitrary and painful. They often undermine the personalistic goods of reason, understanding, memory, and responsible freedom. That is precisely why medical science exists – to remedy the deficiencies of nature. If humans can take some genuine responsibility for their actions, and if the processes of nature often seem to be random and tragic, and if they can be controlled without the risk of causing great harm, it might seem reasonable to control them. The growth of cancer cells is a process of nature, but most would accept that it should be frustrated for the sake of the health of a human being.

It cannot be true, then, that whatever is natural is right. We have to separate the natural from the good. As T.H. Huxley said in a famous essay 'Evolution and Ethics', the processes of evolution must often be opposed, since they produce monsters and aberrations as well as amazingly complex functioning organisms. Nature is, as Tennyson said, 'red in tooth and claw'. It is simply false that 'Nature, in all its works, aims at what is good', as Thomas claims (Aquinas, *De Veritate* 16, 2). Does that render natural-law ethics obsolete?

It does, I think, render obsolete belief in any universally benevolent purposiveness in nature – that is, a providence that ensures that every event that happens is designed to bring about good. But we can retain the Aristotelian/Thomist claim that goodness is what all rational creatures would choose. We can retain the belief that humans are distinctively rational, sensitive, creative, social animals, who have been produced by evolutionary processes that are partly random, but also may be generally directed towards the emergence of just these properties. We can think that, insofar as humans have responsibility, they should develop these properties, not because they are what nature actually does, but because they are what God may be aiming at in ordaining the otherwise morally neutral processes of nature.

Natural law can be what brings happiness by fulfilling the personal natures of human beings, for these are properties that any fully rational and sensitive being would choose. In other words, we may think that nature needs to be personalized, freed so far as is possible from random, undirected physical processes, in order to generate self-regulating conscious intelligences ordered more responsibly towards good.

Such a view does not presuppose an Aristotelian view of all things having inherent final purposes. It is not a view of nature as ordered wholly to good by God, and therefore being completely in order as it is. It is an evolutionary view of nature, as possibly created and generally directed by a cosmic intelligence, but as open and emergent. It is open because it is not eternally determined in every detail by God, but is partly indeterminate, an indeterminism that allows human freedom to develop naturally. It is emergent because new personal properties emerge from it, as it develops towards a future goal that will be partly shaped by the creative acts of the beings it produces out of itself. It is a universe that can grow towards the good – and so, though in quite a different sense, it is still Aristotelian in realizing its primal potentialities successively through time. Compelling statements of such a view can be found in the writings of the Jesuit palaeontologist Teilhard de Chardin and the early twentieth-century English philosopher F.R. Tennant.

This is a very clear instance of the way in which changing views of nature can suggest new approaches to morality. If such an evolutionary view is accepted, morality will not be seen as conformity to the natural processes of the universe, which are wholly good and inviolable because created by a wholly good God. Morality will more probably be seen as the shaping of a morally neutral biological nature towards future personal goals, which God lays down as ideals for an open, emergent, and partly self-shaping cosmos. In that case, of course, many moral questions will be settled by asking what acts make for the greatest health and well-being of intelligent, creative, sentient agents. Those questions are unlikely to be settled by asking what the usual processes of nature are. The relevant question will be how such processes can be best adapted for promoting health, well-being, happiness, and the fullest realization of personal powers – a very Aristotelian aim in a very different scientific context.

Since what is at stake here are deep beliefs about the nature of God, of divine providence, and of the nature of the created world, such issues are not going to be easily or lightly settled, and I do not pretend to have done more than sketch the outlines of one possible theistic view, which tries to be fully cognizant of and consistent with modern evolutionary biology. There will be some theists who would reject many views common in modern evolutionary biology. There will be many evolutionists who will hold that nature is even more ruthless and random than I have indicated, and who will think this rules out the existence of an intelligent and benevolent God at all. They could fall back on the humanist default position of moral self-realization without there being any objective motivation for adopting it. They are more likely, I think, to adopt a sociobiological explanation of morality, which may not stress self-realization very much. Either way, the issue of what nature is like is important for deciding what the foundation and nature of morality is. There is an affinity between worldviews and moral views, and religion usually includes a worldview that will generate some distinctive moral features. Religion and morality will be intertwined, sometimes in conflict and sometimes in mutual support. This is a limitation on the idea of the autonomy of morality. Though moral views cannot be deductively derived from scientific or religious views, moral views will and should be modified by relevant changes in scientific or religious views, and it is impossible to say in advance how deeply these changes may go.

THE ENLIGHTENMENT PROJECT

The Platonic/Aristotelian viewpoint sees morality as the pursuit of an ideal goal of human nature, with social principles being meant to sustain a society in which such a pursuit will be encouraged. In seventeenth-century Europe, Hugo Grotius and Thomas Hobbes illustrate a major conceptual change in thinking about morality. The Grotius/Hobbes viewpoint sees morality as instrumental in enabling partly or wholly self-interested people to live peaceably together, without there being any one ideal of the good human life.

For the former view, if there is a God, it is a God who sets a goal for every individual human life, and whose perfection draws all things towards it. For the latter view, if there is a God, it is a God who is the impartial spectator of the human scene, who lays down general rules that will hold a society of diverse egoists (and perhaps of largely sinful and irrational persons) together. An 'ideal goal' morality has a natural affinity with a theistic metaphysics, because it works with the idea that there is an objective purpose for human life. A 'rational rule' morality is more easily detachable from any theistic belief, even though it often appeals to a God who is seen as the supremely rational creator of nature.

Alasdair MacIntyre, in his influential works on the history of morals (1985, 1988), calls this conceptual change the 'Enlightenment Project'. The project is to provide an objective and impersonal justification for moral beliefs, which will be 'acceptable to all rational persons whatsoever' (1988, p. 8). MacIntyre argues that this project fails, and that both of its most developed major forms – Utilitarianism and Kantian rationalism – suffer from irremovable defects.

He argues that it is better to see moral views as essentially embodied in historical traditions of thought. They develop by encountering internal problems of coherence and also by encountering competing traditions, and seeking a more comprehensive view that looks to overcome those problems, or to reconfigure them in a way that renders them less acute.

However, MacIntyre sometimes speaks in rather apocalyptic terms about the language of morality in the modern world being in a 'state of grave disorder', consisting largely of remnants of past moral theories, 'fragments of a conceptual scheme', which has been largely forgotten or abandoned (1985, p. 2). 'We are all already in a state so disastrous that there are no large remedies for it', he says (ibid., p. 5). I am not convinced, however, that there was once a sort of moral Golden Age from which we have descended into moral chaos, or that the Enlightenment Project has failed entirely, or that there is any realistic hope of finding a more Aristotelian remedy for our moral ills.

It seems to me that ancient Greek views of morality were just as pluralistic and diverse as are views in the modern age. Socrates and Protagoras had very different views, as did the Stoics and Epicureans. There never was an age of universal agreement about morality. There have always existed very basic options between theism and atheism, between moral objectivity and subjectivity, and between basing morality on reason and on desire. We need not regard our present inability to agree on basic moral principles as anything new or surprising, or as a sign of some sort of conceptual decadence.

Moreover, there were always at least two major coexisting types of morality in Greek city-states. There was a minimal morality enabling people of different classes to live together more or less harmoniously, and a more ideal morality for the aristocratic elite to live excellent and happy human lives. Thus, the polarity of 'ideal goal' and 'rational rule' morality is not so much a case of historical change and collapse as a more or less permanent feature of any complex human culture. Those two types of morality are probably both necessary in any well-developed culture. The main problem of the Enlightenment, with regard to moral theorizing, was how some sort of ideal-goal morality could survive the collapse of Aristotelian metaphysics, and whether that could be done without recourse to some form of religious view. That is another way of describing the Enlightenment Project.

It is not obvious, either, that the Enlightenment Project has 'failed'. Its attempts to find a justification for morality certainly do not and probably never will convince everyone, and perhaps that might be called a sort of failure, from the point of view of its own highest ambitions. There are ultimate disagreements, as MacIntyre points out, about such topics as justice and equality, and about pacifism and just war. But that seems to be a virtually inevitable part of the human situation, not something that could ever be resolved by some moral theory. The best one can do is work out a relatively coherent ethical system, in the knowledge that it will never be universally agreed, but that at least it makes an attempt at consistency, coherence with all well-established facts, and openness to rational criticism.

The demise of Aristotelian teleology was virtually inevitable, given the rise and overwhelming success of law-based experimental science. There may be hope of restoring a teleological view of nature in a different form, and, if so, it will probably be allied with something very like theistic belief (a mental or personal reality that can build purpose into the nature of the cosmos). As such, it will probably always be disputed, and therefore will not ever be made into a universal basis for morality, despite the hopes of some natural-law theorists.

In Aquinas, Aristotle's view was allied with a conception of a divine law that imposed categorical obligations on humans. That sense of being absolutely obligated to do God's will was unlike anything to be found in Aristotle. And yet the idea of obligation was far from unknown in ancient Athens and Sparta. The virtue of courage, for example, called for the strongest of obligations, the obligation, when called upon, to die for one's city or country. Not all virtues are ideals that one may or may not strive for, and that one is not expected fully to achieve. The virtue of courage imposes a moral obligation to face danger and death for the sake of one's friends. This may not be thought of as a divine command, in any literal sense. But it is more than a personal choice. It is something that is felt to be incumbent upon the agent, whatever their present desires, and even at great personal cost. I think that this is a distinctively moral sense of 'ought'. It may be true, however, that theism provides a firm foundation for the objectivity of moral obligation, and even that a sense of moral obligation is one experiential indicator of the existence of God. The history of post-Enlightenment moral thought shows a continuing struggle between such a view and the attempt to found a rational morality on a purely secular basis.

As a matter of fact, the Enlightenment Project seems to me to have largely succeeded in gaining widespread acceptance for the view that moral claims need some sort of reasoned justification, and cannot just be accepted on the authority of tradition or religious revelation. Such justifications, however, will operate within wider worldviews or general metaphysical pictures of human nature, and those worldviews are, and I suspect always will be, widely disputed. It is not a failure, then, when one does not achieve universal agreement. The Enlightenment did lead to the increasing respectability of relativistic views of ethics – views that are sceptical about seeing moral claims as true, and even more sceptical about seeing them as universally or absolutely true. But that is precisely because traditional theism and Aristotelian science both faced up to, and in the eyes of many fell before, the reasoned criticisms of a more scientifically oriented philosophy.

On good Enlightenment principles, however, that philosophy itself must face up to critical enquiry, and to the charge that serious moral and metaphysical questions cannot be answered simply by dogmatic reiterations of a presently fashionable worldview. There can be no return to pre-Enlightenment philosophies. MacIntyre's own proposal is that historical traditions all possess internal puzzles and tensions, and that they progress by a dialectical process of argument and insight. Close attention to the historical process in the West by which thinking about morality has developed does, I think, suggest that present secular views of morality do not have particularly strong foundations, and that an appreciation of the ways in which metaphysical and theistic views have interacted with moral views in the past may well hint at new ways of understanding both the diversity and the depth of what may be called transcendental interpretations of moral utterance, even in what can sometimes seem an almost wholly naturalistic (non-transcendental) age.

So, my own view is that 'the project of an independent rational justification of morality' (MacIntyre, 1985, p. 39) did not fail, but it produced a number of rational justifications of slightly different types of morality. One (itself containing a whole set of subclasses) of these is transcendental or theistic morality. I do not think that 'moral judgments are linguistic survivals from the practices of classical theism which have lost the context provided by these practices' (ibid., p. 60). I think that there are, and always have been, diverse forms of the moral life. Between them we have to choose, and such a choice will be made partly, but not entirely, on moral grounds. Theistic moralities are distinctive types of morality, capable of having their own internal criteria of rationality and intelligibility. In that sense, morality is not autonomous, but is closely intertwined with metaphysical and religious beliefs. Naturally, religious believers can have reasons for the greater adequacy of their own view of morality, but those reasons will not be found convincing by all. One reason will be that religious moralities provide a coherent account of objective values and goals, which is able to see humans as moral agents of great intrinsic worth with a responsibility for shaping their lives for good or ill. The more instrumental moralities tend to see moral agency as less decisively important, and principles of social ethics as more a perpetual compromise between diverse human projects, and less a matter of achieving a common good. There will still be differences about which broad view of human existence is more adequate to the facts. But, for a theist, the facts of moral experience will provide one sort of good reason for thinking that there is a God. It will never be universally convincing. That is not a failure; it is simply the human condition.

QUASI- AND REAL REALISM

I am inclined to agree that there is an irreducibly moral element that cannot be deconstructed and explained in entirely non-moral terms. Yet I also think that morality does need support of some sort from a wider metaphysical context, whether this is some form of 'natural law' theory, a more Platonic view centred, perhaps, on an existent ideal of the Good, or a fully theistic view, which makes the foundation for morality, and indeed for all reality, more personal or mind-like in nature. At this point, I call in aid a rather improbable ally (improbable for any religious believer), Simon Blackburn (1993), who rightly sees a basic division between moral realists – who think that moral assertions are true or false, and make assertions intended to be about objective reality – and moral projectivists – who think moral assertions are projections of subjective human attitudes onto reality. Having made this distinction, he proceeds to argue for what he calls quasi-realism, which is the view that there is nothing in objective reality except facts known to the natural sciences and psychology, yet moralists can quite correctly *speak about* moral facts, moral truths, and moral values as being parts of the fabric of reality.

This theory is to be distinguished from John Mackie's 'error theory', for which moral assertions look and feel (phenomenologically, or in experience) as if they are asserting facts about objective reality, whereas they are not. Moral facts are too 'queer' to exist objectively, and the extent and non-resolvability of moral disagreements militates against any of them claiming truth. Moral statements are no more than expressions of attitudes, and perhaps our moral vocabulary should be revised accordingly. Blackburn does not think that any revision is needed. Moral assertions can have every appearance of being proper beliefs, and quite properly so, but they require no ontological commitment to the objective existence of especially moral entities. They are quasi-realistic.

Where I agree with Blackburn is in thinking that there is a basic, and real, division between moral realists and anti-realists. I do not think either of these positions can be formally refuted. Both can be supported and attacked by arguments from adjacent non-moral areas of discourse. In his case, he clearly states his preference for gaining some view of the human world that fits comfortably into the scientific worldview. He is not a reductive physicalist, explicitly including human needs and desires in his preferred worldview, but he does like an elegant and economical worldview that does not need to appeal to entities that cannot in the end be wholly accounted for in terms used by the natural sciences, including psychology. He is a naturalist by nature. The point is that he is sympathetic to finding external, metaphysical, reasons for deciding which of moral realism or anti-realism is true. One of them is, though there is no conclusive experimental test, and no way of ensuring the agreement of all informed disputants.

It should be obvious by now that I am a committed moral realist. I think there are more things in heaven and earth than the natural sciences can deal with. I am as committed to the scientific worldview as Blackburn is. I just do not think that the natural sciences can say all there is to be said about reality. Yet where do I differ from Blackburn, if he is a quasi-realist, and accepts that we can speak of truth and falsity in morality without deception?

I agree with him almost entirely on the question of how we come to believe that certain moral assertions are true. We do not just have a quasi-perceptual 'intuition' of a moral truth, rather like just inescapably seeing the colour yellow if our sense-organs are working properly. We carry out a thought-experiment, asking about ideal conditions for considering possible good states (including elimination of partiality, the cultivation of calm dispassion, critical self-evaluation, and comparison with alternative states), and paying attention to the judgements of others whom we judge to be wise and experienced. Then we make a personal judgement as to what state we think is worth choosing for its own sake. All these things Blackburn can do. He can even say, being a quasi-realist, that in the end he, like me, is capable of coming to a true belief.

What is missing in his account that is present in mine? Well, in the end he has to say that nothing objectively exists apart from physical and psychological facts. Just as we can pick out chairs without believing that in reality there is some special 'disposition to create chair discriminations', so we can pick out good states without believing that there is some special feature of objective reality that is (like a McDowell secondary quality) a 'disposition to evoke a moral attitude', and thus a real and independently existing feature of the world. We can see how the physical features, plus some psychological facts about human needs and desires, give rise to talk of objective chairs and objective values. But there is no need to think those values exist without us, or independently of our desires, or that we would have to mention them in a complete description of the objective world. We pick those features out because our needs select them out of perfectly natural features of the world.

However, as McDowell and Griffin have pointed out, 'objective reality' does not have to be reality independently of our perception of it. An actualized value, a worthwhile state, would not exist unless it was appreciated by some mind. But that does not entail that all value is contributed by our minds, while objective reality remains value-neutral. A property can be objective if it is such as to arouse a specific mental state in any properly functioning mind. We can say that state A really is (objectively) more worthwhile than state B, in that it is more worthy of choice by a free rational agent. But the value is only realized as a value when it is apprehended by some mind. The mind does not project the value onto reality. Using an analogy from quantum theory, we might say that the mind 'collapses' the possible value into an actual value.

Unlike chairs (which are not special dispositions in things to produce chair-like appearances in consciousness), possible values are precisely dispositions to evoke apprehensions of value, and need to be characterized as such to be understood. In other words, what is missing (for a realist) in Blackburn's account is a distinctive sense of obligation, of moral pressure, of 'ought-to-be-ness', which is lying in wait for mental agents who perceive the facts as they are. There is no 'complete' description of the objective world that fails to mention these facts. For a moral realist must say of the world that it does not contain mention only of actual desires and interests. It must also mention desires that humans ought to have, and states at which humans ought to aim, which are worthwhile whether or not individual humans think they are.

They are indeed very queer facts, if one insists that all facts must fit into a scientific/neutrally descriptive framework. But why should there not be facts which in themselves are apt for evoking a sense of obligation when apprehended by free agents? To be a moral non-realist is to deny there are any such facts. To be a moral realist is to affirm that there are some. We find out what they are when a sense of obligation is evoked (though, of course, we could be mistaken. Moral knowledge does not have to be infallible). To be a quasi-realist is to say there are no moral facts, but it is all right to talk as if there were some. Like many people, I have an uneasy feeling about quasi-realism. How can it be all right to talk as if there were moral facts, yet declare there are none? I do not say this is a refutation – I would not be so rash. But I do think that such a view is at least as queer as saying that moral facts actually exist, that we can quantify them, and do so in an intentionally and fully existential sense.

I would be happy with saying that every meta-ethical view is queer, from other perspectives, and that what seems queer is relative to what metaphysical or ontological view one finds appealing. Hilary Putnam does not seem to me to be right when he says that we can have ethics entirely without ontology. Putnam regards attempts to provide an ontological explanation of the objectivity of ethics as an attempt 'to provide reasons which are not part of ethics for the truth of ethical statements' (2004, p. 30). But I think this is significantly mis-described. Ontology, as I understand it, is an attempt to provide reasons that are not part of ethics for speaking of ethical statements as true and as objective in a more than trivial or merely quasi-real sense.

6

THE OBJECTIVITY OF THE GOOD

THE NATURALISTIC FALLACY

One way of trying to capture an element of objective value in morality is found in the work of G.E. Moore. In *Principia Ethica* (1951), he argued that, when I say something is morally good, I mean that some object possesses an indefinable, simple property of 'goodness', which is not to be identified with any other property or thing. Moore calls the identification of goodness with any other property 'the naturalistic fallacy'. It might have been called 'the definist fallacy', since it objects to defining 'good' in any other terms at all.

Moore thinks that goodness is a non-natural property. He defines a natural property as one 'which is the subject-matter of the natural sciences and also of psychology. It may be said to include all that has existed, does exist, or will exist in time' (ibid., p. 40). Goodness, he claims, does not exist in time and is not a subject-matter of any natural science. That is why it cannot be defined in terms of any natural object, and why he termed any attempt to do so the naturalistic fallacy.

What he says about this is very hard to understand, and I am not sure that it makes sense. Goodness, according to Moore's definition, is a non-temporal, ultimate, unanalysable property. It is 'a property of certain natural objects' (ibid., p. 41). Yet he says it is 'a predicate which neither does nor can exist' (ibid., p. 125). Is goodness, then, a non-existent property? That hardly seems possible. To help us understand this, Moore produces an analogy from mathematics. He says 2+2=4 is a non-natural truth. Yet numbers and equations do not exist in reality: 'Two *is* somehow, although it does not exist' (ibid., p. 111). In fact, he says, 'no truth does, in fact, *exist*'. His use of italics suggests that 'exist' is being used in a special sense. Such 'being without existing' is, he says, characteristic of all mathematical truths and truths about what is intrinsically good.

I can only make sense of this by supposing that, by 'exist', Moore means 'having a place in space and time'. There are in addition, he says, metaphysical objects, supersensible realities that are talked about by metaphysicians, and he concedes that metaphysicians tend to think that such realities exist supersensibly. But his own view is, apparently, that such realities 'do not exist at all' (ibid., p. 112). Does this mean that they are fictions? Or just that they are not things that we can move around or experiment upon? Of course, no metaphysician ever thought they were. So it is difficult to see just what Moore can mean by saying that there are properties which can be known, but which do not exist in reality.

This puzzle is not helped by the fact that Moore sometimes uses 'X is good' interchangeably with 'X ought to be'. It is doubtful whether these do, in fact, mean the same. If I say that X is good or intrinsically worthwhile, that does not entail that I think it ought to be. An 'ought' implies an obligation on some personal being to bring something about, and we can believe that something is worthwhile without thinking that anyone has an obligation to bring it about. There might be many good things, and it might be good if they existed, and yet it need not be true that they all ought to exist. Indeed, we can think something is worthwhile and that a person is obligated not to bring it about, if, for example, bringing it about would involve breaking a promise, or if it would conflict with some other good thing.

It is this assertion of equivalence between 'X is good' and 'X ought to be' that has given rise to the common confusion of the naturalistic fallacy with Hume's alleged argument that you cannot derive an 'ought' from an 'is'. Moore not only thinks that 'good' cannot be defined in terms of any natural object or property. He also thinks that it cannot be defined in terms of any supernatural or non-natural object, such as God. Such definitions he calls 'metaphysical ethics', and rejects all such ethics on the ground that it tries to define 'good' in terms of some other property. He thinks that metaphysical ethics commits the error of thinking that 'some knowledge of supersensible reality is necessary as a premise for correct conclusions as to what ought to exist' (ibid., p. 114).

This is not in fact so, since, even if X is defined as identical with Y, it is possible for someone to know Y without knowing X, or that Y is identical with X. But, supposing it is so, Moore might be taken as saying that you cannot derive an 'ought to be' from an 'actually (supersensibly) is'.

That sounds like an 'is-to-ought' move. But it is very different from saying that you cannot derive an 'ought to do' from an 'actually is'. To say that you ought to do X is like saying that it is right to do X. And Moore says that 'it is right to do X' is definable in terms other than itself – it means that X will produce a greater amount of good than any other action we can do. I doubt if Moore was right about this, but, even if he was, it would follow that 'X ought to be' (which is indefinable) cannot mean the same as 'X ought to be done' (which is definable), and so we can sensibly say that something ought to be, without implying that we or anyone else ought to do it or that we can do anything about it.

The upshot of all this is that the naturalistic fallacy (that good cannot be identified with any other property) is quite different from Hume's 'is to ought' argument (R.M. Hare called it 'Hume's Law': we cannot deduce an obligation from any description). Unfortunately, both these different arguments are widely misunderstood. Both of them in fact allow an inference from 'is' to 'ought', in the following way: Moore says that, if state X is good, then it follows that one ought to aim at X, if one can and if there is nothing better to aim at (this follows from his axiom that 'it is right to do X' means 'it is right to bring about the greatest possible good'). Hume argues that you cannot derive an obligation from a purely rational premiss, but, given that a right action is one that produces a feeling of pleasure (unlike Moore, he is a naturalist, and identifies 'good' with some state of mind), the factual statement that X produces most pleasure implies the moral statement that one ought to aim at X. Neither the naturalistic fallacy nor the 'is–ought' argument rules out inferences from the right sort of facts to moral conclusions. And, in any case, they are both saying quite different and incompatible things.

MOORE AND PLATONISM

Moore (but certainly not Hume) seems to believe that we can have indemonstrable knowledge of some 'non-existent', indefinable, non-temporal, simple property. The naturalistic fallacy is committed by anyone who tries to define this property, 'goodness', in terms of any other property. But, if 'good' really is a simple property, then saying 'X is good' *is* a descriptive fact. Perhaps it is a purely propositional truth – the analogy with mathematical truths and the occasional use of the phrase 'X would be good if it existed' as an equivalent for 'X is good' suggests that possibility.

Do propositional truths, truths, generally speaking, about possible states of affairs, such as truths of logic, mathematics, and some moral truths perhaps, exist? I think Moore suggests that they do exist, but in a different way than truths about material things in time exist. Thus, the contemplation of beauty would be good (hypothetically good, good if it existed and was contemplated), even if nothing beautiful existed, and there was no one to contemplate it.

If this is to make sense, we have to think of propositional truths somehow existing. Among these truths will be the truth that certain states, if they existed, would be good – or even, says Moore, that they 'ought to exist'. But this does seem to contradict what Moore clearly says, that it is an error to think 'that to be good *means* to possess some supersensible property' (1951, p. 123). For he would be saying that to be good is precisely to possess a supersensible property – the indefinable property of 'goodness', which is, of course, non-natural or *non*-sensible, and *super*sensible, in that it will be a necessary and eternal (non-temporal) truth, not just a contingent and temporal one.

This property is not to be identified with any other property, either natural or supernatural – that is the naturalistic fallacy. But the assertion that goodness is a property that does not exist in the same way as objects exist is itself a metaphysical assertion, and so Moore's analysis of 'goodness' will be, ironically, a metaphysical ethics of just the sort he declares to be impossible.

Moore thinks that the truth of what things are intrinsically good can be discerned by 'intuition' – though he remarks that he simply means by this that they are incapable of proof (ibid., Preface, p. x). He does think, however, that it is true that certain objects possess this simple property, and that we can know this to be true. In other words, it is not just a free postulate or axiom, which could be anything we choose. It is a matter of discovering truth. To find out what these objects are, we must carefully distinguish exactly what the thing is, and then look to see whether it has or has not the unique predicate 'good' (ibid., p. 223). By using this method, he claims to know two, and only two, such things – the contemplation of beauty and natural affection between persons. We might say, slightly more grandly, beauty and love.

Most philosophers, reading Moore, have felt that there is something odd about apprehending a non-temporal property. Moore draws analogies between moral and mathematical truths. But mathematical truths are purely abstract, founded on the relations of purely intelligible objects. Moral truths are about particular sensorily apprehensible objects like (for Moore) beautiful pictures and human friends. It is those objects that are said to possess the property of 'goodness', and so they are a peculiar conjunction of temporal and eternal, particular and universal.

This suggests, surprisingly, that Moore is a sort of covert Platonist, finding a universal, eternal 'value' or 'goodness', instantiated to a greater or lesser degree in particular temporal entities. Seeing the goodness of something is seeing something of eternity in it. It is to see value as objectively existing in reality, and mediated in specific types of object.

Moreover, to discern goodness is not to remain unmoved. If one sees that something is good, one is moved to desire it, to aim for it, or to keep it. This is not a matter of neutral description. To see the good is to be attracted to it. Not to be attracted is not genuinely to see and believe that it is good. Discerning something eternal and intrinsically motivating is a very special sort of apprehension.

Moore does not believe in God, saying that there is no evidence for a supernatural person, and that the existence of any evil at all is incompatible with a good God. But the apprehension of an eternal and intrinsically motivating quality of being *is* evidence for the existence of a non-natural eternal and objective value that evokes reverence and delight. And that value in some way becomes attached to objects in a complex world in which good and evil are mixed, and in which the specific sorts of goodness that exist (for instance, the sorts of paintings we produce) are won by struggle with the resistances and obstacles posed by the obdurate resistances of matter and the natural incapacities and weaknesses of human character.

There is a metaphysics of the supernatural here – something which can embrace an eternal reality of greater value than anything natural, yet which realizes itself precisely if partially and with difficulty in the natural world, and through the medium of human awareness and action. Moore may have argued for the supremacy of common sense over idealism (in his British Academy lecture 'The Refutation of Idealism'), but he had not, I think, entirely escaped the spell of a metaphysical idealism of some sort.

KNOWING THE GOOD

Critics are not slow to point out that people differ in their intuitions of goodness. W.D. Ross, for example, claims to intuit three things that are good – pleasure, knowledge, and virtue – none of which features in

Moore's very short list. He also rejects Moore's 'ideal consequentialism', his construal of 'right' in terms of production of the greatest good. Ross finds it self-evident that there are duties of fidelity, reparation, gratitude, justice, beneficence, self-improvement, and non-maleficence, which create *prima facie* obligations, whether or not they conduce to the greatest possible good in particular situations (1930, cf. p. 21). They are independent limiting factors on the realization of good states, not just means to producing such states.

If there is no possible way of 'proving' the truth of such conflicting intuitions, how are we to decide between them? I think it is clear that Moore and Ross are not just appealing to clear intuitions, as if they were both staring hard at the same colour and trying to decide what it was. They both present arguments, and try to produce a conceptual scheme that will include all aspects they deem relevant in a systematic and comprehensive way. They engage in rational reflection on the data of complex human feelings and on the reality of reciprocal social relations with others, try to formulate basic general principles from which more specific ethical conclusions can be drawn, and try to decide what things are intrinsically worthwhile. This is an activity of reasoning, not of simple intuition. Like any reasoning about complex matters, it will involve creative insight and mastery of various conceptual schemes, and will be undertaken within a specific cultural tradition and social context.

Such reasoning is not just a matter of deducing valid conclusions from clearly formulated premises. In reasoning, we seek new ways of describing things, devise new concepts, and assess them for adequacy to the perceived facts. Of course, there must be perceived facts. But understanding those facts is a matter of devising apt descriptions, making conceptual distinctions and connections, and seeing possible fruitful implications. It is an imaginative and creative activity of mind, directed towards arriving at a more adequate grasp of truth. It is, in short, a more than deductive rational activity, and it is undertaken for the sake of finding truth and consciously directed to that foreseen goal. It is not surprising that reasoning will produce differences and disagreements.

Moore and Ross seem committed to the existence of a realm of necessary and eternal moral values. They are objective parts of reality, and, though of a 'non-natural' sort, they are closely connected with particular states of affairs in the natural world, particularly, perhaps, with mental states and activities (beauty and love, knowledge and virtue). They are knowable by intellect, though not infallibly, and they constitute a distinctive area of human knowledge that requires no reference to either metaphysics or religion. One can, they assume, work out what is meant by 'good' and 'right' simply by attending to those concepts themselves. In fact, however, they both make a very large assumption. They assume that there is a good and a right to be discovered by reasoning, and that in the end close introspective analysis of what these concepts 'mean' or stand for will inform one about how one should live.

This is not at all self-evident. The status of moral facts – whatever it is in objective reality that makes moral truths true – is obscure. They do not exist in anything like a physical sense. Moore wonders whether they can really be said to exist at all. If they exist, they seem to do so in some quasi-Platonic conceptual or intelligible realm, along with logical and mathematical facts, and possibly with some basic and ultimately necessary laws of physics. This is a realm of necessary truths and possible states of affairs, knowable if at all by intellect alone.

THE DEMAND OF THE IDEAL

Such a quasi-Platonic belief in the existence of necessary and eternal values receives some support in more recent philosophy. Russ Shafer-Landau (2003) argues that moral principles are 'as much a part of reality as the basic principles of physics'. It is interesting that some mathematical physicists, such as Roger Penrose, agree that a Platonic realm of quasi-mathematical truths is, if anything, more real than the physical world we seem to inhabit. They do not usually speak of God, however, rather preferring to say that necessary conceptual truths, perhaps including moral truths, are just 'part of the furniture of the universe' (Wielenberg, 2005), and require no personal being to support or enforce them.

I think it is extremely difficult to know what the existence of eternal and necessary truths would require. It is not at all clear to me that they could just exist (or, as Moore might say, not exist while still being there). Of course, it is always possible to say that anything at all 'just exists' without further explanation. But that seems a counsel of defeat for any attempt to understand or explain the universe. The peculiarity of eternal moral truths is that they are, some of them and to some extent, instantiated in physical reality, and apprehended by human minds. And they are apprehended not in some purely abstract conceptual realm like pure mathematics, but in the contingencies and particularities of physical and social existence.

A similar situation does exist in mathematics, where purely conceptual truths appear to fit the world with amazing precision. The mathematician Eugene Wigner wrote, 'The appropriateness of the language of mathematics for the formulation of the laws of physics is a wonderful gift which we neither understand nor deserve' (1960, p. 14). It is almost incomprehensible, he wrote, that the truths of mathematics should just happen to fit the physical universe. The fit is too precise and elegant to be accidental. The equations of quantum mechanics, for example, which are selected, as the Cambridge quantum theorist Paul Dirac said, largely for their abstract mathematical beauty and elegance, turn out to reveal the structure of physical reality with uncanny precision.

So, Plato in the *Timaeus* introduced a Demiurge, a cosmic intelligence, to shape the world in accordance with the Forms. Aristotle said that the Prime Mover – a perfect intelligence – moved the physical world to imitate it because of a mysterious 'desire' for it. It is more comprehensible to think of the physical world as formed as an image of the intelligible world than to think of there being some accidental correspondence between them. But how the physical world gets to exist at all, or how it is to some extent 'formed by' the intelligible world, remains mysterious. One may just have to put up with that. After all, humans cannot explain everything.

The world of necessary and eternal moral truths has as its conceptual content possible states in the physical world. Some of that content is instantiated in the physical world, in good and beautiful things. The content comes to be apprehended by minds that are parts of the physical world. And that content exercises authority over those minds, inviting them to make some possible futures actual as a matter of distinctively moral obligation.

All this suggests that 'seeing what is there' in the physical world includes seeing the non-physical (might we say 'spiritual'?) aspects of reality that are embodied in it, and that, precisely as embodied and apprehended, make specific futures worthy of choice. In other words, it is intelligible to see the conceptual world as *expressed in* the physical world, not as just contingently existing alongside it. Furthermore, when embodied, it 'urges' that world towards a specific future possibility, through being apprehended and responded to by parts of the physical world (human persons). It is causally effective, if only indirectly and in a passive way, through being known and responded to.

Because they call for knowledge, emotional response, and commitment of the will, the morally demanded futures can be seen as fulfilments of distinctively human capacities, so that they favour a move of the physical towards wider and deeper expressions of goodness, and to a greater actualization of capacities that were potential in the structure of the physical world from its beginning. They seem to be causally effective or at least to call for causal effectiveness in the world, through the medium of human awareness and response. The conceptual possibilities of what would be good, if contemplated and appreciated through knowledge and feeling, become actual values and forms of goodness through human co-operation. The history of the cosmos can thus be seen as a movement from potentiality to actuality, in which possible values become actualized through free creative action, and lay down a certain 'direction' or purpose for the physical cosmos insofar as the cosmos is open to a sense of the attraction of goodness.

This type of grand metaphysical view would be too much for Moore and Ross, who were temperamentally indisposed to indulge in such speculations. It might be seen as a tentative attempt to integrate the conceptual, mental, and physical worlds that seem to be implied in their accounts of goodness and morality. Though they did not make such attempts, Iris Murdoch did, and she explicitly introduced a Platonic notion of 'the Good'.

CONTEMPLATING THE GOOD

It must be admitted that the expressions of goodness in the physical world are fleeting, ambiguous, and short-lived. They will, so cosmologists tell us, inevitably end in failure and the final extinction of the cosmos. In view of this bleak outlook, perhaps talk of purpose or fulfilment needs to be set aside as a piece of wish-fulfilment now demolished by a scientific awareness that no moral direction can be found and no final moral fulfilment can be hoped for in this physical cosmos.

Iris Murdoch accepts that this is the case. In fact, she believes that to accept it is important for anyone who wishes to have a truly moral outlook. She adopts Plato's idea of 'the Good', construing it as a 'single, perfect, transcendent, non-representable, and necessarily real object of attention' (1970, p. 55). It is single, because all values and virtues form a unified and interconnected whole. It is perfect, because it is absolute or unsurpassable. It is transcendent, because it is not tainted with imperfection or transience. It is non-representable, because infinitely elusive. And it is necessarily real, as an object of selfless loving contemplation.

The Good is known by 'a refined and honest perception of what is really the case, a patient and just discernment and exploration of what confronts one' (ibid., p. 38). It requires a 'selfless attention to nature' (ibid., p. 41), and 'true vision occasions right conduct' (ibid., p. 66).

For Murdoch, the Good is 'a transcendent magnetic centre', an idea that does not exist in the sense in which physical objects exist, or in which people used to think that God existed (ibid., p. 75). But in beauty and in love, which both subordinate the selfish ego to something that is intrinsically beautiful and worthy of admiration, when seen truly, we grasp intimations of the Good. It is possible to come to think that 'the only thing which is of real importance is the ability to see it all clearly and respond to it justly which is inseparable from virtue' (ibid., p. 87).

What we are seeing can be called transcendent, because it regards more than the purely physical, scientifically measurable, and describable aspects of things. Yet the permanent and incorruptible is not some sort of independent supernatural reality. It is certainly not connected with any sense of purpose in nature, as the idea of God is. It is a sense of objective value that is known in and through transient reality, the eternal known in the temporal. As William Blake put it, in *Auguries of Innocence*, 'I hold infinity in the palm of my hand, and eternity in an hour'.

The idea of the Good comes, of course, from Plato, who saw the Good as the supreme Form, or even the source of all Forms, actualizing in itself perfect goodness. It can be very difficult for modern readers to see what Plato is getting at in his talk of the Forms and of the supreme Form of the Good. Pure mathematicians can often sympathize with what he says, for they, or some of them, can feel that the pure world of mathematics is changeless, beyond time, and the intelligible basis of the physical world, which we see in a confused and often misleading way with our senses. But mathematicians rarely associate this underlying intelligible reality with morality. There may be beauty in a pure mathematical world, but what does that have to do with value and goodness?

However, is beauty not a value? Is what we value not what we call good? And is the pursuit of that beauty, the desire to see it clearly and fully, not a worthy purpose for rational beings? That may be so. There may be deep connections between the ideas of a fully intelligible reality, the beauty of an intelligible world, entailing its possession of a sort of goodness, and therefore the existence of a worthwhile purpose or goal in contemplating that goodness. And yet mathematicians are probably not people to whom one would turn to find examples of supremely happy lives (regrettably, many brilliant mathematicians have been desperately sad), much less people whom one would trust to manage political affairs, as Plato desired.

Mathematics, for Plato, is part of the training of the mind. But there must be something more. That something more is perhaps best expressed in the Dialogues by the great celebration of love put into the mouth of the wise woman Diotima in *The Symposium*. The sort of love in question here is love of what is supremely beautiful, supremely desirable, and supremely good. It is the purest sort of love, and what it seeks and what it sees is a beauty that is 'eternal; it neither comes into being nor passes away... but absolute, existing alone with itself, unique, eternal, and all other beautiful things as partaking of it' (Plato, 1973, p. 94). One who 'contemplates absolute beauty with the appropriate faculty and is in constant union with it... will be able to bring forth not mere reflected images of goodness but true goodness... and becoming, if ever a man can, immortal'.

Part of what Plato is saying is that, in order to be truly just or moral, one has to escape from the entanglements of the senses and contemplate the Good as it really is. Morality is not at its heart a matter of making necessary or expedient or wise decisions. It is a matter of contemplating the supreme intelligible reality, so that the soul will be nourished and made happy by the contemplation of truth.

Beauty can be found in many forms, in beautiful persons, works of art, in mathematics and natural science, and in morality. But for Plato the final wordless object of contemplation and union is something that he calls 'Beauty itself', and it is clearly identical to 'the Good'. True knowledge of such Beauty requires a conformity of the mind to what it knows, so that the mind that truly contemplates beauty becomes a beautiful mind. Then what that mind undertakes, its actions in the world, will be good and beautiful. That is the source of morality, the mediation of absolute Beauty through minds that have attained union with it, to transform the world by acts of beauty and love.

THE WORLD VIEWED *SUB SPECIE AETERNITATIS*

Talk of 'Beauty itself' is too much for some philosophers. Stewart Sutherland protests that the Good is not, as Iris Murdoch says, single (an individual entity) or an object of attention, 'not something other than the world and experience' (Sutherland, 1984, p. 99). He wishes 'to establish the intelligibility of a notion of transcendence which is essentially ethical in character' (ibid., p. 125). In this, he is expressing similar concerns to those of Moore and Murdoch. But he does not want to localize this transcendence in an individual or personal being that could be an object of knowledge or contemplation.

He is adamant that the objects of ethical concern are items in the world, and not some reality beyond the world. Thus, he suggests that what used to be thought of as God, a transcendent reality of supreme value, is best thought of as a (now obsolete) way of preserving the possibility of seeing the world '*sub specie aeternitatis*'. It is the world, and the particularities of the world, that provides the objects of our attention. 'Eternity' functions as a sort of regulative ideal or, as Kant puts it, a *focus imaginarius*, for helping us to see the world in this special way.

'Eternity' is given a special meaning in this formulation. It does not just mean what is beyond time (like Moore's non-natural properties), or what is immutable, uncreated, and objective (not invented by human minds). It is essentially connected with a 'transcendent order of values', values that are eternal. Like Moore, however, Sutherland is unhappy with saying that such values 'exist'. I think one reason for this is that existent things may carry the implication that anything that really exists must have some causal power or influence, and, like Murdoch, Sutherland does not wish to give values causal power over future events.

It seems clear, however, that, if there is a transcendent order of eternal values, then they must be parts of the fabric of the universe, and they cannot be caused by any merely contingent realities. More can be said about them, too. They function to defeat egoistic concerns, and, like a 'demand from without' (Sutherland, 1984, p. 120), they call for altruistic concern for others. They are, in other words, spoken of as objective (not products of contingent human minds) and categorical or intrinsically demanding. They are also unitary, in the sense of being interconnected, and forming an ethical and integrated totality rather than being a haphazard collection of unrelated demands.

I think this view expresses very well the sense of objectivity and authority that is felt by many to characterize truly ethical commitment. It is a very tentative ontology of value, but it is an ontology nonetheless, which gives values transcendent existence and, if not independent causal power, at least a power to incline perceptive minds towards particular possibilities of action and concern. It would not be too much after all, for this view, to speak of the Good as a transcendent ideal, by attention to which humans can find an authentic possibility of being.

The distancing from theism, which is characteristic of Moore, Murdoch, and Sutherland, is due to two main factors, which Sutherland powerfully outlines. One is the existence of horrendous evil in the world, and the other is the difficulty of giving an account of how a personal God could act in a world that seems to many people to be causally closed and complete without any reference to divine acts. It is God's causal power, or apparent lack of it, that is the main problem with the idea of God. What Sutherland calls the 'legacy of theism' nevertheless remains of great importance, in positing the objectivity of eternal and transcendent values, and in believing that morality is a matter of 'seeing justly what is there', which is something in addition to purely physical realities.

MORALITY AND PURPOSE

Though Sutherland is sceptical of what he sees as Murdoch's tendency to regard the Good as an individual object of knowledge, there are deep affinities between the thought of the two philosophers. Murdoch believes that great art, or music, or literature, opens the mind to depths of reality, aspects of the natural world that are not captured by the analytic procedures of natural science, but that show us what is truly there. This is a sort of 'moral sensibility' that is not shared by everyone. But it is a way of seeing the world of human experience as disclosing commanding values that call for dispassionate attention and the sacrifice of self.

This talk may be reminiscent of the God that people used to believe in, she says. But it is definitely not a personal God, and not a personal being at all, who acts in the world, comforts the oppressed, and makes everything all right in the end. 'The Good has nothing to do with purpose, indeed it excludes the idea of purpose. "All is vanity" is the beginning and the end of ethics. The only genuine way to be good is to be good "for nothing" ' (Murdoch, 1970, p. 71), she writes. It is not only that science tells us there is no finality in nature. It is, more importantly, that we must choose the Good for its own sake alone, and not for any reward or fulfilment it may bring.

It is hard to pinpoint exactly what is being said here. If you choose the Good – say you choose, for instance, to help an injured person – you are naturally concerned with a purpose (that the person be actually helped), and with its fulfilment. There may be no final causes in nature, but there are final causes in persons. That is, persons do things for the sake of some end, and, if that is a moral end, naturally they hope for its realization. Purpose and its realization are internally connected with moral action. Every rational action has an end or purpose, which you want to realize. If you tell the truth, you aim to bring it about that some other person's mental state is one of knowing truth, and not being deceived. The Good does not exclude the idea of purpose. In fact, it entails the idea of purpose. To know the Good is to have a moral purpose; it is not mere contemplation without responsive and appropriate action.

There is a real question of whether it is possible always to do what is good, or whether you can guarantee that your long-term purposes will be realized. There are many reasons why they may not be – because others frustrate them, or because chance intervenes and makes them impossible, or because you lose heart and give up trying. If you say, 'I want to bring about world peace', this will immediately be seen to be too big a project for one person to undertake. You can do something towards it – take part in a demonstration outside the Ministry of Defence, perhaps. You can do that. That is your purpose. But it may not, and almost certainly will not, have the desired effect. But that is because your purpose is an instrumental one. It is part of aiming at a greater good. You might say that you cannot guarantee that goodness will ever flourish in the world. But you can still have moral purposes of doing little bits of good, and making some things less bad than they might have been. Those are your real purposes. They are not very grand, and you may fail even at those – but at least they are purposes that you want to, and often can, realize.

Perhaps there is no moral purpose in the world. Perhaps it is not inevitably getting better, and goodness will never triumph. Perhaps there is no purpose for your life, written in the heavens, or no purpose in the existence of humans at all. Or perhaps you will always fail to do the things you ought, so that you will never be wholly good. Perhaps, as Murdoch herself concedes, 'a glance at the scene [of human evil and violence] prompts despair' (1970, p. 73). In that case, acting for the sake of goodness may be a tiny flicker of moral purpose in a largely indifferent universe, which will not be greatly affected by your pitiful and ambiguous flicker of goodness.

It will still be true, despite what Murdoch says, that on her view moral agents will have purposes, and they will not simply invent or make up those purposes. They will discern them, as moral possibilities for their own situations. I think Murdoch must therefore mean that the Good has no direct causal power. Human knowledge of it may generate an idea of purpose, but humans will have to initiate action to realize that purpose, and human power alone will determine how far that purpose can be realized.

So Murdoch's view is of the Good as demanding something that will only scintillate for a moment in the cosmic scene, that will probably fail in many cases, and that will always fail in the long run. She says, 'Of the very small area of "freedom", that in us which attends to the real and is attracted by the good, I would wish to give a . . . perhaps pessimistic account' (ibid., p. 75).

ART AND BEAUTY

It is not surprising that she seems more confident in speaking of Beauty and of art than of love and of goodness. Her view of art seems to me almost desperately (I fear I would also say often falsely) romantic, seeing it as implying 'love and detachment', as 'without any point beyond itself', as 'totally opposed to selfish obsession', and as affording 'a pure delight in the independent existence of what is excellent' (Murdoch, 1970, p. 85). The good artist is 'brave, truthful, patient, humble'. Art is 'a sacrament'. Art 'shows us the only sense in which the permanent and incorruptible is compatible with the transient... pierces the veil and gives sense to the notion of a reality which lies beyond appearance' (ibid., p. 88). 'The enjoyment of art is a training in the love of virtue', enabling one to forget self and see justly.

The fact is, however, that great artists are not usually known for their moral heroism, much less for their patience and humility. Wagner with his arrogance, and his odiously racist views, seems to me to be a great musician, but a rather poor example of a saint. His music is sublime, but some aspects of his libretti were morally ambiguous enough to be loved by Hitler and the Nazis. If you walk into any gallery of modern art, you will find irony, satire, the desire to shock and offend and to express personal visions of life that are often disturbing and despairing.

Murdoch's view of art is very idiosyncratic, and much contemporary art is not concerned with the idea of Beauty with a capital letter, at all. I nevertheless find what she says about art suggestive, and think she is right in saying that it has no point beyond itself, that it expresses creativity and uniqueness of vision, and that it has a sense of meaning, a semantic dimension, of pointing beyond appearance to a perceived transcendent depth. But that depth is not always Reality seen as excellent and worthy of contemplation. It sometimes expresses reality as seen by the artist, who may be egoistical and obsessed and spiritually myopic (I refrain from citing the most obvious examples). Plato was opposed to all forms of poetry that did not express the true and the noble – which was most of them. So it is odd that Murdoch, who sounds rather like Plato at times, turns art as such into a sacrament of reality and truth. It is not. It is the expression of the artist's vision. It may reveal much that we had not perceived, but what it reveals may not be beauty or goodness at all.

I believe Murdoch is correct in saying that art can be a sacrament, though it is very much still bound by human misperceptions of reality, and often has little relation to truth and goodness. It may not matter much that art, as an expression of human creativity for its own sake, has no point or future, that it flickers into life for a moment and is then gone. But that is exactly where morality and goodness differ from art. It matters if goodness flickers, fails, and is extinguished forever. If there is no hope that your actions will be for good, or that you will ever be truly good, and if it seems likely that goodness will always be defeated by evil, it is not so sensible to say that you will nevertheless celebrate pointless goodness just for its own sake. In particular, if moral action is not necessarily beautiful, but often painful, cruel, and even agonizing, it can seem unduly Stoical to say that you should still do it just because you ought. A clear perception of the pointlessness of action for the good is almost bound to qualify and limit moral commitment, and lead to despair about the real worthwhile-ness of human existence. Even though there will be objective reasons for acting in accordance with moral ideals, it may well seem more reasonable to fall back on limited self-interest and limited altruism as life principles for those who are in any case morally sick and facing inevitable failure and death.

So, even if there is a conceptual realm of values – and it is easy to dismiss it as an imaginative fiction – why should it have any effect on my conduct? It certainly provides a good reason for moral action, and it articulates our natural belief that such things as the contemplation of beauty and personal affection are intrinsic goods. But such considerations may seem as relevant to this largely ugly and violent world as dreams of Utopia are in a military dictatorship. Talk of intrinsic goods, especially talk like Moore's of sharing beautiful experiences with beautiful friends in London art galleries, can sound almost offensive in a world in which billions lack the basic necessities of life, and have to fight for their survival in hostile conditions and with ruthless enemies.

This suspicion is not helped by the fact that Aristotle's recommendations for the life of virtue are apparently aimed at proud and 'great-souled' men who have slaves and enough wealth to be magnanimous. There is a danger that the reasons for action that Moorean values provide will not prove to be very compelling for the poor and downtrodden of the earth, and will not motivate the privileged to care too much about them. Plato, too, it must be admitted, saw justice as lying in people knowing their place, and the contemplation of the Good was something available only to a small elite. I think, then, that more is needed from a Platonic view of the Good than the thought that moral action is pointless and unconnected with any belief in purpose or the possibility of moral success. Yet, if the objectivity and authority of morality is to be defended, Moore, Sutherland, and Murdoch seem correct in saying that there must be moral values that can be known, and that are not naturalistic in the reductive sense of being identical to facts of the sort with which the natural sciences deal.

There are problems about how and where objective moral truths (or the facts that make them true) exist, and about how such a realm of eternal truths relates to the physical world in which they are partly to be expressed. The intriguing Ideal of one supreme Good-and-Beautiful has a puzzling ontological status. Sutherland is sceptical about saying that it exists as any sort of individual. Murdoch regards it as part of a naturalistic view, perhaps because it has no direct causal power. Moore would not hypostasize it, but would be prepared to speak of moral values as non-natural, and as certainly non-physical or non-material. It seems that talk of objective moral truths requires some sort of metaphysical foundation, and for that reason moral discourse will, while employing distinctive and irreducibly moral concepts, in some sense, depend upon a wider metaphysical view.

7

TOWARDS THEISTIC MORALITY

FROM THE PLATONIC GOOD TO A PERSONAL GOD

It is important to try to find a wider conceptual scheme for interpreting reality into which both moral and scientific facts will comfortably fit. Moral realists do need to give some account that makes the existence of moral facts less queer. At least we have some idea of what moral facts are. They are facts that give rise to obligations and that make some possible states intrinsically worthwhile. Supposing there are such facts, what metaphysical schema might make them more intelligible?

I do not want to suggest that there is just one such schema. Some things, however, might be said about the sort of schema that is likely to prove plausible. It will not be a materialist schema, for there will exist entities (namely, values) which are not amenable to scientific measurement, observation, and experiment. It will not be a determinist schema, for moral agents will have alternative possible futures between which to choose. And the cosmos that it attempts to describe will not be a physically closed causal system, for some events will be causally influenced by reasons, rather than solely by unconscious physical entities and laws.

Whether one calls such a schema 'naturalistic' or not does not much matter, as long as the term natural is used in a rich or extensive sense, to include non-physical data with which the natural sciences do not directly deal. Fiona Ellis (2011) provides a good survey of the way in which expansive naturalists are able to include what were once called 'non-natural facts' within a naturalist scheme. Expansive naturalists are not usually overt Platonists, but, if one is prepared to go so far, a Platonic interpretation begins to seem fairly appealing – Platonic in the sense that there exist conceptual realities underlying physical phenomena, and these conceptual realities may bring about, or may contribute to bringing about, causal events in the phenomenal world. This is because 'betterness' or 'worthiness to exist' is a conceptual, not a physical, property, and because future possibilities can be assessed by comparing alternative scenarios, some of which are better than others. Since these are being considered as objective possibilities, not merely human constructions, one can conceive of a set of possible worlds, differing in respect of the sorts and degrees of value they possess, and able to be accessed and compared by human thought. This thought of an existent array of possible worlds is quite a familiar one, in terms of the history of classical philosophy, from Plato to Spinoza, Leibniz and Kant. It is also deployed in modern mathematical physics, so it is certainly not just a matter of 'faith' as opposed to reason, or of 'fantasy' as opposed to 'science'.

That some possible worlds, or particular states in such worlds, are better than others provides a good reason why they might actually exist. It is minds (human minds, in our case) that actualize possible worlds, by conceiving such worlds and seeing which are of value. One possible ontology suggested by moral experience, then, is that the set of all possible worlds, with the differing values they possess, exist as conceptual realities. They are conceived or understood, at least partially, by minds, which have the power to actualize some of them. The actual world in which we live is a product of physical causes, conceptual possibilities (Plato's 'Forms') with their inherent values, and minds that understand and can actualize some of those possibilities (presumably the better ones, other things being equal). In this world, some things come into existence for a reason, and the reason is likely to be that it is intrinsically good that those things exist.

The Platonic world itself, being purely conceptual, is not to be thought of as conscious and aware of its own content. Though some possible states are of greater value than others, this value can only be experienced and understood by something rather like a human mind. Though it may also be very unlike a human embodied mind, it must at least be conscious – possessed of conceptual objects of awareness. Perhaps it could be called, still in Platonic fashion, Intellect (*Nous*), so as not to presume that it will necessarily be an embodied human mind. If something is to operate as a reason for existing, it must be understood as a reason, and deployed as a reason, by an Intellect that is capable of understanding and of acting in accordance with that understanding. In addition, the value can only be experienced as an actual value by an Intellect that is aware of its value.

Merely possible values, even though they must in some sense exist, are not actual values. They are conceptual entities that become actual values when they are entertained and actualized by some Intellectual substance. A reason for the existence of a good state, then, is that some Intellect sees it as a reason (a good possibility in a conceptual world), decides to make the state actual, and enjoys the state, realizing it to be good.

If a naturalistic view of ethics is so 'expansive' and 'enriched' as to include normative values, it becomes difficult to see how, in principle, that view could exclude the reality of the Good as a transcendent and non-physical supreme focus of values. If the Good is then thought to be a necessary and eternal reality (by analogy, perhaps, with mathematics), it will be hard to think of it as caused, or emergent from, or brought into being by, matter. Then there would be a radical dualism between the conceptual or intelligible world (eternal, its elements uncaused, and necessary), and the physical world (temporal, its elements caused, and contingent), which would deprive the naturalist hypothesis of the major advantage of having to deal with just one real world.

A more fully Platonic thesis suggests that the obvious move to make is to see the causally constituted physical world as brought about by the uncaused intelligible world. The only available form of causality between the eternal and the temporal is a non-temporal relationship of dependence. There needs to be a selection from the set of possible worlds, which implies conscious knowledge of those possible worlds, and conscious selection, presumably for the sake of the values that would become actual, of this actual cosmos. Such a scheme would provide an intelligible place for values in 'the fabric of reality', and provide an intelligible relationship (of 'embodiment' or 'participation') between values and physical facts.

Whether such a Platonic view could still be called naturalistic is unclear. The eternal and necessary consciousness and actuality-selection-principle of the Platonic Good seems very unlike a popular view of God as a supernatural person who interferes in the universe in often apparently arbitrary and miraculous ways. Perhaps it will turn out to be a rather partial or inadequate concept of any God who is actually worshipped in the world's religions. However, it is an intelligible idea of God, and it gives causal priority (though not of a temporal sort) to the non-physical. Modern physical concepts of the origin of this space-time from a realm governed by deeper quantum laws of intelligibility and beauty is not so different from the Platonic view. The main difference is the attribution of some form of consciousness to the Good. But the eternal and purely rational consciousness ascribed to the Good is very unlike that of human temporal, embodied, and evolved consciousness. A Platonist – certainly, a Platonist like Plotinus – might also want to say that the intelligible world would in some way be incomplete without some form of necessary actualization in a physical world. Then the Good would be seen not as an entirely separate reality, but as the inner reality of this physical world. That could be called an expansive naturalism, though it should be clear that it is far removed from classical materialism or reductive physicalism, and it is recognizably a form of theism.

This is not intended to be a 'proof of God'. It could be that the Platonic conceptual world exists, and there are no intellects in existence except human intellects. Then possible worlds and their values would not be known until human beings, or at least complex conscious animals capable of intellectual thought, come into existence. At that point, and only at that point, some possible future states could be understood to be objectively good, could be causally brought to be in the actual world for the sake of their goodness, and could be enjoyed as actually good.

It is true, however, that this scenario does introduce the possibility that there could be intellects other than human that exercise moral causality in the world. It would seem to become intelligible that there could exist one Intellect that eternally (timelessly) conceives and understands the whole world of Platonic Forms, and that sees in it a reason for making actual some specific cosmos, even this specific cosmos, for the sake of its distinctive goodness. Platonism can lead (and, historically, it has led) to belief in God, as conceiver of all possible worlds and creator of one or more of them.

Both Moore and Murdoch see this possibility and discard it. They see no evidence of purpose in the cosmos, and they see too much evil and suffering in the cosmos for it to have been brought about for the sake of good. For Murdoch, the Good remains precisely an object of attention, a conceptual and asymptotic idea, which has no direct causal impact upon the world, except insofar as it affects human minds that are attracted by it. If the idea of God is in some way internally incoherent (perhaps because we can only think of minds as embodied in a physical world), or if the cosmos is too random and non-purposive, and too filled with suffering and evil to be consistent with being created by a God, then that idea will be of no help to moral realism. There are strong and well-known arguments against the existence of God. I will assume, however, that they are not strong enough to be overwhelming, and that there is a coherent concept of God that is consistent with the nature of the cosmos as we observe it.

I have already argued that the modern scientific view of an evolutionary universe is consistent with an idea of divine purpose. Writers such as

Simon Conway Morris, Paul Davies, John Polkinghorne, Francis Collins, and Arthur Peacocke are all leading scientists who find in the whole process of cosmic evolution a directionality towards consciousness and intelligent life. It is not, to say the least, an established conclusion of science that there could be no purpose in the cosmos.

Though the problem of suffering and evil is notoriously severe, I do not think it can be shown that the existence of suffering is inconsistent with all ideas of God. For instance, a Platonic God, surveying all possible worlds, might see that there was a possible world in which beings of overwhelming value could come into existence, able to enjoy endless and intense happiness and fulfilment. That world, because of the general laws governing its existence, might necessarily contain much beauty and happiness, but might also necessarily contain much suffering and the possibility of much moral evil. Perhaps there is some necessity in God by which some such world has to be actualized. In any case, God could be justified in actualizing such a world, perhaps on the condition that all suffering beings would subsequently be able to enter into endless happiness. It could be argued that this is such a world, in which every suffering being would assent to existence, when they saw the nature and extent of endless happiness, the necessity of the general laws of nature, and the impossibility of their existing, as the precise individuals they are, in any other possible world.

Of course, there is much work to be done if we were to show why God may necessarily create such a world (a world of free and partly self-shaping intelligent beings who had to learn love through struggle and discipline), why the laws of nature must be as they are (perhaps the laws of nature must be precisely as they are to enable the human species to emerge), and how suffering beings can live after their bodily deaths (in new forms of embodiment, and in a different kind of cosmos?). Maybe it is beyond our capacities to show these things. But, even as thought-experiments, they show that there are possible ideas of God, a personal ground of being, which may not avoid the problem of evil, but which may not be defeated by it.

A MORALLY CONDITIONED GOD

There are many concepts of God, which have been worked out in some detail by various religious thinkers. I do not wish to consider the whole question of general philosophical arguments for God or for specific concepts of God here. My purpose is rather to ask what difference the existence of God would make to concepts of morality, or whether morality is autonomous in being unaffected by questions of God's existence. This may also, however, involve asking how specific concepts of God may be affected by independent considerations of the nature of morality. If my general account of morality is correct, we can already see some implications for a concept of God, which would suggest making some choices among differing concepts of God.

The first point I would make is that if God is the creator of the cosmos, the one who makes it actual, and if free choice exists, God cannot be the all-determining cause of everything that happens. There must be room for free creaturely actions. If humans are to be held responsible for their actions, able to choose either for the sake of objective goodness or for self-interested desire, then God cannot make those choices for them. The cosmos must be such that some futures are not fully determined, either by physics or by God.

This does indeed mean that such a God will not be fully in control of the cosmos. If things are indeterminate at the point of moral choice, then they cannot be fully determinate at all. Before rational choice comes to exist (a very long time after the origin of the cosmos), there will be elements of chance in the way things go, for that is what indeterminacy entails. When rational choice does come to exist, many things may happen of which God disapproves – presumably, all self-interested choices. So it cannot be said that everything happens in accordance with the will of God. Many things happen by chance, and some by flouting the will of God. That is the cosmos God has created. There is a sense of autonomy in which it means that humans decide their own future, at least morally speaking. They choose good or evil, and nothing outside them or in their formed psychological characters determines their choice. It is autonomous and they bear responsibility for it. Any concept of God that takes moral freedom seriously is, I think, committed to thinking that God's purpose can be frustrated by creaturely actions, and that God will not force the future to be as God wishes. Such a God creates a genuinely open universe, whose future is not wholly determined in advance, and which is not wholly under the determining control of God.

This entails that God does not, after all, just select a complete universe from the list of possible universes that exists in the divine mind. God will be continuously responsive to free creaturely actions, and God's specific purposes will adapt to such actions, perhaps positing a range of good possible futures for finite agents at each stage of free choice. This may appear to such agents as 'the will of God' for those occasions, but again they may well be free to accept or reject even such apprehension of God's will as they have. If this is so, there will be much change and contingency in God's setting of purposes in the history of the cosmos. All such contingency, however, must be constrained both by God's overall purposes in creation, and by the general moral constraints inherent in God's necessary nature. The nature of God will be dipolar, necessary in general respects (in being loving, just, and maximally knowing and powerful), yet contingent in the selection of a specific universe to create, and in particular divine responses to free creaturely actions. That may seem an unfamiliar idea, but in fact I believe that it has always been inherent in the traditional Christian view that God exists necessarily yet creates a contingent universe.

The second point follows from this. If God creates the universe for good reason, God must have a purpose in creating the universe, a final cause or goal at which God is aiming, for the sake of which the cosmos is created. But God's purpose does not compel human obedience to it. Indeed, God's purpose includes human moral freedom, so that humans may freely choose the Good or reject it. God's purpose may therefore be to some extent frustrated, though, if the purpose is that some should freely choose the Good, it is unlikely to be wholly frustrated.

It seems reasonable to think that God would not create a universe that would wholly fail to realize its intended purpose. So the cosmos must be such that God's purpose will in some way ultimately be realized. Presumably, this means that evil and suffering will be eliminated, and at least some free creatures will reach their intended moral fulfilment. How this is to be done is another matter. The crudest view is that there will be a Judgement Day when all evil will be destroyed, and a renewed cosmos when the just will live in Paradise. But this is a rather crude and preliminary view, and much more needs to be said. What does seem morally important is that God will somehow bring about the fulfilment of the divine purpose in creation, by something more like persuasion than by divine fiat. The moral purpose of the cosmos will not fail.

THE DIVINE-COMMAND THEORY

A third and related way in which this conception of morality is relevant to concepts of God is that God cannot be conceived as arbitrarily commanding adherence to certain rules, which we have to obey on pain of punishment. What is called 'divine command' theory is often stated in this way, even though it is a way that most philosophically minded believers in God have decisively rejected. Those who support a 'divine command' view in recent times state it in a more subtle way. Philip Quinn (1978), for example, has shown that versions of divine-command theory are compatible with moral autonomy, as long as one holds that God never commands anything evil. A person can conscientiously approve of whatever God commands, if God is necessarily good. It should be clear that the basic truths of morality are necessary – in the Platonic conceptual world, possible states necessarily possess the values they possess, and even God cannot change that fact. Indeed, God is to be conceived as the intellect that conceives of the set of all possible worlds, and that set, being exhaustive of possibility, is necessarily what it is. Just as God cannot change the laws of mathematics, so God cannot change the laws of morality, though God necessarily knows what they are.

Plato's Euthyphro dilemma – in its modern form, it is put as the question: does God command something because it is good, or is a thing good because God commands it? – is not a dilemma at all. Plato clearly argued that God commands things because they are good. That is, moral values are necessarily what they are. There should be no objection to this, from a theistic point of view. The proposed objection is that God would be unnecessary to moral goodness, and we could know what is good without reference to God. But it is just true that we can know what is good without referring to God. That does not mean that God is unnecessary to moral goodness. For it may be that possible worlds, with all their values, only have existence within the mind of God. It is not necessary that people should realize this, but it may be true, and necessarily true, all the same.

It may also be true, as I will argue later, that God instantiates in the divine being a great number of actual values, including the personal virtues of creativity, sensitivity, understanding, and love. Unless God knows, is conscious of, and appreciates values, they will only exist as possibilities, not as actualities. God is needed if value is going to be actual, as opposed to being necessarily possible. That, of course, is a very important function that God possesses – that of actualizing values in the divine being, and making some created values actual.

Robert Adams (1999) has defended a revised form of divine-command theory. He does not mean that a divine command makes morality what it is, and he thinks that God is necessarily, not contingently, good. So, he avoids some of the usual objections to divine-command theory – that

God's will is morally arbitrary, and that morality must be subject to divine whims. He argues that it is the commands of a *loving* God that are to be obeyed. The notion of a loving God builds necessary moral values into the concept of God. God is necessarily loving, and does not just decide to be loving, when God could have decided to be tyrannical or repressive.

There are necessary moral values in God. As I have put it, all moral facts (all values as possibilities) exist in the mind of God, and they are necessarily what they are. In addition, God actualizes in Godself all com-possible virtues in a supereminent sense. Why, then, appeal to divine commands at all? A main reason is because God selects which possible values to actualize by creating a universe. This is an active choice, and so adds something to a purely Platonic (non-creating) conception of the Good. Nevertheless, God can only select what is good, though that may leave many possible choices open.

A sense of moral obligation arises when free creatures are faced with a choice of good or evil. It is plausible to say that obligations such as 'do not lie' arise when agents are confronted with the possibility of lying or telling the truth, and the moral fact that knowledge is intrinsically good, which implies that deceit is intrinsically bad, gives good reason for not lying. In other words, obligation arises from the existence of objective goods, when those goods are perceived as relevant to the possible action of a free agent. This does not entail a consequentialist view that actions are only right if they promote the greatest amount of good. It simply asserts that 'moral rightness', whether conceived in absolutist or strongly *prima facie* terms, is logically dependent upon beliefs about intrinsically good states. Thus, the belief that it is categorically wrong to lie is logically dependent on, and only makes sense in the light of, the belief that knowledge is good.

Adams holds that obligations are identical to divine commands. It does seem that, if there are obligations that necessarily follow from necessary values in the divine being in specific situations, then God is bound to assent to them. Robert Audi (2011) has suggested that we might say they are necessarily commandable by God, even if God does not actually command them by some specific speech-act. But God will not merely assent. If God has purposes for human lives, and cares for the good of human beings, God will positively desire that they fulfil their obligations, and intend that they do so. Perhaps the word 'command' is not the happiest word to use here, because it suggests the order of a superior officer, whereas we are thinking of the desire of a being of supreme value. But the word is rooted in the tradition, and God does after all command that evil be avoided. So, we can say that 'X is obligatory' is identical to 'Y is a content of the divine mind that, when apprehended by a moral agent, entails X'. The divine mind entails obligations when apprehended by moral agents in specific circumstances. If so, it is important to stress that God's commanding does not *make* an act into a duty, whereas otherwise it would have had no moral import. God may make that duty relevant to me, but it derives from a value that is necessarily and eternally in God, and so will necessarily entail duties in specific situations. In addition, however, God will desire that we fulfil our obligation. That is, of course, an additional reason for doing so, since, if we love God, we will want to do what God desires.

Good states morally necessitate of themselves, and they need no extra divine command to become obligations. I cannot see that, as Mark Murphy claims, God must be introduced to explain 'the power of . . . properties to morally necessitate' (2011, p. 90). But Murphy is right to say that 'facts about God figure in an account of why some set of properties morally necessitate' (ibid., p. 60). That is not because God must contribute some undifferentiated necessitating 'power' that can be mysteriously channelled into a specific form. Rather, the relevant facts about God are that it is in the being of God that objective moral facts reside, and that God positively desires (commands) that we fulfil our obligations. Obligation then follows from both those facts, and, though only the former is available to atheists, theistic belief does add something important and overtly theistic to the experience of obligation, which is what Murphy wants.

It is not that we need a divine command before we can have a genuine obligation. If God is (necessarily) supereminently good, and if God (contingently) selects a specific world for existence, and sometimes selects specific futures for humans to realize, then that precisely these things are obligatory for us is due to an act of divine will, which probably could have been otherwise. In that sense, Adams is right; what is right for us is what God commands us to do; though God's commands are constrained by God's necessary goodness.

In addition, if I am a theist, my failure to meet an obligation will be the breaking of a personal relationship with a loving God. It will be a moral failure even if there is no God. But, if there is a God, there will exist an additional level of failure. God, as a being of supreme value and the creator of all for the sake of good, will add love and gratitude to sheer obligation. That is what we will fail to give. Such failure may be in itself, if and when we come to see it clearly, a form of punishment.

DIVINE PERFECTION

I have said that all values exist in the mind of God. Of course, God is *ex hypothesi* aware of all disvalues as well as of all values. That gives them a sort of reality, but it would be unacceptable to say that God 'enjoys' disvalues, or that all possible bad things have become actual in the mind of God. We need a distinction between those things that God merely conceives and those things that God makes actual, in the sense of having independent and more than conceptual existence. We can say that God's conceiving of all possibilities is in a way detached, in the way that our conceiving of, or imagining, some terrible catastrophe, even in full detail, can be entertaining rather than horrifying. After all, we are only thinking about the catastrophe. It is not actually happening, and nobody is actually being hurt.

God's making values actual is not just God conceiving them. It is God giving them real existence, as opposed to existence as possibilities. One major reason for creating a universe is in order to make values actual, and therefore enjoyable to any intellects that become aware of them, including the divine intellect.

In this conceptual scheme, there are (necessarily) some things actual already, before God makes them actual. The main such thing is the being of God itself. The divine intellect cannot bring itself into being, for it would already have to exist in order to do that. We have to say that there is an intellect that knows all possibilities, and that is able to actualize many (we may not know exactly which and how many) possibilities, and that is not capable of being brought into being by anything else. God must be an eternal being with the greatest possible knowledge and power (we may not be sure exactly what that 'greatest possible' is), who always and only acts for the sake of goodness. If God is an Intellect, this is a unique and uncreated Intellect (for the religious, 'uncreated wisdom' might be a better expression).

I have sketched a tripartite Platonic world whose three coexisting elements are: an eternal and necessary world of possibilities ('Forms' or essential natures), an eternal intellect, and a physical cosmos. In Plato, these are all present, but remain rather disconnected, or at least not connected in any coherent way. That is not surprising, since Plato wrote Dialogues expressing many different points of view, and did not present just one systematic 'Platonic' doctrine. It was Augustine who formulated an elegant integration between these elements by placing the world of Forms in the mind of the primordial intellect, and making the physical cosmos a 'moving image of eternity', a world selected by intellect out of the world of Forms for the sake of making many sorts of goodness actual.

If God necessarily acts for the sake of goodness, it follows that any cosmos God creates will exist for the sake of the types and degrees of goodness it actualizes. If there are sentient beings in such a universe, God will necessarily intend their well-being, and intend that they should fulfil their purpose in being created. The being of God itself manifests a high degree of compossible values, because God is rational, and all rational beings will, other things being equal, aim at what brings self-fulfilment, at what is good for them. If and when God creates other things, the highest form of fulfilment for these beings will be attained by a form of mutually reinforcing relationship that may be called 'loving communion'. Such fulfilment may also obtain between finite creatures and God, and in that way God's perfection may express itself, not only, as Aristotle thought, in contemplation of perfection, but in self-giving love. No form of evil or suffering by others could be directly chosen for its own sake by God, because God will have perfect and intense knowledge of all finite experiences exactly as they are, and because personal relationships of mutual regard create one of the most intense worthwhile states. God will necessarily be, as Adams says, 'loving'.

In general, God will instantiate in the divine being the highest set of values that could possibly exist, not only being the source of every good thing, but also including in the divine being every actualized and enjoyed form of goodness. For God not only knows all possibles. God also knows, in the fullest, richest, and most intimate and intense way, every actual form of good that ever exists. So, if we could know the mind of God, we would know every form of actualized goodness, in a complete, integrated way, purified of all imperfection and evil. God is a condition of all other goods existing, the divine existence is necessary to the overall goodness of the cosmos, and God experiences in the divine being every actual good. It is appropriate, therefore, that we should revere the perfection of God and be thankful that such a being exists. That adds another dimension to a morality of obedience to divine commands. For these commands will be the necessarily good and wise commands of a God who deserves unreserved reverence and gratitude. We will obey, not out of fear, but out of grateful love. That is to say, we will do what is right, not only because it is right, but because it is set before us by a being whom we revere and love.

A CONCEPT OF GOD

G.E. Moore held that beauty and love are intrinsic values, and (though Moore did not hold this) as such they must exist in any God who incorporates the highest possible values. If these were just hypothetical values (stating that *if* beauty was ever contemplated and loved, *then* that would be good), nothing much might follow. But suppose there is a supreme *actual* beauty that is known and loved for itself, then it would follow that there is a mind (or mind-like reality) that knows and loves it. And, if love (personal affection) is an intrinsic good, this mind would desire to express love in personal relationship, and so to share its love of beauty and perhaps the creation of new forms of beauty and forms of appreciation by and with other personal beings. That is one reason one might have for thinking that some form of creation is necessary for a loving God.

I am supposing, as Moore does, that beauty and love are intrinsic goods. I am going beyond him in suggesting that, if they find supreme realization in an eternal and necessary mind, this will resolve some of Moore's problems about the status of moral truths and 'non-existent' properties, and it will make an enormous difference both to what humans see to be good, and to the authority that they take moral truths to have for them.

Moore denies this when he says that 'no truth about what is real can have any logical bearing upon the answer to the question ["what is good?"]' (1951, p. 118). But he also says that 'love of God' is good if there is a God, but it is 'misdirected affection' if there is not (ibid., p. 194), and that 'we should hesitate to encourage the love of God, in the absence of any proof that he exists' (ibid., p. 196). That entails that the truth about the existence of God has a logical bearing upon whether 'love of God' is good. And the difficulty about this is that it is not easy to know the truth about God, so it may be that the answers to some moral questions depend upon facts that are not conclusively verifiable.

The situation seems to be that we can – in general and in the abstract – see that beauty and love would be very great goods. If we now suppose that there exists a supremely beautiful and loving (and eternal and necessary) mind, we will naturally and justifiably love it for its own sake, not for the sake of any rewards or punishments it may intend for us in some afterlife. Its reality, if rightly perceived, will evoke in us both desire and freely given obedience, and impel us to make its purposes our own and to share insofar as we can in its perfections. Moral truths will exist objectively in this supreme mind, and they will have authority because I will see them to be good and worthy of loving and obedient response.

Morality will have an objectivity and authority that is firmly rooted in reality. Clearly, the truth (if it is a truth) that God exists has a bearing on the question of whether the love of God is good. And a Moorean insistence upon the objectivity and authority of ethics will be a major factor helping to determine the mind to assent to the existence of such a God (of an Ideal, eternally and necessarily existing, of Supreme Beauty and Love). This conclusion would surprise and possibly distress Moore, I have little doubt. But it would ease his metaphysical puzzles by a proposal that makes the Ideal of Beauty not a hypothetical and probably unrealizable dream, but an actual and rational metaphysical basis for an objective morality.

A theist will therefore see moral rules as set before us by God. But they are not just rules that we have to obey, without reference to considerations of human well-being. They are means to fulfilling the purpose our lives have – more than that, they are part of what our fulfilment truly is. There is a theistic answer to the question 'Why should I do what is right?' The answer is, of course, primarily because it is right. But, in addition, it is because that rectitude is part of our cosmically intended fulfilment. And, for a theist, that fulfilment is guaranteed. It is not guaranteed as a sort of long-term prudence, as though we could aim at fulfilment just for ourselves, independently of being concerned about objective goodness. Our aim must be coincident with the divine aim, a distinctively moral form of fulfilment, one that is possible for all who do not consciously and wilfully reject it.

These two factors, the love of what is supremely worthwhile and the attainment of personal fulfilment, not just for us but for all who accept the offer of it, are bound together. That is because human fulfilment is to be found in God, in union with the life of God, and in leaving the ego-bound self behind.

This is one way of working out a metaphysical worldview that makes a coherent place for objective and irreducible moral values. It connects moral values closely with the mental understanding and appreciation of them, with libertarian conceptions of human free moral choice, and with ideals of human flourishing or fulfilment. All these things are topics of controversy. This is a view of morality that I hold to be reasonable and plausible, but that I do not expect to be universally convincing (though I am quite sorry about that). I also think that it is reasonable to seek a metaphysical context for this view of morality, one that seems consistent and coherent, and that fits both our scientific knowledge of the cosmos and our most general ontological intuitions.

To do this is to reverse the naturalistic or Ionian enchantment completely, and examine, if only as a thought-experiment, the non-naturalistic or Platonic enchantment. I have presented a form of Platonic theism, for which moral values exist irreducibly in a conceptual realm conceived by the primordial intelligence of God, who creates the cosmos in order to actualize many diverse and distinctive forms of goodness. Of course, there are many possible objections to such a conception. Some people simply hate Platonism, some think it a vacuous myth, and some find the cosmos too full of randomness, suffering, and evil to be a consciously intended image of a supremely good eternity. So this is no proof. There is, however, a distinctive conception of morality. If one believes in God, one may be led to such a distinctive view. Conversely, if one has that view of morality, one may be led towards belief in God, or, if one already believes in God, to an idea of God that is distinctive in some respects. Either way, morality will not be autonomous in the sense of being wholly self-contained and self-explanatory without reference to background metaphysical beliefs, some of which will be sympathetic to some forms of religious belief.

Part II

AN OUTLINE OF A THEISTIC MORALITY

8

MORAL COMMITMENT AND MORAL PURPOSE

KANT'S NOTION OF CREATIVE RATIONAL WILL

I have argued that a theistic morality will see moral principles as ultimately aiming at the fulfilment of an objective and universal purpose for human lives. Those who do not believe in God will probably deny that there is such a purpose. Those, like Iris Murdoch, who believe in an objective and transcendent Good, may feel similarly sceptical about purpose in the cosmos or in human existence. And those who accept a strong view of the autonomy of moral discourse – namely, that ethical beliefs do not depend upon broader metaphysical beliefs – would hold that moral commitment has no relevance to beliefs about whether or not there is an achievable purpose in human life.

There is one major philosopher who has argued that moral commitment of itself provides a strong reason for believing that there is an objective moral purpose in the cosmos, and that such commitment would be in danger of collapsing if it could be shown that there is no such purpose. That philosopher is Immanuel Kant.

This is odd, since Kant virtually originated the idea of the autonomy of morality. He argued that moral assertions do not and cannot depend upon divine commands or revelation. He is thought to have argued that moral action cannot depend upon any appeal to consequences (and purposes are surely consequences). He is often said to have refuted all possible arguments for God. So how could he have produced what many people call a 'moral argument for God', which is widely regarded as almost laughably inept, and in obvious conflict with almost everything else he said? What I aim to show in this chapter is that Kant is successful in arguing that the acceptance of categorical imperatives in morality does entail a hope for the fulfilment of a moral purpose, and that something very like God is needed to provide a firm foundation for such hope. Moral commitment does imply hope for the triumph of the good. And that is a good reason for postulating the existence of a God who alone can match commitment and hope in one intelligible framework.

One of the most important sentences in Kant's *Critique of Pure Reason* is this: 'I have found it necessary to deny knowledge in order to make room for faith' (Kant, 1781, Preface to Second Edition, p. xxx; Kemp Smith, 1952, p. 22). The basic principle of the Critique is to deprive theoretical reason of any insight into the nature of things-in-themselves, either positive or negative, and to confine reason, in its theoretical use, to the world as it appears in human experience. Nevertheless, there is a world of things-in-themselves. Reason belongs to it, and exercises a legislative authority over the phenomenal world, issuing laws of thought that actually help to constitute the world as we know it. Kant is a transcendental or, as he later calls it, a 'critical' Idealist – the world we know is partly mind-constructed, and of reality as it is in itself we know nothing, theoretically speaking. But we do know something about reality, though not in a testable, experienceable, experimentally confirmable, scientific way. We know that we must think of it as consisting of many rational minds helping to construct the phenomenal world, existing in a non-material and wholly intelligible (rational) way. This non-scientific necessity of thought is what Kant calls 'faith', the rational but not verifiable postulates we must make to render our scientific knowledge possible.

His view of morality must be seen in this context. As well as legislating the basic categories of scientific thought, reason legislates the supreme formal principle of morals, the categorical imperative. This does not directly tell us the content of what we should do, but it lays down what R.M. Hare called the principle of 'universalisability' as a condition to which all specific moral rules should conform. From this, Kant thinks we can infer all our actual moral rules. The moral 'ought' must be thought of as legislated by supra-empirical reason, expressing moral authority over the phenomenal world of desires and aims, and presupposing that we must think of human agents as free to determine their acts by reason, and as not wholly determined by physical causes or desires.

This is familiar doctrine to philosophers, but I have wanted to emphasize the rationalist and idealist nature of Kant's view of morality. He really is committed to seeing moral obligation as rooted in a supra-empirical, not scientifically accessible, reality, which we must think of as a community of rational agents (a 'kingdom of ends') underlying and expressed in the world of human experience.

There is another aspect of Kant's thought that sometimes goes unnoticed. Kant describes reason as 'the power of setting purposes as such' (1797, Introduction to the *Doctrine of Virtue*, p. ix; Gregor, p. 56). 'The power to set an end . . . is the characteristic of humanity' (Kant, 1797, *Doctrine of Virtue*, p. viii; Gregor, p. 51), he says. It is sometimes said that Kant advocates doing your duty, whatever the consequences, or without regard to what you desire or aim at. That is not quite right. For him, reason is not some sort of bloodless and passionless calculating operation. Reason sets goals of human action, and to do so it has to take human desires and interests into account. Reason decrees that we should become capable of 'the fullest realization of all possible purposes of which we are capable'. Reason is a creative power that sets positive goals for human action, and the only limits it sets on these is that we should 'act according to a maxim of ends which it can be a universal law for all to have' (Kant, 1797, *Doctrine of Virtue*, p. ix; Gregor, p. 55).

For many people, reason is not a transcendent power that is worthy of reverence and awe. It is either an accidental by-product of evolution, or an instrumental slave of basic human passions and sentiments (à *la* Hume), or (on a common but misplaced interpretation of Kant) a rather austere and abstract calculating faculty that omits any consideration of feeling and imagination and creativity. This is not what Kant means by reason. It is truer to Kant's own conception of reason to think of it as creative rational will, as a creative and dynamic generator of all possible good purposes, as a consciousness that expresses its inherent capacities of wisdom, feeling, imagination, love, and sympathy to the fullest degree, and that fully and sensitively appreciates all the positive values that it creates.

It is not merely the fact that I can legislate universal laws that gives me dignity and value. It is the fact that I can freely create and appreciate many possible worthwhile states (ends), develop my own value-creating capacities through struggle and self-discipline, and do so in co-operation with others as a member of a community of creative rational wills who shape their own futures as sources of consciously apprehended states that are of value in themselves. On this interpretation of Kant, the basic conception of human nature is that humans are creative rational wills in a universal community of similar agents. As such, they are not just parts of a deterministic and materialist system of nature. It is personal agency, creating for the sake of good, that gives value and purpose a place in the world.

Kant holds that humans are essentially rational beings – that is their noumenal nature – who appear in the world of sensibility and appearance as desiring and emotional beings. So, in conforming to reason, humans are realizing their 'true' natures, and subordinating the world of sensibility to the rational nature that is that world's true, yet hidden, reality. This is what is of great, even unqualified and unconditional, intrinsic value – that a person can escape determination by the world of appearance, and manifest the reality of his true rational nature in the world of sense. Creative rational action – the 'good will' – is of supreme intrinsic value, and is worth having just for its own sake. So, it will be wrong ever to fail to respect one who has a capacity for such action.

To respect persons as ends-in-themselves is not just to respect the freedom of people to do what they want, to choose freely whether to be good or bad. It is to respect the intrinsic value of creative rational action, which aims at many different purposes by free choice, a choice limited only by its compatibility with respecting the similar value of all other personal, rational, agents.

This is not far from saying that all intrinsically good states are states of mind, or of the exercise of the distinctive capacities of mind. The reason persons are to be respected is that they are the sources of creative action, sensitive understanding, and compassionate co-operation, all of which are intrinsic goods. Persons are the loci of intrinsically good states, and in this sense they are ends-in-themselves, instantiating goods that are worth pursuing for their own sake. Importantly, all persons equally are such loci, and so each person limits the freedom of all others, being an 'end', which must not be treated merely as a means to some individual's good.

Kant cites the generally obligatory ends as the fullest realization of one's own powers and the happiness of others. Clearly, we need to know what our own powers are and what makes others happy in order to pursue these goals. We also need to know what is possible for us, and what the means of obtaining happiness are. In that sense, even to deploy the categorical imperative, Kant has to think about desires and consequences. He wants to make desires and purposes conform to moral conditions, rather than making moral action depend on the existence of desires. But he does not want to impose some abstract formal rules on people regardless of their consequences, or their relation to deep and natural human desires and capacities.

THE MORAL PURPOSE: HAPPINESS IN ACCORDANCE
WITH VIRTUE

There is, nevertheless, and Kant sees that there is, a major problem with this view of morality as presupposing the existence of a noumenal world comprising a kingdom or union of free rational agents, who will the flourishing of all possible purposes that are universally agreeable between them. The problem is that the phenomenal world does not seem consilient with this view. Kant says that a moral agent 'must judge that he *can* do what the law commands unconditionally that he *ought* to do' (Kant, 1797, *Doctrine of Virtue*, p. i; Gregor, p. 37). But there seems to be a radical predisposition to evil in human nature, which makes it impossible for us to be wholly good. Kant says as much in *Religion within the Limits of Reason Alone*, a late work that is often neglected, but is very significant for his view of morality. This creates what John Hare (1996), in his perceptive book on Kantian ethics, has called a 'moral gap' between the categorical demands of morality and the inability of humans to meet them.

Furthermore, morality is essentially concerned with the happiness of sentient beings, and reason recognizes that happiness is a necessary part of any universal goal of human actions, and in the case of the happiness of others it becomes a morally obligatory one. Reason also requires, on reflection, that such happiness should not be indiscriminately distributed, but that it should be proportioned to virtue, to the pursuit of self-perfection and benevolence. Yet, even if we are morally perfect, it does not seem that these goals can be attained in human life. Chance, misfortune, the evil actions of others, and death ensure that the evil often flourish and the good find only suffering for their pains.

That is, of course, only to say that the world is unjust, which we all know. The problem this raises for Kant is that, for him, moral action expresses what the world in itself is really like. The phenomenal world should be an appearance of that reality. 'The world of understanding contains the foundation of the world of sense, and consequently of its laws also' (Kant, 1785, Third Section, 'How is a Categorical Imperative Possible?'; Abbott, p. 88). Yet appearance seems to be in conflict with reality. One ready solution would be simply to drop all talk about noumenal and phenomenal worlds, and write a demythologized Kantian ethics, where we are just told to act impartially, whether or not we have any metaphysical beliefs. This is arguably what R.M. Hare did with his universally prescriptive view of morality. But it does not represent Kant's own thought, and it does raise a severe question about why anyone should act impartially in a world that may be full of self-interested and intensely competitive human animals.

For Kant, moral commitment requires an assertion of full autonomy or freedom of the will. That is already a metaphysical commitment. He holds that such freedom cannot be established empirically. It must be a presupposition of taking moral responsibility and affirming the moral dignity of human persons. Thus, he believes that moral action does presuppose metaphysical truths, and that such truths can be reasonably accepted because they are necessary conditions of the possibility of morality, and not because they can be theoretically shown to be true.

Kant seeks to close the moral gap with his so-called 'moral argument for God and immortality'. When that is discussed, it is often presented in something like the following way: Kant begins by saying that we must do duty for its own sake, without considering the consequences – he is not any sort of consequentialist. But then he contradicts himself by saying that we must aim at a state in which happiness is proportioned to virtue, the *summum bonum*. This state does not exist for most people in this life; therefore, there must be an afterlife and a God who can ensure that 'happiness in accordance with virtue' will exist.

When the argument is put like this, it seems a rather lame form of wishful thinking, unworthy of a major philosopher. If duty is for its own sake, we should not be considering future happiness – that would be a form of self-interest, after all. The oddity of the argument is that it seems to undermine everything that Kant has said at such length and with such strenuous effort. We might wish there was a God who could reward good works. But to make that any sort of condition for moral action would be to revert to the worst sort of heteronomy – making moral obligation depend upon the happiness it will ultimately bring.

That form of the argument cannot be right. And it is not. Earlier in his life, in the *Lectures on Ethics*, Kant had discussed what he called Stoic and Epicurean moralities. Stoics, he said, insist on doing one's duty without regard to the consequences. Epicureans make morality subordinate to the desire for happiness. He rejects both views. Human persons are rational agents. As he was to put it in his later Critical philosophy, 'It is only in that [intelligible] world, as an intelligence, that he is his proper self (being as man only the appearance of himself)' (Kant, 1785, Third Section, 'On the Extreme Limits of all Practical Philosophy'; Abbott, p. 94). Yet humans are also sentient beings, existing in the world of appearances, desires, and inclinations. The laws of morality are laws for any rational beings whatsoever. But, when they are applied to humans, they must take into account the general nature of what it is to be human, to be a member of both intelligible and phenomenal worlds.

In the phenomenal world, reason legislates necessary goals of action, and one of them is happiness. Kant says that he does not, like the Epicureans, make moral rules depend upon some independent conception of happiness (which might vary from person to person, and is almost impossible to establish with certainty). But neither does he, like the Stoics, think that happiness is unimportant to phenomenal human beings.

What has often been overlooked is that Kant does believe that morality necessarily aims at happiness. It is in the quality of happiness, and the conditions of its existence, that Kant differs from both the Stoics and the Epicureans. He does not think that a man can be happy on the rack. What he thinks is that there is a specific sort of happiness at which moral principles aim. That is 'happiness in accordance with virtue'. It is not that you aim only at virtue, and then hope that happiness will follow as a reward. You aim at happiness in a sense, but only at the sort of happiness that accompanies virtue.

It may be helpful to recall Aristotle's definition of 'happiness' (*eudaimonia*, now more often translated as 'fulfilment' or 'well-being') as unimpeded activity in accordance with virtue. If we think of intellectual virtue as the capacity of humans to realize as many personal powers as possible, and of moral virtue as the disposition to universal benevolence, then happiness is not just a contingent consequence of the exercise of such virtues. Rather, the exercise of those excellences is what happiness – true happiness – consists in. That, I think, catches the sense of what Kant is saying.

It is in this sense that Kant does take consequences into account. He looks to specific good states – especially the existence of a 'good, morally directed, will', a fully developed intellectual life, and a happy life – as morally obligatory ends of action. The point is, however, that he does not first of all think of those states, and then devise moral rules as means to achieve them. It is the one basic moral principle, the categorical imperative, that necessarily legislates these general ends of human action. It legislates that we are obliged to seek intellectual virtue and happiness as ends, because these are ends that must be adopted by any rational being that is a member of both the 'kingdom of ends' and a phenomenal world of potentiality and desire.

As so often in Kant, the main point turns on a very fine but vital distinction – the distinction between adopting a moral maxim because it leads to an independently identified happiness and aiming at a sort of

happiness that is in accordance with virtue because the categorical imperative (the principle of universal co-legislation) enjoins it. It is the 'order of
moral incentives' that is important. The former view is, Kant says, the
essence of radical moral evil. The latter is definitive of moral goodness
(Kant, 1794, Book One, 'Concerning the Propensity to Evil in Human
Nature'; Greene, p. 25). Human actions have both a form – for morally
good actions, this is given by the categorical imperative – and an end or
aim – which, at its most general, is also given by the categorical imperative when it takes the phenomenal nature of humans into account.

The necessary end of moral acts is thus a sort of happiness that is in
accordance with virtue. Whatever is obligatory must be possible. So, in
committing ourselves to moral action, we commit ourselves to a belief
that happiness in accordance with virtue is possible. Now Kant asks, what
are the conditions of the possibility of this belief? They must be that
the world is such as to make the *summum bonum* possible. Human agents
may have the power to act autonomously, but they do not have the power
to ensure that the necessary ends of moral action can be realized in the
phenomenal world. Only a supreme Reason who orders the phenomenal
world in accordance with rational principles could have that power. So
far, it may have seemed that Kant affirms the existence of a community
of rational agents as the 'real' or noumenal basis of the phenomenal
world. But, since human beings are not the creators of the phenomenal
world, it is a requirement of Reason that there must be one supreme supra-
human Reason that can ensure that the ends of moral action are obtainable
in the world of appearances, precisely because it is itself the supreme
ground of appearances.

This has in fact usually been implicit in any Idealist philosophy. If
the intelligible world is a kingdom of ends, one 'King', one supreme
'End-in-itself' is required to establish the unity of the kingdom and the
nature of its phenomenal expression. Reality is not, after all, an unthink-
ing, unconscious, undirected material realm. It is the realm of reason,
which is not subject to sensibility, but orders sensibility to be what it is,
an appearance to finite agents of a purely intelligible reality.

God, conceived in this way as supreme Reason, has always been
implicit in Kant's notion of a noumenal world. His 'moral argument', that
reason legislates ends of action in the phenomenal world that must be
possible of realization, is just a spelling out of his critical idealism, which
the whole Critical philosophy seeks to establish. God is not some sort
of afterthought to Kant's system, brought in at the last moment to act
as an incentive to moral effort. God, in the sense of supreme Reason,

is fundamental to the idea of a kingdom of ends as the realm of things-in-themselves. God is the reality that makes autonomous action in the world possible, that enables reason to have practical effect. Therefore, God, and only God, can and will make the moral end, happiness in accordance with virtue, possible.

THE *SUMMUM BONUM*

John Hare has a very interesting take on Kant's 'moral argument', which is rather different from this, since it does not appeal directly to God, and it does not stress as much as I do the way in which the happiness aimed at in moral action is internally related to moral virtue, and is not just an added reward for virtue. I have suggested that Kant's crucial principle is that moral action must be seen as leading to (a special kind of) happiness, such that the happiness is constituted by a virtuous life, plus success in that life and satisfaction in living it. Kant would also hold, I think, that immoral action should be seen as leading to misery, again of a special sort – the sort of misery that results from the pursuit of egoism and hatred of others.

John Hare reduces Kant's principle to the claim that 'an agent's virtue [is] consistent with her happiness' (1996, p. 87), which is different from claiming that virtue leads to happiness in proportion to the amount of virtue. The morally committed person should, Hare says, believe that, even if there is no God, I will be happiest if I try to be moral, and that 'I do not have to do what is immoral to enjoy future happiness' (ibid., p. 92). The trouble with this reduced principle is that it seems to be false. Leaving aside life after death, a martyr cannot believe that virtue is consistent with future happiness. Moreover, I will only be happiest by being virtuous if I am the sort of person who finds happiness in virtue, which already implies that I am virtuous by nature. If we are all, as Kant says, radically evil, this is unlikely. It is more likely that I will find happiness in being immoral, even though that is not the sort of happiness a virtuous person – one who would be happy only on condition that they were, and knew themselves to be, virtuous – will prefer.

Hare argues that, if we add belief in a generally Christian God to these purely rational arguments, we would have a much stronger case. We could say, for instance, that 'living a morally good life requires . . . belief in extra-human assistance' (1996, p. 270), that the moral order of the world would be much more likely to be secured, that we could place reliance on personal experiences of divine help and moral empowerment, and that we could hope more justifiably for an eventual triumph of the good. In that sense, belief in God would add support and greater coherence to the beliefs we might obtain from pure reasoning. He is well aware, however, that Kant does not appeal to prior theoretical or revealed beliefs in God, which is why he reduces the Kantian argument to something less ambitious but also, it seems to me, less convincing.

What Kant wants is that 'virtue and happiness are thought of as necessarily combined, so that the one cannot be assumed by a practical reason without the other belonging to it' (Kant, 1788, Book 2, Chapter 2, 'The Antimony of Practical Reason'; Beck, p. 117). That is, I cannot aim at virtue, and then hope that some sort of happiness will be given to me as a reward, though it may not be. I must aim at virtue-and-(moral) happiness inseparably combined, which is the same as aiming at happiness-as-conditioned-by-virtue. It is such a goal which only God, or an ordainer of the order of the world, could ensure. The lesser ('less ambitious', Hare says) goal of thinking that happiness is compatible with virtuous action seems to be true only as a generalization about already virtuous people who are very lucky in their lives. It does not seem to be any sort of necessary moral goal of action.

It looks as though Kant's argument would not succeed without appeal to God. It also looks as though the *summum bonum* is not possible in this life, because of what Kant calls 'the foul taint of our race'. What Hare calls the 'more ambitious' claim that it is possible for everyone to be both virtuous and happy may be true. But it could only be true if somehow human radical evil could be overcome, and that does not seem to be possible by human effort alone, or in this life. Therefore, some form of hope for immortality is also implicit in our commitment to morality, when that commitment is seen as a commitment to the intelligible reality and authority of the noumenal realm and the kingdom of ends.

Kant's moral argument must be seen in the whole context of the Critical philosophy. Then it can be seen as expounding Kant's claim that theoretical, experimental, verifiable knowledge – the sort of knowledge the natural sciences give – is limited to the phenomenal world, and has no place when thinking of ultimate reality. It can neither prove nor disprove God, freedom, or immortality. Understanding constitutes the phenomenal world, and reason postulates an intelligible reality of things-in-themselves beyond it, as its ground. Though we have no theoretical (that is, scientific) knowledge of that world, and no theoretical access to it, reason compels us to think of it as a world of rational agents united in a community under the rule of reason itself. In moral action, we express the rule of reason in our own actions, and thereby we are justified in thinking of the intelligible world as one of active, practical reason. God is this Reason with the power to bring into being a phenomenal reality and make moral action effective in the world, if not wholly in this life, then in another transcendent and intelligible realm of being.

Kant's 'moral argument' is not that if you are good you deserve to be happy, so it is not worth being good unless there is a God who will make you happy when you are dead. That is the prudential argument for morality of which Kant is consistently contemptuous. In the *Groundwork*, he totally rejects any idea that we can derive our moral ideas from God or from some divine revelation, remarking that, on the contrary, we must form our idea of God in accordance with our independent moral judgements. He also rejects the idea that morality could be based on a prior belief in immortality, and on the fear of divine punishment or the hope of divine reward. 'Any system of morals erected on this foundation would be directly opposed to morality', he writes (Kant, 1785, Second Section, 'Classification of all Principles of Morality which can be founded on the Conception of Heteronomy'; Abbott, p. 74).

Nevertheless, Kant is quite clear that 'the moral law . . . defines for us a final end . . . and makes it obligatory upon us to strive towards its attainment. This end is the *summum bonum*' (Kant, 1790, para. 26; Meredith, p. 118). The moral agent 'must adopt the assumption [that the final end is possible] if he wishes to think in a manner consistent with morality' (Kant, 1790, para. 26; Meredith, p. 119). 'No man can possibly be righteous with having the hope . . . that righteousness must have its reward' (Kant, 1782, 'Reward and Punishment'; Infield, p. 54). So a moral agent cannot be moral *because* he thinks there is a God who will reward him. But if 'he resolves to remain faithful to the call of his inner moral vocation . . . he must assume the existence of a God' (Kant, 1790, para. 26; Meredith, p. 121).

The argument appears to be that one ought to be moral for its own sake. But if one thinks through the implications of giving morality that authority in one's life, one will see that it presupposes that one is a free rational member of a kingdom of ends, that this kingdom is one in which reason has authority and power over the whole phenomenal realm, and that the moral goal of a morally qualified happiness and personal fulfilment is therefore a possible goal for human beings, if only in a post-phenomenal or intelligible world. Morality does not need religion 'either to know what duty is or to impel the performance of duty' (Kant, 1794, Preface to 1st edition; Greene, p. 3). But morality leads inevitably to some form of religion, in the sense of a belief in the sovereignty of reason, the reality of the intelligible world, and the nature of the phenomenal world as a temporal appearance of intelligible reality. Morality is the capstone of the Critical philosophy.

A KANTIAN 'MORAL ARGUMENT'

What are we to make of Kant's widely maligned argument today? I suppose we must rein in his universalistic claims a little. Few people will accept wholesale Kant's programme of critical idealism, with its sharp disjunction of noumenal and phenomenal reality. Few will think the categorical imperative provides an answer to every moral question. And few will think that Kant's view of morality will be accepted by all rational beings – in fact, we know it will not. But I think his 'moral argument for God', rephrased as a claim that a specific sort of categorical morality requires metaphysical backing, and that moral commitment can provide reasons where purely theoretical considerations must remain agnostic, is compelling.

A categorical morality is one that presents some moral claims as providing an overwhelming reason for acting simply because the states at which such acts aim are objectively (whatever people think) worthwhile. Kant suggests that these are states of happiness in accordance with virtue. They are conscious states that manifest happiness in realizing to the fullest practicable extent the distinctive capacities of free rational agency – primarily states that manifest knowledge, wisdom, creative ability, and universal benevolence.

Human agents are under obligation to bring about such states. This presupposes that reality contains objective obligations to what Kant calls the *summum bonum* – happiness in accordance with virtue. Kant then argues that, if this is so, we must postulate that humans are autonomous, in being free from purely physical or divine determination, and free to aim at the basic moral goal, universal happiness in accordance with virtue. If we are free to aim at this goal, it must be possible to attain it. The objective moral ideal must be possible.

One thing we might do at this point, John Hare says, is to reduce the moral demands that we seem to encounter. We could say that our only

9

KANT, EVIL, AND REDEMPTION

KANT AND AUTONOMY

There is a major problem with believing both that moral demands are unavoidable and authoritative, and that it must be possible for moral agents to meet those demands. The problem is that it seems clear that hardly anyone manages consistently to do what is right. It is what John Hare calls the problem of the moral gap between duty and performance. This might be thought to be a problem for religion, but, in fact, it is the place where most major religions take root. One very general issue with which religions attempt to deal is that of finding some way of closing the gap between what humans ought to be and do, and what they actually are.

In Christian terms, it is the issue of the ubiquity of sin and the possibility of salvation from sin. Kant was well aware of the problem. He was not a Christian in any ordinary sense, even though John Hare does his best to suggest that he might have been. Hare, in *God and Morality* (2007), brings out very well the way in which Kant's views on religion and morality were suffused with Lutheran insights. But I tend to agree with Allen Wood that Kant was more of a Deist than a Christian. Kant refused ever to enter a Christian church, even when it was his duty to do so at the University of Konigsberg – rather ironic for the 'apostle of duty'. He regarded worship as servility, religious experience as 'the moral death of Reason', miracles as magic, and attempts to make faith depend upon historical claims about Jesus or anyone else as morally worthless.

Yet he did think there should be a 'moral church', a voluntary, universal, and enduring union of hearts, which would be the vanguard of a true ethical commonwealth. It would consist of people who recognize their duties as divine commands (Kant, 1794, Book Four, Part One; Greene, p. 142), and hope and strive for the coming of a perfectly moral society. He also regarded Christian concepts as symbols for the realities of the intelligible world, of which we can have no theoretical knowledge, but the existence of which moral commitment ('moral faith') compels us to affirm.

The Christian concepts are skewed by his insistence that we ourselves are self-legislating rational beings, not accepting the authority of any other being than ourselves. This leads inevitably to paradox. We cannot, he thinks, theoretically reconcile the belief in creation (dependence for existence on something other than ourselves) with belief in complete human autonomy and self-direction. This remains an ultimate mystery. Kant calls it the mystery of 'creation'.

Kant's suggestion that persons are free in the noumenal world, but determined in the phenomenal world, that they are purely rational in the former, but swayed by natural inclinations in the latter, verges on the incoherent. If human moral decisions are free, this must mean that some events in their lives are physically under-determined (I am assuming, as Kant does, the inadequacy of the sort of compatibilism that interprets freedom as doing what one wants). And, if reason and desire are often in conflict, this conflict must occur in the phenomenal world, so that the self who chooses between reason and desire does so on particular temporal occasions. Freedom will be the freedom to choose between reason and desire, not, as Kant holds, the freedom to act out of pure reason.

If there is a purely rational being, a 'holy will' as Kant calls it, it is not us. Why can we not then say that God is the holy will, which is not our will, but other than our wills? Our calling is to become like God, to share in the nature of God (of absolute Reason). This God does not give a set of arbitrary commands that we must obey, or make us do things we do not choose to do. This God is the impartial and purposive creator, who leaves us free to see what reason requires, and try to do it. If we say this, God becomes the only fully pure and rational will, who sets the standard for what morality requires. This would mean, of course, that humans are not wholly autonomous, in Kant's sense. They are morally free, but not the creators either of their own existence or of moral values.

We can then see God, as Pure Reason, aiming at universal fulfilment for created beings, generating finite persons who ought to be rational, but who subject themselves to desire, who struggle to meet the requirements of rational universality, to attain a distinctive sort of happiness that follows from moral endeavour. God, and only God, can make the attainment of this goal possible, and thus realize the purpose of creation through the struggles and development of a community of self-shaping wills, in relation to which, perhaps, the full nature of reason itself is expressed. Persons are autonomous in two senses: first, that they work out their moral principles for themselves by asking what impartial reason would require. Second, that they freely shape their own lives for good or evil in accordance with their moral choices. Yet they are not autonomous in the sense of being the authors of moral law. They are dependent on God for their existence, whose necessary and fully rational will objectively defines what is rational and right, and who will ensure that the way they choose to live will have appropriate consequences.

The moral law is rooted necessarily and eternally in the mind of God. Humans do not invent it, they discover it. They discover it by reasoning, by critical reflection on human nature and the conditions of its possible fulfilment in all human beings without exception. Insofar as humans reason correctly, they may discern what is in the mind of God. It seems right to say that there are true (and false) moral assertions. So reason does not just prescribe moral recommendations. Reason tries to work out what the ultimate moral truths are.

RADICAL EVIL

However, even a superficial examination of actual human existence shows that we do not manage to fulfil our moral obligations. There is a 'Fall' from moral perfection into a state in which we are ruled by passion and desire instead of by reason. This, Kant thinks, must be a supersensible decision that we have made, before or outside of our phenomenal and temporal existence. We are born in radical evil, and yet we are responsible for our actions. We cannot do what we ought, and yet the imperative of 'ought' remains categorical, and so it must be possible to do what we ought.

Kant seeks to resolve this difficulty by supposing that, as well as a supersensible fall into radical evil, there is also a supersensible 'conversion of the will', which is expressed in time as 'an endless progress to holiness', in which we must continually strive for goodness by our own efforts alone – 'man must proceed as though everything depended upon him' (Kant, 1794, Book Three, Division One, 'The Idea of a People of God can be realized only in the form of a Church'; Greene, p. 92).

Human life in time thus expresses a basic duality – the 'death of the old man', by which life is 'a sacrifice and an entrance upon a long train of life's ills', and the birth of a 'new man', by which we strive for holiness and liberation from the radical evil of our own wills. Kant seems here to be heavily influenced by the Lutheran doctrine (with which, of course, he was perfectly familiar) that humans are simultaneously sinners and redeemed, *simul justus et peccator*. But he allows no 'external God' to condemn in judgement and to redeem by divine action. Instead, he insists that it is our own proper, noumenal selves who fall into a world of natural ills, which are now seen as the punishments for our radical evil, and who are at the same time redeemed by our own efforts and cleared of guilt. Only this view of a double, but unitary, intelligible act of self-wrought fall and redemption 'makes hope possible in the situation of constant moral failure' (Kant, 1794, Book Two, Section One, 'Difficulties which oppose the reality of this Idea, and their Solution'; Greene, p. 71).

The mystery here is how a perfect reason can fall into radical evil, or be subjected to passion and desire. I think a reasonable reduction of this mystery can be found by distinguishing between the perfect Reason of God and the created wills of humans. God cannot fall into selfish desire, but humans evolve in a world in which selfish desire is a real possibility for them. Evolutionary theory gives a good account of how evolving humans would necessarily form dispositions to rape and kill (to reproduce and exterminate competitors), as well as form dispositions to limited altruism and benevolence. The evolutionary process had to take the general path it did, including randomizing elements and the occurrence of disease and death, because of the fundamental physical laws necessary to produce an emergent universe that could contain intelligent and morally free beings like humans. For humans contain a genetic inheritance that has been built up over generations of evolutionary adaptation, and is now an essential part of their constitution. That general path of adaptation permits choices between egoism and altruism to be made, when something like human consciousness evolves. It is plausible to think that humans could have gradually brought their passions under the control of their more rational and compassionate capacities. Regrettably, they consistently failed to do this, and so they increasingly fell under the sway of their more destructive tendencies. Even their highest moral and religious ideals were corrupted to some extent by this failure. Thus, all human lives became enmeshed in 'radical evil', which now makes it virtually impossible to meet the demands of morality.

Kant did not have this evolutionary account available. It is a much more helpful way of explaining how humans came to be involved in radical evil than an appeal to some non-temporal 'choice' made in a noumenal reality. Either way, however, there is a major problem in thinking both that moral fulfilment is obligatory and that it is impossible. Kant clearly doubts that there ever could be a moral commonwealth in this world. 'We can never hope that man's good will will lead mankind to decide to work with unanimity towards this goal', he says (Kant, 1794, Book Three, Introduction; Greene, p. 86). Failure seems inseparable from human existence. All he is able to propose is that 'endless progress' towards perfection might be possible, and could be seen, from a noumenal point of view, as the actual attainment of final perfection.

This hardly seems a satisfactory position. If there is a perfect God, and absolute moral obligation as a condition of attaining human fulfilment, and humans continually fail in their obligations, there must be some way of remedying that failure that does not just consist in seeing progress as though it was achievement. It is Kant's refusal to think of any external help to fulfilment that prevents him from seeing this. But it is not absurd to see the possibility, and the necessity, of external help to moral striving and human fulfilment. We know that we can be helped by the encouragement and example of other people. If there is a perfect loving God, then there may be some way in which that God could encourage and help us. And there may be some life beyond this in which conditions could be so different that we were not left wholly to our own resources, but could be so united to the divine presence and power that it would become possible to live a truly just life.

Many major religions can be seen as proposing ways in which this might be accomplished. The sense of a complete human fulfilment (in religious systems, it is often called 'salvation' or 'liberation'), in the face of widespread, perhaps universal, human failure to achieve it, may lead to a path of liberation that can be found in religious practice. And indeed religious ideas, for Kant, are necessarily generated by reflection on moral commitment. While morality does not depend on religion, it necessarily leads to religion. But this, for Kant, is a very 'thin' sense of religion – one not concerned at all with historical or experiential claims, or with the sacramental conveyance of grace by some ecclesiastical authority, but only with accounting for our sense of moral demand, guilt, forgiveness, and hope, by offering non-picturing models of the transcendent reality that morality requires, but that understanding cannot fully comprehend.

Morality, for Kant, attests to 'a feeling of the insufficiency of the contingent for realizing the moral destination of human existence'. But he is too wary of a God who is an external and tyrannical being, undermining morality by turning it into prudence and fear, to introduce God as a redeeming power. It may well be thought, however, that the only rational response to the fact that humans are faced with categorical demands that they are unable to fulfil would be to posit an external power that was able to renew human nature and enable it to become what it was originally meant to be. God can be seen both as the objective reality in which moral values and demands are located, and as the liberating power that alone can enable them to be fulfilled in human lives.

Immanuel Kant is often thought of as the Enlightenment philosopher who finally divorced morality completely from religion, and insisted on doing one's duty for its own sake, without any thought of the consequences or any appeal to God as the author of the moral law. In fact, however, he was keenly aware of the moral incapacity of human beings, and insisted on the necessity of grace for the attainment of human moral destiny, and on the necessity of belief in God as the ultimate metaphysical foundation of the moral law.

Kant stressed the absolute authority of the moral law and the necessity of some extra-moral way of remedying human moral imperfection. In doing so, he illuminated one distinctively religious element of ethical thinking, which is unlikely to be found in any purely secular view of morality. He also showed how ethics has an important relation to metaphysical thinking. A religious conception of morality – one, for instance, that thinks of moral demand, sin, and salvation as involved in any adequate perception of the moral life – could be undermined by a materialist metaphysics that refuses to accept personal agency as of absolute value, and refuses to accept that purposive action for the sake of good has any real causal input into the world in addition to the mechanical causes of changing brain-states. It could be strengthened by a metaphysics that makes personal consciousness and agency a primary reality with causal power, and that gives creative rational will a foundational place in the order of being.

THE LIMITS OF AUTONOMY

Kant's concern is that God should not be thought of as a dictatorial tyrant, arbitrarily saving or condemning whomsoever he will, and requiring unceasing worship to satisfy his egoistic demand for praise. Perhaps Kant found something like that notion in the Pietistic faith of his parents and in his early education, and he rejected it vehemently. Kant thinks of a

God who wills to act through creatures, though without depriving them of their freedom. God is the power of absolute reason, which is freely accepted and adopted by persons whose proper role it is to be the vehicles of Wisdom in the world. God will ensure that morality will attain its goals without favour or favouritism, and as a validation of a genuine moral striving for goodness for its own sake, not a reward for believing lots of improbable things on very weak historical evidence.

What in effect Kant is saying is that the concept of God must meet the highest moral standards we can think of. Some concepts of God fail to meet these standards, and must be amended or even discarded. Some of the obscurities and paradoxes of a Kantian account can also be eased if the notions of an unknowable noumenal reality, and of a radically autonomous human reason, are discarded. Then God can be seen as a being in whom all values are instantiated to a supreme degree, while humans are evolved animals with the freedom to choose between good and evil, but who remain under the authority of an objective good, rooted in the necessary being of God. Humans are free to obey morality or not, but not free to invent it.

A number of different meanings of the idea of autonomy have been deployed in these chapters. There is a broad general distinction between the autonomy of moral discourse and the personal autonomy of moral agents. With regard to moral discourse, morality may be called autonomous if it is conceptually self-contained, independent of and irreducible to any other forms of discourse. I am disposed to accept autonomy in that sense, but not in the stronger sense that moral beliefs do not depend on divine commands, laws of nature, or purely rational considerations. I have tried to show that there can be irreducibly moral concepts, which yet have a metaphysical backing in beliefs about human nature and God, which entails that some moral claims, and even a general understanding of the moral life, may depend importantly upon wider metaphysical or religious beliefs.

At the outset of this book, I mentioned the *Oxford Dictionary of Philosophy* statement that the autonomy of morality means that views of morality cannot depend upon the commands of God, facts about the processes of nature, or the alleged pronouncements of pure reason. It should now be apparent that this statement is true under one interpretation, and false under another. It is true that we can know moral truths without believing in God, without deriving them from scientific claims about evolutionary psychology, and without thinking that there is such a thing as 'pure reason'. But it is false that belief in God will make no difference either to the moral truths one believes or to the way in which one sees the moral life. It is false that our understanding of human beings as by-products of a long, unguided evolutionary process or as creatures of a loving God will make no difference to our view of morality. And it is false that a belief about what an impartial and benevolent reason would decree will be irrelevant to our beliefs about what is morally right and wrong.

With regard to the autonomy of personal agency, the primary meaning of autonomy is to assert that moral agents are self-determining. But this has a number of possible interpretations. In one sense, having autonomy is being able freely to choose between good and evil. This entails lack of determination by anyone or anything else, but it has no implications for how we come to know or decide what is good or evil.

Immanuel Kant's definition of autonomy is 'that property of the human will by which it is a law to itself' (Kant, 1785, Second Section, 'The Autonomy of the will as the supreme principle of morality'; Abbott, p. 71). John Hare rightly says that this does not mean that persons can propose any laws they like, and simply invent or make up moral rules (2007, pp. 145–56). Hare suggests that we think of autonomy as 'putting ourselves under the moral law', or 'endorsing' it. The law is necessarily what it is, and, when we 'give it to ourselves', that means we freely subject ourselves to it.

While this is true, I think there is a little more to it. If one follows my construal of reason legislating the moral law (and of the subject as legislating the ideas of reason, the categories of understanding, and even the forms of sensibility), then it is not the person as an isolated and phenomenal individual who does the legislating. It is reason that legislates the same principles in and through all individual persons. What the phenomenal person does is to allow reason to act through him or her. The moral law is being 'given' or legislated by reason, taking into account the empirical circumstances in which the law is to be applied.

This sounds, ironically, like heteronomy, like the law being given by another, by reason, and persons just submitting themselves to it. What makes it autonomous, truly self-legislation, is that persons, in their noumenal, real, essential nature, *are* reason. They are the phenomenal appearances, partial and imperfect, of noumenal reason in which they participate. Humans, as truly rational, rule over their sensual natures, and are not determined by the laws of those sensual natures.

If this is right, Kantian autonomy is not merely a personal endorsement of a necessary moral law. It is a submission of one's phenomenal nature to one's true nature as a rational agent in a community of such agents. We become vehicles of creative reason (which, as noumenal, can be said to be neither one nor many) in the phenomenal world. Thus, we become most truly ourselves in moral action.

There may not be 'moral facts' lying around somewhere, that we just intuit. Kant consistently rejects such an idea. But the basic moral fact that Kant postulates is the autonomy of the will – the fact that we are rational agents existing as fragmentary phenomenal expressions of creative reason, necessarily bound together in one self-manifesting whole.

That vision is probably opaque to most modern philosophers, which is why Kantian autonomy has to be translated by them into something different, perhaps a thinner concept of universal, but thoroughly phenomenal, moral legislation like those of John Rawls, R.M. Hare, or Christine Korsgaard in slightly different ways. Then one may doubt whether it can bear the weight required of it in the original view, of grounding a universal, perfectionist (fully self-realizing), categorical morality. And so the morality changes from Kant's unconditional commitment to something more relative, mutable, and hypothetical.

Kant's sense of autonomy may seem to be a submission to pure reason, but it is not a submission to what is actually the most reasonable course of action, given our empirical human situation and its probable consequences. It is a submission to a supreme impartial and universally benevolent reason, and to universal ideal goods that could only be realized in a perfectly morally ordered world of morally good agents. It is grounded on the irreducibly moral axiom that one ought to obey such reason. So it preserves a sense of the irreducible nature of morality. And, in identifying the true person with reason itself, it preserves a sense of autonomy or self-direction. Yet it is clearly not autonomous in being independent of all metaphysical or ontological claims. Indeed, the Kantian principle of autonomy is itself a grand metaphysical claim.

The Kantian idea of autonomy, in its full metaphysical dress, is not very common today. A more common sense of autonomy, especially in the world of education, is that someone is autonomous if they recognize for themselves what is morally good or right. The psychologists Piaget and Kohlberg, in their studies of the development of a sense of morality in young people, distinguished between acting out of fear of punishment or hope for reward, following unquestioned conventions, just obeying the laws of a particular society, and acting for the sake of good, or doing something just because it is right. Kohlberg calls the latter choice a fully autonomous choice. It involves recognizing what is right. Such recognition is, of course, compatible with deciding to do what is evil.

There are various ways in which this recognition may be thought to occur. There could be intuitions of goodness or rightness. There could be rational consideration of what makes for human happiness or fulfilment. There could be consideration of what could be commended by an impartial spectator (or by what R.M. Hare called an archangel). There could even be recognition that some divinely revealed moral rule was right, even though one had not thought of it previously. There could be some combination of these ways of recognizing goodness, or there could be as many ways as there are moral philosophies. But they all presume that there is a good to be recognized in some way.

A more radical sense of personal autonomy would be that each person invents for themselves a set of moral principles, principles that they would be prepared to recommend to everyone, perhaps. This sense naturally could not be accepted by anyone who thinks there are moral truths, whether located in the mind of God or not.

What makes these views similar is the thought that we cannot accept moral rules just because they are claimed to be revealed or issued on unthinkingly accepted authority.

I doubt whether autonomy is an unqualified good, in any of these senses. There are other principles that may be balanced against it. Kant recommends, in his essay 'What is Enlightenment?', that you 'think for yourself'. But if we are more sceptical about what principles people would actually invent, or if we are less certain that all humans would be able to work out what an impartial and omniscient spectator might decree, we might want to place some limits on this piece of advice. If everyone thought for themselves, starting from nowhere, and put their principles into action, the result might be moral chaos.

One may certainly encourage agents to reflect on their moral beliefs, and not accept moral rules unthinkingly. It may be true that many moral beliefs are not reasonable and do not take account of human desires and interests. It is important to insist that moral beliefs be justified by their power to reinforce human flourishing and happiness. The great legacy of the Enlightenment is not, as is sometimes said, a call to let reason rule in all things, or to insist on sufficient evidence for every belief. It is rather the call to informed critical enquiry, in morality as well as in science and philosophy.

It is not reasonable, however, to insist that everyone just makes up their moral beliefs *ab initio*, without paying regard to long-established traditions, born of long experience, or to social obligations that they might not make up themselves, but that function to hold society together. It is not reasonable to recommend that everyone tries to think out everything, from nuclear physics to basic moral principles, wholly by themselves. We all start from values and principles that we have been taught and that at first come naturally to us. What seem to us to be direct moral intuitions are mostly attitudes that we have been taught, or that we have picked up by osmosis from our families and social environments. Notoriously, conscience can err, and people sometimes have alarming moral intuitions if left to themselves. All of us need to take moral advice. We need to seek a wide knowledge of moral opinions and ways of life, and to begin with the wisest advice we can find.

A modified sense of autonomy as 'thinking for yourself' might take the form of insisting on a right to criticize when a serious claim exists that a culturally specific moral tradition is deficient in some way, perhaps with regard to human flourishing, and that a more expansive and fruitful form of flourishing is possible.

We should, then, think for ourselves; but we should also be sure to understand the reasons behind our moral traditions, and probably learn from others the reasons why they stand under challenge. I do not think it is true to say that we should just make up our moral beliefs for ourselves. If there are moral truths, we need to learn how to discern them, and some of us may be better at that than others. It may therefore be wise for many of us, perhaps for most of us, to be members of a moral community within which some moral truths are centrally established. What is needed is the freedom to challenge these truths when there seem to be good reasons to do so. That, I suppose, was implied in the Protestant Reformation, when certain beliefs or practices of the Church were put in question, and many people were compelled to make a choice between differing systems of belief.

The challenge, however, came from a few outstanding individuals, who managed to make a convincing claim for some sort of authority, based on allegedly superior knowledge of relevant data. Such challenges arise in particular historical circumstances, and they pose new living options when knowledge of them becomes widespread in a particular society. At such points, people need to examine the sort of justifications that are being offered for moral beliefs. But it is unrealistic to suppose that everyone will be able to make wise decisions about competing moral opinions. There needs to be a balance between accepting reputable authorities (who claim to have beliefs they are prepared to justify with reasoned argument) and thinking out moral issues for oneself. Perhaps one should accept the guidance of a moral tradition with which one feels, in general, comfortable, unless on some issue one comes to have a very strong sense that the tradition is inadequate in some way. In other words, freedom of conscience, freedom to dissent, is an important value (though it will have limits in any stable society), but an acceptance of a traditional authority that is prepared to offer reasons for its judgements is important too.

It may be that revelation based on the superior knowledge and experience of some wise and holy teacher will genuinely extend our accepted moral insights and redirect our rational reflections. But it may also be that traditional religiously based moral rules can act as a brake on moral progress. Both sensitive attentiveness and informed criticism are needed in religion and in morality. There is no precise algorithm for getting the balance exactly right. Practical wisdom is needed. But it seems to me that there is no necessary incompatibility between moral autonomy, in some of its major senses, and acceptance of revealed moral beliefs. Persons could endeavour to recognize for themselves what is good and right, and they could find that the good is disclosed to them by some specific communicative act of God, which deepens and extends their existing moral beliefs. Autonomy and revelation are after all not as opposed to one another as Kant thought they were.

10

THE RELIGION OF HUMANITY

There is a possible conceptual space for divine revelation within a moral view that gives full rein to autonomy. But any such alleged revelation – and, of course, claims that God has spoken do not establish that God actually has spoken – must be tested against the basic moral criterion of conduciveness to human flourishing and happiness. A religious revelation may deepen and extend our moral views, but it cannot ever be allowed to undermine or contradict them.

John Stuart Mill, like Kant, gives basic moral concepts epistemic priority over religious beliefs. In his essay 'Utilitarianism', he suggests that the Christian revelation was intended to enable people 'to find for themselves what is right, and incline them to do it', and that 'we need a doctrine of ethics . . . to interpret to us the will of God' (1861, ch. 2, p. 20). He accepts that religion may provide external motivations to moral conduct, in the thought of afterlife rewards and punishments, though, of course, he does not think that there will be such divine judgement.

Mill's thesis is very persuasive, that obligation is founded on 'the social feelings of mankind', and on 'the feeling of unity with all sentient beings', which, he says, should be 'taught as a religion' (ibid., ch. 3, p. 30).

This, he holds, is 'a natural basis of sentiment' (ibid., ch. 3, p. 29), and 'the ultimate sanction for the greatest happiness morality' (ibid., ch. 3, p. 31). But it needs to be inculcated by education and example, so that our feeling of unity with all things will come naturally and easily to outweigh our selfish interests. As society becomes more advanced, people will see that the interests of all must be consulted, that all should be regarded equally, that all should feel compassion with the injuries of others, and realize that actions are more effective as they are co-operative and collective, so that finally our aims are identified with those of others, and we desire to pursue the interests of all, and 'the service of humanity'. Every political improvement will remove oppositions of interest and level inequalities of legal privilege, and bring this desirable state nearer. It is, even now, 'in the comparatively early state of human advancement', an ideal that can possess any 'mind of well-developed feelings' (ibid., ch. 3, p. 31).

Having said that happiness is a matter of being satisfied with a life of many various pleasures mixed with a few transitory pains, and of cultivating intellectual capacities, he remarks that 'the present wretched education, and wretched social arrangements, are the only real hindrance to its being attainable by almost all' (ibid., ch. 2, p. 12). The happy person will have a life that balances tranquillity and excitement, that cultivates the social affections of fellow-feeling and the pleasures of intellectual understanding and appreciation in science, history, and art. Poverty and disease can be overcome, and one may hope that 'all the grand sources . . . of human suffering are . . . conquerable by human care and effort' (ibid., ch. 2, p. 14).

This is a happy, even inspiring, picture of human life, and it can motivate a commitment to social reform, so dear to Mill. But is it true that scientific progress and social reform will issue in this happy state? It is just at this point that most religious views present a much darker picture of human nature, and do not hold out much hope of the existence of an ideal society. We need to ask what would happen to Mill's view if there will be no progress to an ideal society, but only wars, famines, tyrannies, social collapse, and the destruction of the planet by the very technologies that were supposed to bring us progress. Would he then say about morality what he does say about self-sacrifice, that if it will not bring about greater fulfilment it is in vain? Can Mill's Utilitarianism found commitment to a morality for a broken and doomed world? I only raise this as a question, and it may be that he would still say it is better to work for small temporary improvements than to do nothing. I am sure that is true, but would his foundation of morality in the culture and relaxed social affections of a civilized society survive in a darker world of global anarchy, famine, and conflict?

Mill's 'religion of humanity' – partly deriving from Auguste Comte – does not stick to the facts as they are, to a relentless and steady examination of the absurdities, tragedies, and barbarities of human nature as they appear throughout our world. It constructs an idealized picture of human nature, with a goal that may well be impossible to realize, the goal of a society of equal, fully sympathetic, and highly cultivated agents freely co-operating in the service of the unity of all sentient beings. This goal is an ideal aim rather than a factual description. It is, in fact, almost exactly the ideal of that just and humane society that the Christian Gospels call the 'kingdom of God'. For it is the society of *Shalom*, of peaceable flourishing, which the God of Jewish and Christian faith is said to command and desire.

Mill's is a wholly admirable vision; he is one of the moral heroes of the English Enlightenment and of modern liberal thought. I fear, however, that his view of human nature is altogether too sanguine, that it does not take full account of the power of hatred, pride, and greed in human life, and a feeling that the goal he proposes is impossible may undermine the rigour of its internal binding force. In short, I feel that the binding force of morality should not depend upon a calculation of its beneficial social effects, or upon our feelings of unity with all humanity. Perhaps we are obligated to seek justice and benevolence even though the world collapses around us in ruins, and though our feeling of unity with others is mitigated by our awareness of the sheer human malevolence that stalks the world.

The religion of humanity has dangerously weak foundations, for humanity seems to be what Kant called 'crooked timber', and though we should respect and care for all, even our enemies, I cannot love them for what they are and rejoice that they are as they are. Even less can I revere society or humanity *en masse*, which seems to compound the worst human vices by enrolling them into one fearsome Leviathan (Leviathan, remember, is the terrifying sea-monster that is the enemy of harmony and security in the Bible).

Religious views, Jewish, Christian, and Muslim, are usually careful not to let this critical assessment of humanity be the last word. For the world is encompassed by the mercy and compassion of God, who forgives and remoulds human lives and touches the broken world with the healing power of divine love. That is why, for believers, love for God must precede love for humanity. It is God's love that wills the redemption and fulfilment of humanity, who makes it possible, and who draws out of each person the good that they are unable to realize by themselves. Thus, we are enabled to see people as God sees them, as souls to be made whole by the divine love, not as humans might see them, as the scavengers and destroyers of the earth.

If we are to love humanity, not for what it is, but for what it may or shall become, then I think that the only hope of this being true is that God will make possible what is impossible for human strength. We can indeed desire a sense of the unity of all sentient beings. But, if there is to be any hope of it, we must first desire a lively sense of the power, wisdom, and compassion of a supremely good God who can bring that unity into being. Even in religion, which in practice divides humans as much as it unites them, this is a difficult path, found by few. But, if that reality grasps us, it will never let us rest until we follow it.

What intrigues me about Mill is that the ultimate sanction of his morality is an ideal conception of human nature and human possibility. It is a sense and hope for the unity of all persons in a society marked by universal sympathy, intellectual creativity, and co-operative understanding. I feel the attraction of that ideal conception. It is precisely what, taken in conjunction with a realistic appreciation of human nature and society as we see it in the modern world, leads me to a more transcendental, less purely humanistic, religious vision of human nature. For me, it is when the ideal of the unity of all humankind is placed in the context of a transcendental reality that is able to bring that ideal to realization, despite the manifest failure of humanity to do so, that it can motivate the heart to respond to morality as categorically demanding.

GOD AND HUMAN WELL-BEING

Mill says, 'The essence of religion is the strong and earnest direction of the emotions and desires towards an ideal object, recognized as of the highest excellence, and as rightfully paramount over all selfish objects of desire' (1874, p. 109). This ideal, for him, is a future possibility, not an existing reality. He maintains that the 'religion of humanity' fulfils this condition better than any supernatural religion. For, he says, its devotion to goodness is purely disinterested, and is free of the contradictions of belief in an omnipotent and benevolent God who creates earthquakes to torment the living and Hell to increase these torments after death.

So far, this is what we may expect of a non-believer. But then Mill interestingly adds an unexpected twist, both here and more so in his essay on 'Theism' (in its fifth part, entitled 'General Result'), when he advocates a doctrine of a benevolent but non-omnipotent God, who struggles against a recalcitrant power of evil, and asks our co-operation in this struggle. Mill advocates this, in the sense of conceding it as a possibility founded on hope, though it has insufficient evidence to establish it securely. Yet, in a foreshadowing of William James, he writes that hope, if it does not contradict reason, may be a 'legitimate and philosophically defensible' ground for belief (1874, p. 249). Lack of positive evidence for religious beliefs of a high moral character 'is more than compensated by the greater truth and rectitude of the morality they sanction' (ibid., p. 255). So, in the end, he seems to think that belief in a supernatural God 'may still contribute not a little' to the religion of humanity, which calls humans to take part in the great battle of good and evil, and contribute to the final victory of Good by a 'religious devotion to the welfare of our fellow-creatures as an obligatory limit to every selfish aim' (ibid., p. 256).

We cannot fail to note that the religion of humanity itself is largely founded on hope, not on evidence. The victory of Good is not in sight, and I think probably never will exist on this planet. Moreover, a belief that the overcoming of selfishness and the promotion of devotion to our fellow-creatures is incumbent upon all humans is rather like a belief that there is an objectively existing ideal reality that makes such a thing incumbent upon humans, whatever they happen to think about it. For Mill, supernatural religion is more of an optional extra than a Kantian necessary postulate of practical reason. Yet, in stressing the imperative character of morality, and the element of hope that is involved in serious moral commitment, Mill shows how morality and religion can be closely interwoven, mutually supportive, and even coincident, if only a consistent and coherent account of their metaphysical status can be given.

If and insofar as religion militates against a humanistic understanding like Mill's, religion is to be rejected – and it has been so rejected in the works of Nietzsche, Marx, and Sartre. In that sense, Mill's philosophy can purify religious morality. But it cannot replace it, for, in the end, for many, perhaps most, people the religion of humanity offers nothing that can adequately ground what they feel to be the absolute demands and ultimate hopes of moral commitment, which, as absolute and ultimate, are transcendental because they are rooted in a supra-human reality.

Mill's hope for a sense of unity between all sentient beings, and for the cultivation of a universal impartiality and sympathy by individuals, would certainly be strengthened by the belief that there is an impartial and sympathetic spectator of human lives, who has compassion for all sentient beings, and gives humans the task of seeking to help all sentient beings towards an appropriate fulfilment and a sense of communion with one another.

As a matter of fact, I think that Buddhism may have done better at encouraging these attitudes than many forms of belief in God. The compassionate spectator is the Buddha, the Enlightened One, and the Buddhist belief is backed by a sophisticated view of the unity of all sentient life. However, insofar as God is unequivocally thought of as a supremely loving being who cares for all created life, theism can as easily serve as a motivation to universal benevolence.

Can a sense of universal sympathy and a feeling of the unity of all sentient life incline a rational agent to a religious belief? I think that it can, for, while such ideals can be powerful without any metaphysical backing, in suggesting that these attitudes are appropriate to the way things are, they suggest that there is something special about conscious life and about centring one's life on care for other sentient beings. This might counter reductively materialist views, and suggest that consciousness and person-centred morality have a fundamental place in the structure of reality. Consciousness is not just an accidental and fundamentally pointless by-product of blind material processes. Seeing what it is evokes the thought of a moral goal – the goal of understanding, empathetic feeling, and action to achieve liberation from pain and suffering – which is built into the nature of sentient life and of the cosmos. Morality would then have a sort of objectivity, suggesting that something like a purpose or goal is inherent in reality itself, and is not just an invention or subjective feeling of some human beings.

Some modern ecological movements embody this vision of the unity of all things, which will evoke a response of compassionate action, confirming that moral action can follow from a way of seeing what reality is. But that way of seeing is itself a specific evaluative stance, so that the world-view and the moral commitment twine together in a mutually reinforcing spiral of experience, evaluation, and action. In that way, finding a specific moral view attractive can reasonably incline someone to find a consilient worldview plausible. The 'religion of humanity' easily broadens out into a religion of the unity of all things, and into a high evaluation of sentient life that is fundamentally opposed to reductive materialism.

It has to be said that many Buddhists and some ecologists find the idea of God superfluous, morally difficult (because God is sometimes seen as a tyrannical dictator), and metaphysically puzzling (largely because of the existence of suffering in the cosmos). But one can think of God as a supremely perfect consciousness who is unable to create a universe like this, with evolved, free, and responsible human beings in it, that does not contain suffering. Yet the universe would not have been created at all unless there was the certainty that sentient beings could be liberated from suffering. Mill's conception of God is very like this, and his often over-looked reflections can be helpful in discovering more morally acceptable formulations of theism than have sometimes been promulgated.

GOD AND HUMAN RIGHTS

I have tried to show how belief in God, conceived in a certain way, does provide strong support for a 'religion of humanity', or for what might be called a transcendental humanism (which is, arguably, humanism's original form, in Erasmus, for example). I want to go on to suggest that it also provides strong independent support for a doctrine of human rights – a notion which poses difficult problems for Utilitarians (though I am not saying they are insuperable).

Human rights are founded on a sense of the unique value of each human person, and on a view of persons as irreplaceable moral agents who freely and responsibly shape a unique pattern of experiences in the exercise of their distinctive creative and cognitive capacities. This view of persons cannot be taken for granted, and it is probably true to say that it grew up, slowly but surely, in the Hebrew tradition. The view can be maintained simply as a moral intuition that requires no metaphysical backing. But it would clearly be strengthened by a belief that persons are *meant* to be morally free, unique, and irreplaceable, and that each person has a unique destiny that is capable of being realized. Belief in a God who plans such a destiny and can ensure its eventual realization, but who also permits and encourages moral freedom and creativity, is fully supportive of the moral view. It would mean that to see persons in this way is not simply a matter of personal choice. It would be the recognition of a truth about human existence, which would carry with it the absolute obligation to respond to this recognition by respecting the freedom, uniqueness, and irreplaceability of human persons in thought and action.

To give a high value to human life is to say that human life is object-ively worthwhile, and uniquely so. What can give it this objective value, which is not subjectively assigned by us, but which is felt to stand in judgement over all our subjective evaluations? Nicholas Wolterstorff, in his book *Justice* (2008), argues that no purely secular view can really justify seeing each and every human person as irreducibly precious, and so as deserving natural and inviolable human rights. For no secular view can avoid seeing some humans as having greater rational and moral capacities than others. Even saying that humans belong to a species to which it is proper to possess distinctive rational and moral capacities cannot, he thinks, justify giving to every member of that species, however damaged or incapable they may be, the sort of individual rights that belong to mature capable members of the species.

He therefore proposes that the attribution of human rights to every human being is only adequately grounded in the fact that God bestows absolute worth upon them. 'If God loves a human being . . . that love bestows great worth on that human being . . . natural human rights are what respect for that worth requires' (ibid., p. 360). I think this is importantly correct. Humans have rights because God bestows worth upon them, and God does this by loving them for their own sakes. I would only add that God does not bestow worth for no reason. The reason does not lie solely either in the actual possession of distinctive capacities (which he calls the 'capacities approach') or in membership of the human species as such (the 'nature-resemblance view'). It lies in the fact that God wills every individual to realize a set of distinctive capacities (to exist in God's image), to play out a particular vocation in the world (to realize the divine mandate to care for creation), and to share in the divine life. If it is said that some individuals (for example, the brain-damaged) do not have such capacities, the theistic response should be to say that all have the potential to develop them, and God's redemptive love precisely consists in enabling them to realize that potential.

Such redemption and healing in many cases will be fully realized only in the world to come, when all will be made whole by God's love and power. We will all be able to share fully in the divine life only in a world beyond our failures and incapacities in this world. The lives of the brain-damaged are, after all, only more extreme forms of the lives of what seem to us to be the healthy and mature. Each human being is of irreducible worth because God loves created persons and will make it possible for them to flourish as they should by sharing fully in the life of God in the world to come.

Two things need to be added to this account. First, in this world, humans are bound together in special relations of love and care for one another, and especially for the disadvantaged. That is a strong reason for giving to all humans without exception the worth that love requires. Second, God loves all creation, not just human beings, which means that the whole world will find its appropriate fulfilment in God. Continuing self-aware morally free agents (and they are not necessarily confined to humans) will still have a special dignity and role, since they alone are capable of knowing that they continue as the same individuals in the world to come. But their role in this world is to care appropriately for every form of life that God has created and that God also loves.

Wolterstorff suggests that 'the present-day secularist is living on inherited capital' (2008, p. 391). Belief that 'all of us have great and equal worth: the worth of being made in the image of God and of being loved redemptively by God' (ibid., p. 393) is part of the Judaic and Christian heritage. If we seek a worldview that can assign unique value to personal existence, it will be one that sees moral freedom and a personal form of consciousness to be worthwhile in themselves. They will be, if anything is, suitable purposes for the cosmos to realize, ultimate ends for the sake of which other things may exist. Yet, for all persons truly to realize, or even to have the possibility of realizing, a unique purpose that employs their own unique gifts and capacities, this life does not seem to be enough. So we are led to think of a further life in which personalities could truly realize the fullness of what it is in them to be. This would be possible if there were a God who valued persons and could assure them of life after death. It is in this way that a sense of the intrinsic value of personhood may naturally lead to the idea that this value could be fully realized, and that in a theistic universe it would be.

It is not that I selfishly desire to go on living after death. Rather, justice, if it were supreme and had power as it has authority, would require a fuller life in which human potentialities and values could be more fully realized. We cannot know that justice has this objective power. But, in committing ourselves to justice, we may be committing ourselves at least to the hope that personal values will be fully realized in the cosmos. Adopting the moral point of view (respect for persons as of unique value and dignity) is in a way a leap of faith, though not an irrational one. So embracing the hope for eternal life is a leap of faith that is not irrational, and that is encouraged by practical commitment to the objectivity of the moral point of view.

Mill's 'religion of humanity' embraces a hope, not for eternal life, but for a future society of justice and peace, and it is probably true that personal fulfilment is not fully possible except within a social context that sustains and expands it. Though we may seek in Platonic fashion to build perfect justice within ourselves, it cannot actually exist unless a just society, a society of just and charitable people, exists. One way in which religion can strengthen a purely secular moral perception is that the Abrahamic religions promise that such a society, in which evil is eradicated, and humans are renewed and reconciled, will exist. If this is true, it is a great encouragement to moral action.

The moral commonwealth will exist, of course, beyond this life, in 'Paradise' or 'heaven' or a resurrection world. So, if one thinks such a life is impossible, this will hardly strengthen one's moral beliefs. For some people, belief in an afterlife actually weakens moral beliefs by turning them into prudential recommendations. However, that is by no means necessary, and the hope for a just society is by no means prudential or selfish. For it is a hope for the fulfilment of all, not just of oneself. And it is a hope for the flourishing of goodness, not just for the maximization of whatever people think is going to give them the greatest pleasure, however that is obtained. If one has a belief in a God who could create an afterlife in which goodness could flourish, for everyone without exception, this will give the hope for the triumph of justice a much firmer grounding than if one just hopes that humans will go on getting better at some far future time, and for the few who will then exist.

It is, I think, hope for justice, not fear of death, that properly leads to belief in a life to come. Moral commitment naturally leads to such a hope, and we may at least say that the hope of heaven is positively encouraged and reinforced by an acceptance of the absolute demands of justice.

JUSTICE AND DESERT

Hope for life in the world to come is a hope for the sovereignty of justice in the cosmos. It specifically involves an idea of justice as merit or desert, the idea that people should be treated in ways appropriate to their own responsible actions. This idea can be founded, as Hume and Mill argue, on natural feelings of resentment or retribution, and an extended sympathy that broadens those feelings throughout society. It does not need a religious foundation. But those who believe in a God who is the judge of all the earth will see retributive justice as more than a series of social sanctions to encourage good behaviour and discourage bad.

If one believes in a God who is supremely merciful, who judges evil justly, but always offers reconciliation after repentance and penance (whatever exactly that may consist in), one will have an objective foundation for a belief that people are free to act morally, and deserve punishment when they fail to do so. But people can always 'turn from their wickedness and live'. Individuals have real responsibility, and they to some extent determine their own futures. This belief in human responsibility has probably been strongest in Indian-based religious traditions, which believe in reincarnation and *karma*, or an impersonal law of cosmic desert.

There are differing religious views on the topic of desert. Some think that God will condemn people forever for doing wrong. That has always seemed to me unduly harsh, and incompatible with the idea of a loving God. Others think that no punishment will last for ever. Some think that punishment should always be strictly retributive (an eye for an eye), while others think that all punishment should be, in principle, reformative, and aimed at changing the hearts of sinners. Some think that people cannot help what they do, so nobody should be punished at all (though they should be prevented or treated). These disagreements exist among secular thinkers as well as religious ones, and do not just derive from religious sources. They arise from differing interpretations of the relationship of justice and mercy, and of what the character of a supremely good God would be. Both doctrinal and moral considerations are involved in working out these interpretations, and it would be over-simple to say either that some revealed belief – in the Bible, say – determines the moral view or that some independent moral view determines beliefs about God. The fact is that many doctrines supposed to be revealed stand in need of interpretation, and that many moral views are influenced by a consideration of what a supremely loving God – an impartial spectator of the human scene with a concern for the welfare of all sentient beings – would or has been alleged to require.

Views of punishment will partly depend upon views of human nature. Are humans radically free? Are they all reformable? Does punishment exist just to keep society working? Or does it aim at some objective sense of 'fairness', so that individuals obtain the good or harm that they have caused to others? In all these ways, morality is not wholly independent of metaphysical and religious beliefs.

What we think a just God will do partly depends on what we think justice is, before we apply it to God. Religious and moral beliefs interact in continually changing ways. It is clear that a general dislike of purely retributive punishment – most often voiced by Utilitarians or at least by those who think morality must take consequences into account – has influenced much recent Christian thinking about eternal Hell. It has led to a widespread rejection of that belief, in its traditional forms. Yet such a change also came about by theological reflection on what a totally loving God would do, and on what is implied by the life and death of Jesus who was said to 'die for the sins of the world', and maybe the Utilitarian reformers were influenced by that, if not by the official teachings of the Church.

It could be held that divine reward and punishment is retributive, in that it is those who do evil who are punished and those who do good who are rewarded. But, if there truly is a loving God, punishment must also be potentially reformative, or at least aimed at the reformation of offenders. For love is always aimed at the good of others, whatever they may have done and however hard it may be to see how such good could come to them. Furthermore, punishments and rewards could not be just arbitrary consequences determined by the sheer will of an omnipotent absolute monarch. Rather, the quality and amount of human happiness or misery will correlate with the extent to which humans relate positively, creatively, and lovingly to others. The reward of virtue is not any sort of happiness, but a kind of happiness that can be experienced only by those who love and rejoice in the company of others. The punishment of vice is not just some degree of pain (the infliction of pain without any remedial intent being arguably as vicious as the offence for which it is inflicted), but the kind of self-inflicted misery of those who hate, fear, or despise, and are in turn hated, feared, and despised by, others.

So the sanctions of divine reward and punishment are in fact the natural consequences (in a morally ordered universe) of a life of love and a life of egoism, when those consequences are allowed to work out to their fullest and unimpeded extent. It is such an insight that enables one to hold that evil will be punished appropriately, and yet that repentance and return to a loving life always remain possible. For, when agents see the natural consequences of evil, they may well turn away from evil actions and seek the good. They must, however, learn to seek the good for its own sake, and that cannot be guaranteed. In my view, the most adequate moral view to take is that repentance will always remain a possibility, unless and until the choices of free moral agents become inexorably fixed. No one can have a very clear view of what an afterlife is like, but it is part of a morally acceptable theistic view that there are sanctions for morality, and that persons will reap the consequences of what they have responsibly done. It is also, in my view, necessary that repentance and forgiveness must always remain possible, though none can obtain the rewards of virtue unless they have come to love virtue for its own sake.

A belief that all moral acts will be judged by a God who knows exactly what degree of responsibility humans had, and what punishment or reward they deserve, should strengthen a sense of the importance of moral obligation. It should also strengthen a sense of the need for mercy, forgiveness, and reconciliation, since very few of us will turn out to deserve rewards! And that should in turn reinforce a belief that mercy and forgiveness are better than strict retribution, and that may modify our natural human tendencies to exact revenge.

A sense of fairness and moral desert can in these ways orient the mind towards a religious worldview. Such a sense cries out against the injustice of a world in which the evil flourish and the good die young. It cries that there must be a world other than this, a world in which our sense of justice is not in vain, where the efforts of human beings, suffering and dying for the cause of justice, are validated, and where brute power does not rule. It is a world our senses do not see, but that our minds and hearts feel, from which our moral sensibility springs, and to which it points.

This could be a wishful dream. Or it could be an insight into a deeper reality that underlies our world. Our actions, inwardly free and oriented to good, may speak of a reality beyond appearances, and we may risk all on the chance that it does. Either, we may think, morality is a heroic but tragic commitment, doomed to failure, or it is the perception of a deeper reality in our broken world. Such thoughts probably occur to most of us at times, as our moral apprehensions seem to be apprehensions of an ideal reality that actually exists and exerts its own attractive force upon us. This is a specific way of seeing morality that may seem very alien to a determinedly secular perspective. But, insofar as it comes to seem genuine, it prepares the mind for other ways in which such apprehensions of the Ideal may occur. It is in this way that moral perception, especially a sense of fairness and desert, may incline us towards a religious worldview and towards belief in God.

THE VIRTUES AND GOD

Those who believe in God will have a strong motivation for thinking that moral virtues should be cultivated, both because they represent inherent goals and fulfilments of human nature, and because they are means to attaining the supreme goal of love for God, who is supremely valuable and intrinsically desirable, and loving awareness of whom can be seen as the ultimate end of human life. God gives objective purpose and meaning to life, because the purpose of sharing in a perfect and indestructible divine love is one that is supremely worth choosing for its own sake.

In this way, a feeling for the virtues of self-realization naturally inclines many people to think that truth, beauty, and goodness are object-ive ideals rooted in a personal being who is supremely real, beautiful, and good. Pursuing these ideals for their own sakes cannot be opposed to pursuing knowledge and love of God, for God instantiates the supreme case of these ideals, and all their finite forms are partial images of the divine perfection. Persons love God precisely through loving the finite expressions of God's goodness. For a theist, the highest moral perception is to love all these things because they exist in God. To see all things in God, and God in all things, is for such a view the final goal of the moral life.

Thus, out of some important and basic moral intuitions – a feeling for the unity of all things, for universal compassion, for human dignity, for social justice, for the hope of moral flourishing, for the common good, for self-realization, and for objective values – there may arise the idea of a supreme objective Ideal of perfect goodness. If and when intuitions are organized around and focused upon that Ideal, morality can be seen as the voice of God. That voice does not command despotically, and it is not heard infallibly. It attracts through the power of love, when the self is centred on that which is of intrinsic value. It is heard among, and unfor-tunately often confused with, all the ambiguities and misperceptions of human life. Nevertheless, the love of goodness may, for many, naturally lead to the acceptance of some self-revelation of the Supreme Good itself.

Revelation reinforces human moral intuitions, for, in and through specific historical events, writings, or teachings, revelation claims a divine disclosure that there is a God who cares for creation, and that there is a life beyond death, where there is judgement, grace, and salvation, and where goodness will finally triumph. Thus, revelation, for those who can accept it, or to whom it comes as an overwhelming disclosure of truth, does not replace or undermine the natural sense of goodness and obliga-tion. It provides an objective (though not universally accessible) valid-ation (though not indubitable proof) of the metaphysical foundations of an objective, authoritative, and finally invincible morality. For this reason, it is one of the tragedies of religious life that sometimes belief in an alleged revelation leads people to embrace great evils such as hatred of others, narrow-mindedness, and intolerance. That it does so is the strongest argument for thinking that the form of revelation they embrace is radically mistaken.

It looks as though no particular divine revelation will ever be accepted by everyone, however pious or morally committed they are. It is therefore important to insist that morality as such does not strictly require either the acceptance of a particular divine revelation or a general metaphysical view of the foundations of morality of the sort that I have defended. Fortunately, the demands of morality can be perceived and justified in ways like those that Hume and Mill have ably spelled out. In that sense, morality does not depend upon religious faith. Yet there is something distinctive about a faith-based morality, and it is not just the addition of revealed moral rules that no one else knows about. It is a perception of an objective ideal of goodness in the everyday claims of morality, a perception that strengthens the force and the attraction of morality, and that makes moral perception a central strand in building up rational belief in God as the source and goal of all beings.

11

THE ANTI-MORALISTS

NIETZSCHE AND THE WILL TO POWER

I have spoken positively of a certain sort of religious view as strongly supportive of a generally life-affirming and humanistic morality. But I have also conceded that this could be a form of wish-fulfilment, a dream built on deep instinctive feelings implanted in us by blind evolutionary mechanisms, feelings we could not otherwise rationally justify. I have suggested that moral experience itself provides justification for taking some generally idealist or theistic philosophical views as genuine insights into reality. But there are philosophies that, if they are correct, show any such interpretations of moral experience to be illusory and even dangerous. It would be wrong to ignore such protests about a religiously based morality, and it might be important to see what lies behind them, and what lessons they may have to teach upholders of theistic morality.

Three of the most influential accusations made against theistic morality in recent times have been that religion (and especially Christianity) is life-denying, that it supports the status quo and offers the poor only hope for heaven rather than practical betterment in this life, and that it undermines human freedom by making everything subject to the all-determining will of God. These accusations have been strongly stated by Nietzsche, Marx, and Sartre, respectively. It is significant, however, that, while they all regarded themselves as undertaking a crusade against religion, they all extended their crusade so that it was, significantly, against morality as such, at least as traditionally understood.

Ironically, I think what their writings show is the advantage of a firm belief in an objective morality, rooted in a wider religious view of reality.

For their description of what a world without morality and religion would be like is one that might reasonably fill us with foreboding. And their prescriptions for a world of freedom, joy, and creative life are ones that may well seem to be possible only if a certain sort of religious commitment is made.

Nietzsche did not care for either Plato or Christianity. 'The most dangerous of all errors', Nietzsche writes, is 'Plato's invention of pure spirit and the good in itself' (1973, Preface to *Beyond Good and Evil*, p. 14). And 'Christianity is Platonism for "the people"'. It is not just Platonic or Christian morality that is in error. 'There are no moral facts whatsoever. Moral judgment has this in common with religious judgment, that it believes in realities which do not exist' (1977, The 'Improvers' of Mankind, p. 119).

Nietzsche's best-known doctrine is that 'life as such is will to power' (1973, Part One, 13, p. 26). This is the urge to dominate, to overcome obstacles, to be victorious in struggle, to master others. It is present in all humans; in fact, that is what they basically are – blind striving wills to conquer all things. But most humans, in the universal struggle of will against will, are doomed to be unsuccessful. Slave morality is an unconscious invention of the weak, based on resentment against the strong and successful, which takes revenge on them by seeking to impose on them, or, better, persuade them to impose upon themselves, 'moral' standards of kindness, pity, and humility, which will fill them with guilt and subordinate them to moral demands, which are in fact a deeply hidden and unacknowledged bid for power by 'the herd'.

'Behind the basic principle of the current moral fashion: "moral actions are actions performed out of sympathy for others", I see the social effect of timidity hiding behind an intellectual mask' (Nietzsche, 1977, *Daybreak*, 174, p. 96). It is in this sense that Nietzsche is an 'immoralist' – he exposes the hypocrisies of a morality of pity (*Mitleid*, or 'suffering with' others), as a stratagem of the herd to gain 'spiritual' power over the strong, and thus as an expression of timidity, resentment, and the will to power exercised by the weak, who deceive themselves into thinking they are only humble agents of a higher transcendent and objective truth. But they have constructed this 'truth' out of their own devious and disguised expressions of their will to power.

Nietzsche's emphasis on 'will to power' as the fundamental aspect of reality sounds very like Schopenhauer's postulation of the 'will to live' as the mindless, aimless, and non-rational force underlying the endless striving, conflict, and suffering of the world. Both philosophers radically oppose the Hegelian Idealist assumption that the world is fully rational and good, and that it expresses some sort of historical goal or transcendent reason. Both confront the stark reality of suffering and evil head-on, and refuse to see it as sanctified or included in some higher reality. Struggle, conflict, and blind will is all there is. There are no goals or objectives given in reality, and there are no truths that are independent of human needs.

Nietzsche reacts strongly against what he sees as Schopenhauer's pessimism, and against the Buddhist and Christian moralities that in his view deny the harsh realities of life. In *Twilight of the Idols*, he speaks of a 'noble Teuton', a 'blond beast', who has been led into a monastery. He there becomes 'like a caricature of a human being, like an abortion . . . sick, miserable, filled with ill-will towards himself; full of hatred for the impulses towards life, full of suspicion of all that was still strong and happy. In short, a "Christian"' (Nietzsche, 1977; The 'Improvers' of Mankind, p. 121).

He sees Christianity as exemplifying hostility towards life and the will to life, as the product of resentment and failure. When he attacks morality, it is this hostility to life that he attacks. In its place, he puts the 'superman' (*übermensch*), one who affirms the will to life and the will to power without guilt or subjection to some allegedly objective 'table of values' to which he must conform. There will, he admits, be few if any supermen, few who have the courage to put the moral constraints of society and religion aside, and dare to live fully, cheerfully, and happily.

Pity must be put aside, for as 'suffering-with' others, it only adds to the sum of suffering in reality. Yet suffering is inescapable. Indeed, the superman wills suffering inasmuch as he wills victory over enemies. The will to power seeks obstacles and pain, for thereby it adventures, makes trial of itself, disciplines itself, and overcomes. In this sense, suffering must be embraced and affirmed. It will not be the passive suffering that increases misery by concentrating on the pitiable nature of life. It will be an active embracing of suffering, and possibly the imposition of suffering on others, as a necessary part of the will to power. For 'life itself is essentially appropriation, injury, overpowering of the strange and weaker, suppression, severity, imposition of one's own forms, incorporation and, at the least and mildest, exploitation' (Nietzsche, 1973, Part Nine, 259, p. 175).

Nietzsche does not think that it is possible to take a dispassionate view of the world and issue a correct description of it. He has been called a perspectivalist, someone who thinks that descriptions, evaluations, and commitments are closely intertwined. Values are not subjective reactions contingently pinned onto objective descriptions. Metaphysics is not prior to morality, as a more or less firm foundation on which morality could be built. Nor is morality independent of metaphysics, as if we could decide what to do without taking any account of what sort of beings we are. While logically distinct, a general interpretation of experience, the evaluation of it, and practical commitment to a way of living, are inextricably linked. When Nietzsche interprets the world in terms of will to power, he also evaluates it as pointless and without objective meaning, and expresses his practical commitment to an anti-Christian and anti-conventional morality.

Nietzsche clearly reacted against what seemed to him the gloomy, life-denying, other-worldliness of German Lutheranism. But the terms in which he did so – the idea of 'the will', of the noble soul, of 'the death of God' as a supernatural person – owed much to Hegel, Schopenhauer, and the condition of German Protestantism in the late nineteenth century. How could it be otherwise? The point is that Nietzsche's perspectivalism is correct to the extent that no one just has access to the facts as they objectively are, forms moral judgements with complete individual autonomy, and then adds religion (or anti-religion) as another independent element to the mix.

What he calls Dionysian morality can seem life-affirming only for the few, the noble souls who stand out from the herd, whose will it is to dominate, for whom 'severity, force, slavery, peril in the street and in the heart, concealment, stoicism, the art of experiment and devilry of every kind' is permissible, and who think 'that everything evil, dreadful, tyrannical, beast of prey and serpent in man serves to enhance the species' (1973, Part Two, 44, p. 54). Even allowing for rhetorical exaggeration, this is a pretty frightening picture. In Nietzsche, the 'superman' is both one who strives for wealth, strength, health, and beauty, and also one who is a 'blond beast', member of a master race, bent on conquering the world, who says, 'The best belongs to me and mine, and if we are not given it, we take it: the best food, the purest sky, the most robust thoughts, the fairest women' (1961, The Last Supper, Part Four, p. 296), and adds: 'Do not spare your neighbour' (1961, Of Old and New Law-Tables, Part Four, p. 216). Nietzsche thinks of the 'superman' as noble, artistic, and creative. But a man who truly creates whatever values he wishes could equally well be uncouth, uncultured, and destructive, if that is what he chose to be. It is not really surprising that Hitler found something congenial in this philosophy, even though Nazi propagandists were very selective in their use of it.

It is hard not to think that this is Nietzsche's view of what is most appropriate for a being who penetrates the delusions of ideal self-sacrificing
morality, born of vengefulness and resentment, knows that he is in his
inmost essence will for power, and resolves to express his being fully.
That is the gospel of *Zarathustra*. 'Become what you are' – this phrase
from the ancient Greek lyric poet Pindar was one of Nietzsche's favourite
quotations. And what you are is the brute will to power, beyond pity,
beyond the constraints of morality, free to create your own values. This is
what a life that fully faces up to a world without God or objective rationality or morality might be like.

Humans are the chance products of a blind evolutionary process, and
human reason is unreliable and untrustworthy. The species has survived
through manifesting lust and aggression, and there is no goal in life other
than one we make up ourselves, or that is implanted in us as an efficient
(in the far past) survival mechanism. Morality will provide us with social
rules necessary for survival, but those rules will be a matter of negotiation
and compromise, and the powerful will find ways to use or evade them.
There is no such thing as a proper or 'authentic' human life, but the rule
of the strong is seen to be natural and inevitable, and the consolations
of religion are seen to be illusory, and therefore religiously based morality
is not compelling. Utilitarianism pretends to a non-existent love for all
humanity, which is incompatible with human nature. Kantian universal-
ism tries in vain to impose complete rationality on an irrational world. It
is time to move beyond morality to social expediency and personal
prudence, but also to a courageous creation of values in a totally free way.
'All gods are dead; now we want the superman to live' (Nietzsche, 1961,
Of the Bestowing Virtue, Part Three, p. 104). If that is where honesty
leads, so be it.

AFFIRMING LIFE

Is that, however, where honesty leads? Scientifically established facts
must be accepted. But broad theories about human existence may, as
Nietzsche himself suggests, not be timeless and purely theoretical surveys
of all knowledge. They may already incorporate values and commitments
that are generated within and strongly influenced by a particular historical
situation. Can the natural sciences establish that humans are accidental
by-products of blind physical forces? Or is that view influenced by a prior

sense that there is no point or purpose in human life, no transcendent dimension to human experience?

Nietzsche sees the universe as a battleground of conflicting wills, without purpose or value. That is certainly a postulate, very far from common sense. It may be an imaginative one, but it is not a reasonable one, and rejects any claim to be.

This is where interpretation and evaluation come into the picture. Is human life all suffering, conflict, resentment and vengefulness? Nietzsche himself does not consistently think so, for his whole philosophy is one of life-affirmation, even an affirmation of life just as it is, with all its suffering.

What he presents is remarkably like many religious pictures of a world fallen into pride, hatred, lust, and greed. The picture of a world of wills in perpetual conflict, seeking to dominate or to subvert others by secret resentments, is a picture of Hell. And much of our human world is like that. Religions propose ways of liberation from such a world, and so does Nietzsche. His liberation is an affirmation of life, of laughter, beauty, creativity, originality, energy, and strength. It rejects all other-worldliness as a craven escape from life as it is, and so he rejects Buddhism, Schopenhauer, and Christianity as deniers of life and health, and as propagators of a false consciousness or self-deceit about the true motives (resentment and vindictiveness) of other-worldly faith.

His analysis of these matters is acute, but perhaps not acute enough. There is suffering and self-deceit in life. But, for that very reason, it cannot coherently be willed just as it is. What can be willed is life, health, laughter, beauty, and creativity. These things do exist in this world, and the moral task is to realize them in this world. But in this world they are hard to attain, harder to retain, often doomed to disappointment, and always ended by death, which is their ultimate antithesis. It may be good to affirm these things, and to fight for them against all life-denying and self-deceiving forces. But would it be reasonable to affirm, as Nietzsche does, that we should will to live through this struggle again and again, without victory ever being in sight? Nietzsche's philosophy is perhaps not as life-enhancing as it may seem at first, when we consider the suffering and ruthlessness occasioned by the will to power, and the inevitability of failure, resentment, and misery for the majority of the human race.

Nor is Christianity necessarily as life-denying as Nietzsche thinks. If we examine the life of Jesus as recorded in the Gospels, it does not at all seem as Nietzsche depicts it. If God becomes incarnate, as John's Gospel suggests, that is in itself an affirmation of the supreme value of human

life. Jesus spent his ministry in healing and exorcism, in bringing physical and mental health to people. He had a reputation as a 'glutton and a
wine-bibber', and caused scandal by not fasting as other teachers did.
John's Gospel says that he came to bring eternal life, which surely is life,
not death. And he gives eternal life now, not later. He objected forcefully
to inhumane interpretations of religious law, to religious hypocrisy and
self-serving casuistry. He preached freedom, health, and happiness (the
Beatitudes are, after all, about happiness, not misery).

So Nietzsche is unfair to the Gospel records of Jesus – though he
may be right about how some Christians live their religion in judgemental
and vindictive ways, the very things Jesus opposed most vigorously. Jesus
affirms life. But it is true that he also affirms life after death, a life with
God where all suffering and evil will be ended. This, however, does not
have to be a denial of the value of life. It affirms all the good things of life;
it does not deny that those good things are inextricably mixed with striving, with endeavour, with nobility and persistence, in earthly existence.
Liberation, however, if there truly is such a thing, will not include
an affirmation of evil. It will not entail a denial of the good things of life,
but it entails that evil will be overcome, and good will be fulfilled and
completed, so that there will be a goal and an existence that can be
unambiguously affirmed.

Is this an irrational wish-fulfilment? If reality is truly intelligible,
if there is a supremely rational God who has the power to create the
cosmos and whose knowledge embraces all reality, then that God will
be able to realize beyond the life of earth the goal of perfected human
life that has been sought during earthly human lives. The hope of eternal
life, life in God, is supremely rational if there is a rational (or wise) God,
who creates life precisely in order that it should attain fulfilment and
liberation from evil. That is, in my view, the only way in which human
life can be unequivocally affirmed as good – not an eternal recurrence,
with evil never overcome, but an eternal transformation, where the intrinsic goodness of life is freed from the opposing forces of destruction and
death, which have been a necessary part of the 'fallen', disordered world
of will to power.

This is a postulate, just as the will to power is a postulate. But it is
not the postulate of a petty tyrant God who can take revenge on all
our enemies after death. It is the postulate of a supreme Reason that wills
both the eradication and transformation of evil, and a fulfilled life for all
creatures who are capable of it. Nietzsche is right. We have to choose –
Dionysius drunk and debauched, living without point or purpose and

sanctifying evil as well as good; or Christ freely loving and forgiving, giving his earthly life for the sake of beauty, truth, and love, and bringing all who will to eternal life in God. If he had not been blind to the Christ of the Gospels, if he had not been so hypnotized by the will to power, might not Nietzsche have been much nearer to Christian morality than he thought? In *Zarathustra*, his 'Second Dance Song', he writes, 'All joy wants eternity, wants deep, deep, deep, eternity' (1961, Part Three, p. 244). This eternity, for Christians, is the God who is eternal life and joy. Christians can adopt Nietzsche's motto 'Become what you are'. But many religious believers, including Christians, would say that we are beings of transcendent spirit, created by transcendent Love, and the full realization of that is what morality, at its deepest level, invites us to become.

12

THE OPTION FOR THE POOR

MARX AND LIBERATION

Karl Marx, like Nietzsche, rejected any idea of objective moral truths. He wrote that morality is, like law and religion, just a bourgeois prejudice, which is 'but the outgrowth of the conditions of your bourgeois production and bourgeois property' (Marx, 1960, *Manifesto*, section 2, p. 31).

Yet Marx's views have been one of the major intellectual influences of the modern world. They constitute a philosophy that has attracted sophisticated philosophical defenders. They have inspired heroic moral campaigns against oppression and injustice. And, while they may not be religious, they invoke a view of human history which is remarkably like the ancient Hebrew prophetic call to realize a just and humane society as the inevitable goal of history.

Marx was not primarily a philosopher; he was an economist, a social historian, and an instigator of social revolution. But a philosophy underlies his thought, and the main philosophical influences are those of Hegel and Feuerbach. Like Nietzsche, he rejected Hegel's theory of history as the progressive self-realization of Absolute Spirit, saying that he stood Hegel on his head. But he retained the idea that history moved dialectically and inevitably towards the realization of a society in which the 'development of human potentiality for its own sake' (Marx, 1960, *Capital* vol. 3, p. 260) would be fully realized. And he retained the Hegelian idea of alienation, whereby humans objectify and project their own natures, creating an 'other' and alienated form of being, which is then to be overcome and reconciled by a historical process. He followed Feuerbach, however, in thinking that the ultimate driving force of history was matter, and not spirit.

Nietzsche despised the herd, and proposed the way of the noble, bold, warlike, and pitiless superman, hating ideas of equality, democracy, and fraternity with all common people. Marx saw the herd – the proletariat – as oppressed and alienated by the capitalist system, and called for their liberation by overthrowing their oppressors and the institution of a new social order. In fact, it is a basic axiom of Marxist philosophy that we must be engaged in the classwar, on the side of the oppressed, and that all our thoughts and acts must be from a basic 'option for the poor', as the Peruvian theologian Gutierrez was to call it.

This may seem like a fundamental moral conflict between Nietzsche and Marx. Paradoxically, neither Nietzsche nor Marx saw it as a moral struggle, since they both rejected 'morality' as an illusion propagated to support a particular, historically conditioned set of social relationships which pitted one class against another in an essentially competitive social system. They both saw a new age dawning, one the age of the superman, who would be free of all old moral constraints, the other an age of communism, when the state, the family, private property, and the class-system had faded away, and each person would be happy and fulfilled in 'cultivating his talents in all directions' (Marx, 1963, p. 253). They both saw the coming of this age as intrinsically associated with violence – supermen would be beyond pity, and the ends of the communists 'can be attained only by the forcible overthrow of all existing social conditions' (Marx, 1960, *Manifesto*, p. 47).

What unites these thinkers is a perception of present (European) society as oppressive and filled with repressed hatreds and resentments. They agree that there is a need to overthrow old moral and religious values and ideals, and accept violence as a means to establishing a radically different social system. What divides them is what is actually to be done about it now. For advocates of the master race, the strong should master the weak, and lead into a new age of freedom. For communists, the weak, by virtue of their greater numbers, should rise up and eliminate the strong – and lead into a very similar new age of freedom.

It does not take a genius to wonder whether the overthrow of moral values and the use of violence to introduce a new social order is at all likely to accomplish the goal of a society of happiness and peace. Marx, of course, does not believe in a fixed human nature, so he supposes that the introduction of a different social order will produce a different sort of human, with different values. But there are notable internal difficulties with this supposition. If 'communists everywhere support every revolutionary movement against the existing social and political order of things'

(Marx, 1960, *Manifesto*, p. 47), there is no reason to think that this process will ever end. The difficulty is the same as that faced by Hegel when he saw history as a dialectical process from thesis to antithesis to synthesis (although these were not terms Hegel used), which would in turn form a new thesis, and so on, ad infinitum. In a world of perpetual revolution, conflict will always remain, and a truly final communist society will never exist. That means that we are likely to remain for the foreseeable future under the preliminary stage of state socialism, under the dictatorship of the proletariat, which will seek to eliminate all bourgeois ideologies, including religion, and impose atheism by force.

In Marx's visionary description of communist society, he speaks of it as one 'where nobody has one exclusive sphere of activity but each can become accomplished in any branch he wishes, production as a whole is regulated by society, thus making it possible for me to do one thing today and another tomorrow' (1963, p. 110). Apart from the fantasy that anyone could become accomplished in anything they choose, how can one reconcile this aim with saying, in the same breath, that production will be 'regulated by society'? 'The product of freely associated men . . . is consciously regulated by them in accordance with a settled plan' (ibid., p. 120). Who does the regulating? Who draws up the plan? Will there be no disagreements? Will no meetings be necessary to get agreement? And will greed and envy have totally disappeared from human nature? If religion is a wish-fulfilling illusion, so is the communist dream of a society of free and fulfilled persons, which is to be brought about by repressing and eliminating all who disagree with that dream.

Marx always held that his theory was a scientific one, not a moral one. Yet the major appeal of Marxism has always been its moral critique of free-market capitalism as unjust, and its hope for a society whose guiding principle will be: 'From each according to his ability, to each according to his needs' (ibid., p. 243). This has led some to say that Marxism is itself a religion. But it does seem unduly paradoxical to say that a system that seeks to abolish religion is itself religious.

It is true that moral ideas can be used to repress others, and that every system – including a communist one – will be liable to be misused by those who pursue power and greed. But the ultimate communist goal is that people should be free to express themselves, that there should be some means of efficient planning so that social needs can be met, and that personal relationships should not be based on dominance and the submission of women to men. The contrast with the Nietzschean ideal of the 'master morality' that should not be shared by slaves shows that there is a specific ideal of human life present in Marx. It is not a purely scientific conclusion arising from a study of historical laws. It is an evaluative belief that human persons should be free creators who express their potentialities in a social context that makes such development of talents possible for everyone.

This is a fine ideal, but it is in tension with the thought that it can be brought about by a violent process in which, according to Lenin, 'the working class must break up, shatter, the "available ready machinery of the State"' (1960, p. 180), in which there is 'an unshakable and iron discipline supported by the power of the armed workers' (ibid., p. 191), and in which 'the armed workers . . . will scarcely allow anyone to trifle with them' (ibid., p. 238). Freedom is unlikely to be brought about by armed repression of all opposition.

It is also in tension with the view that persons are nothing more than the sum of their social relationships, whose natures are wholly created by the social structures of which they are part. If the moral ideal is of a society that makes free self-realization possible for all, a value is placed on the creative expression of human potentialities that fits uneasily with a view that humans are mere products of material processes without any inherent moral goal at all. If Marxism has a moral ideal, it is one that suggests and relies upon a specific philosophical view of human nature as possessing creative freedom, and as having potentialities that it is good to realize in co-operation with others. For Marx, this is not a moral goal, but just the inevitable end of a blind historical process. However, this form of amoralistic materialism seems, paradoxically, ideological – that is, it disguises as a scientific prediction of how history will end what is in fact a moral affirmation of ideal goodness as the goal of human existence.

Why should that ideology exist? I think it is to disguise the fact that any talk of realizing an essential creative nature, or of a goal of human existence, strongly suggests that there are in reality essential natures and goals, that there is a form of teleology or purposiveness in human existence, that Hegel was (broadly speaking) right after all in giving spirit priority over matter. For, if persons have an essential nature and a purpose in realizing it, this is fully intelligible only when there is something mind-like (spirit) that conceives of a possible goal, and creates persons in order that they might freely realize it (or not).

For Marx, any such 'externally imposed' purpose would be repressive of human freedom. Humans would have to obey and conform, and the foundation is laid for the social structures of hierarchy and authority, of repressive violence and enforced conformity with beliefs and actions deemed by authority to be 'good', against which Marx passionately rebelled.

Religions may be, and often have been, repressive in that way. But there are forms of religion which affirm the realization of human potential (for God may well create humans so that they may freely realize the potentialities God has given), and the duty of working for the common good of society (for God may will humans to live with universal concern and compassion, and with the purpose of sharing with others in achieving common goals).

Such goals do not have to be religious, or to involve conscious participation in religious institutions. But religious belief systems are natural, and virtually inevitable, developments of a view that human societies and individuals have objectively given moral goals, and that they seek, at least for those who have this sensibility, to evoke and sustain some form of appropriate conscious relationship to the cosmic Mind that formulates such goals.

Some forms of religion may fairly be accused of being almost exclusively 'other-worldly', of looking for salvation or liberation beyond this life, while remaining uninvolved in the political affairs of the world, which is the realm of ambition and greed destined for destruction and not reformable by political action. But this is not essential to religion. If we think of the universe as created by God for a purpose, then that purpose will at the very least include a purpose for this planet. It is not unreasonable to see that purpose as the mutual realization of human potential in society. A form of religion that holds such a basic view will emphasize an objective obligation to seek this-worldly liberation from anything that frustrates the divine purpose, which is that all without exception should achieve their potential. It will engage in social and political action to achieve these ends. But it is unlikely that it will approve of violent action to achieve them, except in the most extreme circumstances, if only because violence contradicts the realization of human potential.

Most religions are well aware that the goal of human fulfilment is not easy, and may well be impossible, to achieve. Buddhists see the world as a wheel of suffering and attachment, Hindus as an illusion of the grasping ego, and Christians as enslaved to sin. Marx shares this perception in his idea, derived from Hegel, of alienation, which subjects persons to false consciousness and diminishes their humanity. Under conditions of class warfare, workers are alienated from the products of their labour – they do not produce things they themselves can use, but work for the artificial good of money. They are alienated from their fellows, since they are locked in the competitive relations of the free market. They are alienated from the natural world, being forced to work in factories and on assembly-lines that separate them from nature and the rhythms of the seasons. And they are alienated from their own true natures, as their own creative potential cannot be realized in their work.

It is not only the workers who are alienated. Even though owners of capital have more freedom and power than workers, they are still subject to the alienation of working to produce profit, of separating themselves from the broad mass of workers, and of becoming dominated by a lust for power that frustrates their more natural social affections. Society is in the grip of what may be called 'demonic powers' that diminish humanity, powers created by the social conditions of the capitalist system.

Religious perspectives tend to attribute this alienation to forces within the human mind, and to a possessive attachment to objects, which entails a turning away from the goal of the positive realization of social goods. Buddhists speak of the 'three fires' of hatred, greed, and ignorance, while Christians think of pride – self-assertion and a refusal to serve others or seek an objective good for its own sake – as the root of alienation. Marx rather finds it in the social structure, the means of production and exchange, which characterizes capitalist society. Though he would agree that the love of money and power are symptoms of alienation, he sees them as produced by the structure of bourgeois capitalism. From a religious viewpoint, this is, ironically for Marx, a form of ideology. It projects deep personal moral failure onto society, where it can be seen as an amoral power that is no longer anyone's personal responsibility.

The consequence is that Marx claims that liberation from alienation can be found by a revolutionary change of social conditions, by the abolition of private property and the democratic State. Change society, and you will change the individual. Religions like Christianity believe that, on the contrary, individuals need to be changed if there is to be true social reform. Christians think of alienation as sin – that is, as a turning away (probably unconsciously but practically) from God, the objective Ideal. They then think of liberation as salvation – whereby God forgives and actively rebuilds the self to unify it with the objective Ideal. Marx thinks of liberation as a real political freedom from oppressive structures – and also as freedom from the authoritarian rules of religion and its oppressive God.

Marx believes that real liberation needs to be social and political. You cannot be free unless you have a social structure that allows you to be free, and this freedom must be observable and material. He sees religion as giving only an illusory freedom, an inner and individual freedom that is so imaginary that it is compatible even with being a slave in a repressive society. Yet both Marxism and many religious systems identify alienation and liberation as major factors in the human situation. Morality is thereby embedded in a wider context of ideal goal, alienated existence that makes the ideal unattainable, and some way of liberation that makes the ideal realizable. A crucial question is whether this context is to be interpreted wholly in social and political terms, or whether there is an inner and individual freedom that is not illusory, but fundamentally real. And that, of course, is the question of materialism versus the ontological priority of morally engaged, free but morally disabled, human minds. Those who hold some form of the latter view will want to say that those who seek inner freedom should always aim at social freedom, and hope for it, but never make it a condition, or the sole content, of moral endeavour. For them, Marxism will always be an inadequate account of the human condition, and therefore of morality.

Marxist thought has influenced religion in good and bad ways. Especially in liberation theologies in the economically undeveloped world, it has led to a renewed emphasis on the religious obligation to enlarge the creative freedom of all, especially those who are marginalized by social conditions. Gutierrez's 'option for the poor' was affirmed in the *Instruction on Certain Aspects of the Theology of Liberation*, issued by Cardinal Ratzinger in 1984. That instruction warned, in opposition to Marxist thought, that truth is not just a by-product of economic struggle, that class war is not essential to society, that violence is not a justifiable means to a moral goal, and that history will not inevitably end with a wholly free and just society. Nevertheless, it remains an obligation to seek to establish such a society. Belief in an afterlife in which it will eventually exist (as the 'kingdom of God' or as Paradise) should not undermine the present obligation to try to realize it now, since individual destiny in the afterlife will partly depend precisely upon how far we have tried to meet our obligations.

Such a belief may also encourage people to continue attempts to achieve the goal even in face of continual disappointment. For, though moral efforts may fail in this life, religions usually affirm that they will contribute to positive outcomes in the world to come, and so will never have been in vain. Perhaps the conception of an afterlife that best matches this conception of morality is one in which God's forgiveness and love is never withdrawn, but in which persons have to face up to the consequences of their actions by undergoing some form of penitential process ('punishment'), which leaves them free but never precludes their ultimate reformation.

Marxism has influenced religion most obviously, however, in seeking to eradicate it. 'The only service which can be rendered to God today is to declare atheism a compulsory article of faith and to . . . prohibit . . . religion generally' (*Marx and Engels on Religion*, 1972, p. 127). That is incompatible with freedom of belief and religious practice – though, ironically, the disclosure that atheism can be as intolerant as many religions have been has had the effect on more liberally minded people of making official atheism seem a poor alternative to religion, and of reminding them that liberalism (freedom of belief) is an entailment of any religious morality that genuinely cares about respect for the individual and for freedom of conscience. The right to religious freedom was affirmed at the Second Vatican Council's 'Declaration on Religious Liberty' (in *Dignitatis Humanae*, 1965).

Marxist thought has also influenced some religious groups in ways that are morally dangerous. It has led some groups to think that violence and terrorism are legitimate means to bring about a just and rightly believing society. In arguing against the 'bourgeois' concept of human rights, and in holding that capitalist society can legitimately be overthrown by force, Marxist thought, though perhaps in opposition to Marx's own intentions, has encouraged some religious groups to adopt morally unacceptable means (such as terrorist acts that directly kill the innocent) to gain their ends.

Wherever atheism has been officially established, as it has been in communist (more properly, as interpreted by Marxism, 'socialist') states, it has not proved to be a liberating force making for a more humane society. The major world religions have not always proved liberating either. If we want to take a positive message from Marx, it is that human morality should be concerned with liberating the oppressed and the weak, by changing the social conditions that help to cause their oppression. In order to gain the motivating power that morality needs for this task, a commitment to a higher and morally just cause, and to a higher power (in Marx, the unstoppable dialectic of history) that makes liberation possible, is needed (as the success of communism in enlisting the heroic loyalty of so many shows). Religious commitment to a God or higher spiritual power who wills human fulfilment and happiness is well placed to provide this motivation. And here religion itself is faced with a choice: will religious faith be an escape from this-worldly responsibilities, and a retreat to other-worldly or purely inner consolations? Or will it involve a commitment to liberating the oppressed of the world so that they can realize their full God-created human potential in creative and co-operative action?

For Christians, the words of Jesus must have some force: 'The Spirit of the Lord is upon me, because he has anointed me to bring good news to the poor, he has sent me to proclaim release to the captives, and recovery of sight to the blind, to let the oppressed go free' (Luke 4: 18). For those who hear these words and accept them, the choice is already made.

13

SARTRE AND AUTHENTIC LIFE

'EXISTENCE PRECEDES ESSENCE'

Jean-Paul Sartre in later life became a Marxist, and was always concerned for the poor and oppressed. Yet he is most famous for stressing the total freedom of humans from any objective moral constraints, and so his work, like that of Marx, contains a paradoxical combination of moral fervour and the rejection of morality.

The most accessible philosophical work by Sartre is 'Existentialism and Humanism'. This is a short public lecture for a general audience, and he later repudiated it, so it cannot be called a definitive statement of Sartre's views. Nevertheless, he said it at a certain time in his life, and it has become, whether he liked it or not, a standard manifesto of atheistic existentialist thought. The key statement in the lecture is that 'existence comes before essence' (Sartre, 1989, p. 26), and that statement is definitive of Sartre's radical view of human freedom. Physical objects have essences, properties that define what they are. But a human first of all exists, and 'defines himself afterwards' (ibid., p. 28), so that 'he will be what he makes of himself'.

This means that there is no such thing as human nature, which ordains what a person is bound to be in a deterministic way. Neither is there any ideal nature, something that a person ought to be, like an idea in the mind of God to which humans ought to conform. Man makes his own essence, and that essence is simply the sum of a person's acts, a matter of sheer creative will. In his major work *Being and Nothingness*, Sartre calls for a renunciation of 'the spirit of seriousness' (2000, p. 626), the belief that there are objective moral values that lay down a human essence.

And, after setting out a number of moral examples, which are chosen precisely because they pose very difficult moral choices, Sartre concludes that we simply have to decide what to do, and take responsibility for our choice. There is no correct or incorrect in morality.

There is, however, the possibility of 'bad faith', which is the pretence that our path is laid out for us, and that we must conform to it. If we think this, we reduce ourselves to the status of passive objects, and disguise the truth of our radical freedom and responsibility from ourselves. We lose our true being as free possibility by becoming immersed in the 'given' structures of the world, where other people define what we should do and think. We feel ourselves 'at home' in the world, and become absorbed by its alien and fundamentally trivializing concerns. Paradoxically, to realize what we are, we must take responsibility for our freedom to create meaning in an objectively meaningless world.

The paradox is that, if 'we realize what we are', then we must have a nature after all – our nature is to be radically free, not bound by objective moral standards. If we fail to do that, says Sartre, our lives are inauthentic, they exhibit bad faith and self-deceit. But, if that is so, existence cannot wholly precede essence, for there must be something of a specific nature that exists, and that nature, for Sartre, is unconstrained freedom.

It is hard to see how such a view of freedom can be given by introspection (a phenomenology) of human experience alone. We cannot tell, just by looking hard, that we are totally free. We must bring an interpretation to our ontological analysis. That interpretation will depend upon the concepts, the language, we have and have learned from others, and upon our personal assessment of its adequacy to describe our own experience. It will involve our evaluation of human experience, which will in turn express our practical commitment to certain forms of action in the world (our radically free choices, for Sartre).

If I ask, 'How do I know that I am radically free?', for Sartre, the answer will be that in my actions I commit myself to such freedom. I do not let myself be governed by constraints about a given human nature, whether given by science or by social convention or by religion. Yet that commitment carries an evaluation of my life – an anti-authoritarian determination to express my individuality. And that commitment will have been shaped by my education in a specific culture against which I may be reacting (while it shapes the very thoughts in which I express my reaction). This spiral of personal commitment, evaluation, and cultural placing – which I have called perspectivalism – is inescapable. It means that there is no 'pure ontological description' that is available. Commitment, evaluation, and cultural tradition all play a part in the description we give of our lived experience.

It is probably true that Sartre does not after all describe what it is to be human, as such – as though phenomenology was something that would reveal what is true for all human beings, instead of what is true for people in one tradition, with their own commitments and evaluations. He adopts a practical stance in the world, a stance that is consonant with his own evaluation of what it is to exist as a human being, and with a general (perhaps implicit) descriptive interpretation of human existence.

CHOOSING FOR ALL HUMANITY

Sartre's ontology may then be the result of an introspective evaluation of one personal life that is without any sense of God or of categorical moral obligation. Is it a matter of phenomenological description that there is no sense of objective moral value? It might be more accurate to say that this is the description of a person's life who acknowledges no sense of objective moral value. On this matter, Sartre is, as so often, perplexingly ambiguous. If we are free to decide our moral values, it may seem that we can decide for power and domination over others if we choose. In fact, that is what Sartre thinks that most people do choose, since others are threats to our existence. Yet he insists that, in freely choosing to act, a person 'is responsible for all men' (1989, p. 29), and 'in choosing for himself he chooses for all men'.

This puts a huge constraint on moral choice. It seems to be a sudden reversion to a Kantian doctrine that my choices must be such that I could choose them for everyone. In British moral philosophy, it is paralleled by R.M. Hare's proposal that we freely prescribe moral recommendations, but they are only 'moral' if we prescribe them universally. That seems to be Sartre's meaning. But why should it be so? Sartre suggests that it is because we choose 'an image of man such as he believes he ought to be'. But why should we believe man 'ought to be' anything? We can say, 'This is what I choose', but I am not committed to saying that anyone else should choose like that, or that I think man, as such, ought to be anything. There is no 'ought', and my choice does not create one.

Sartre's remark that 'the moral choice is comparable to the construction of a work of art' (1989, p. 48) belies this thought that 'in fashioning myself I fashion man' (ibid., p. 30). In creating a work of art, I do not say that it is such as all should create. On the contrary, I hope no one else can create a work quite like it. Why should morality not be the same? I imaginatively create my life, and hope that no one else is quite so creative. In fact, however, it seems that, despite everything he says, Sartre really thinks my essential nature is that I should choose on behalf of all persons. This is a constrained choice. It leaves me with many alternatives, much of the time. But I am not totally free to choose whatever I like, even if it destroys others.

Sartre's own political views were always in favour of liberation for the poor and concern for the oppressed (this is the Marxist strain in his thought). But was he just saying, 'This is what I have decided, and I wish everyone would agree with me (though I do not expect they will)'? Or was he saying more, that what I decide should be such that I can (and do) positively will that all decide it also? If each choice has to be such that everyone can make it (that I decide on behalf of all men), then, of course, I could never choose anything that harms others just for the sake of it. I am opting for a choice of total impartiality. But why should I make that choice? 'Take all others into account' is just about the biggest moral constraint there could be on free choice. This is hardly radical freedom.

In any case, the idea of totally unconstrained freedom seems incoherent. If I am to choose anything, I must have an idea of what can be chosen, and so my choice is constrained first of all by the ideas I have. Moreover, when I evaluate some possibilities as preferable to others, this is not a wholly arbitrary selection. I find myself preferring pleasurable events to painful ones, for example; I do not just decide to prefer pleasure over pain. So, my choices are constrained by what seems worthwhile to me, and that comes to me as a 'given'. I may attend to or reflect on that given or not, but I cannot simply decide what is worthwhile and what is not. This does not mean that I have no choice. But I can only choose what I believe to be possible and good.

Moral choice is something that exists within these constraints. When I make a choice 'on behalf of all', I am affirming that this possibility is worthwhile for anyone like me, that is, for all; it is objectively worthwhile, whether they agree with me or not. This is to affirm an objective moral truth. It is set in my nature, by my stock of ideas and the preference-ranking they have when I consider them. My freedom is not totally unconstrained.

Sartre writes that it is wrong to refuse to face up to our freedom to choose. But why should it be wrong, if there is no meaning, purpose, or objective good in the world? I can choose to be a conformist if I wish. Why should that be called 'bad faith'? The only answer Sartre could give is that it refuses to accept my nature. But I am not supposed to have a nature! Do I live authentically if I make a free and unconstrained choice for personal pleasure and power? In that case, an authentic life could be an evil life! In a way, it is authentic; it is a real human possibility, consciously faced and accepted.

What Sartre wants to say is that a choice of evil is a rejection of authentic human nature. But now authenticity cannot be just any free conscious choice. It must be a choice, realizing a potentiality that I can reject, but that fulfils what I am meant to be. I am meant to be not just a free being, but a free being who knows what is good for all, and chooses good for its own sake. Sartre cannot give an account of this without qualifying radically his account of freedom. The sort of human being I become might be brought into being by free choice; but its possibility and its imperative quality is given in human nature.

I do not come across a moral fact, as I might come across a table. But, in reflection, I come across a positively evaluated possibility, and see that in some sense I 'ought' to realize it. I am free not to do so; but I am not free to decide whether or not I ought to do it. The 'ought' might have no force for me. I can say: I know I ought, but I do not care. That, I think, is moral freedom, and Sartre gives no adequate account of it.

Sartre does not acknowledge that moral values can exist without being repressive, without destroying freedom. He himself places a universal value on creative freedom, and on 'self-surpassing' choices that are liberating (1989, pp. 55, 56) and that are made on behalf of all persons. We may agree with him that passive conformity to social custom is 'bad faith', and that we should be creative, imaginative, and actively concerned with the liberation of all persons. But that would precisely be to adopt an attitude of moral seriousness, not one of morally unconstrained freedom.

MORALITY AND MEANING

The root problem, for Sartre, is that he is convinced there is no place for objective moral values, because the universe is without meaning or purpose, and that all human commitments are 'useless' in that they will inevitably end in disappointment and death. 'Man', he writes, 'is a useless passion' (2000, p. 615). Sartre's call is not, in the end, to total freedom, but to creativity, practical commitment, and concern. But this commitment is made, he says, in anguish, abandonment, and despair, because we realize its absurdity (and so we feel anguish), because there is no higher power to help us (and so we feel abandonment), and because all will end in failure (and so we feel despair). That does not seem a strong recommendation for the way of life Sartre set before us as the authentic human possibility.

It is possible, however, to interpret our situation differently. If we ask whether the universe as we experience it is without meaning or purpose, one relevant consideration is the widespread sense of the imperative character of moral experience. It is not really plausible to say that I choose to do something because it is absurd. Then my best choice might be to eat nothing but tomatoes for the rest of my life. I may feel a normative pressure to be rational, to be creative and concerned, because these are possibilities of my being-as-human. They are not just possibilities; they are authentic possibilities, in that they place before me what I ought to be as a personal being with free choice, faced with the possibility of losing my authentic being by sub-rational and sub-moral choices. Human existence places before me the possibility of the creation and appreciation of values that are worthwhile in themselves, and of relating to other persons, not as objects but as subjects of compassion and co-operation. They are not constraints, repressing my humanity (though they are constraints on my egocentric desires). They are ideals that draw out my truest human possibilities, that express my ideal nature, the nature that I am free to realize or not, and am free to realize in different creative ways, but that stands ahead of me as a possibility that is most distinctively human and most properly my own.

If I turn away from these possibilities, I fall into a world of alienation and bad faith. I turn from creative freedom to destructive power, from positive appreciation to negative dislike, from compassion to indifference, and from free co-operation with others to a will to dominate or be dominated by them. Then, having turned from all positive goods, I will become prey to anxiety, despair, and guilt, and will be alienated both from others and from my own innermost being. That is the inner world that Sartre describes so well. The irony is that he wants freedom, but the only freedom he can find is absurd and pointless, for the universe will obliterate it without even noticing that it has ever existed.

Sartre's analysis of what human intersubjectivity is like is bleak. In his play *Huis Clos*, often titled 'No Exit' in English, one of the most memorable lines is 'Hell is other people'. Others are known to me as those who seek to dominate or be dominated by me, whose objectifying gaze seeks to reduce me to the status of an object, to judge and condemn me. In *Being and Nothingness*, he speaks of 'the petrifaction in in-itself by the Other's look' (2000, p. 430). The inescapable paradox, he thinks, is that, though others reveal to me my authentic being, they are always also threats to authentic being.

That is partly why Sartre objects to the idea of God, who would be an inescapable Other, seeing and judging all that I do, reducing me to the status of an object and subjecting me helplessly to external control. But there is something odd about Sartre's combination of the total freedom of the human subject and the threatening fact of intersubjectivity. On the one hand, others confront me with actions that may limit and oppose mine (though, without them, I would not learn to speak or act as I do). Others thereby essentially limit my freedom. On the other hand, when I discover myself as 'for-myself', I am said to be totally free to be and do whatever I wish. How can both these things be true?

For Sartre, there is little possibility of living a truly authentic life. But a descriptive ontology of human being need not disclose only the negative fact of human alienation. It can also disclose that reason, value, and purpose have a primary place in human ontology. Since humans are part of the universe, reason, value, and purpose therefore have a place in cosmic ontology. Morality and rationality both disclose being, as it appears in human awareness, as valuable, purposive, and free. That is a discernment that should be taken seriously in any analysis of human being-in-the-world, and it gives morality a transcendent dimension – a reality beyond purely personal desire or choice.

The place of reason and morality in a seemingly amoral physical universe remains problematic. But it cannot simply be denied, and Sartre's work shows it seeping through even as he overtly denies it. One thing we can say is that the physical cosmos has produced human being, that its basic processes are mathematically elegant, and that it generates spectacular beauty as well as terrifying catastrophe. In aeons of cosmic evolution, being moves from the first manifestation of vast impersonal powers of creation and destruction towards the generation of societies of free rational and moral agents and shapers of the process itself. If we see the process from its end and not from its beginning (though we have not reached the end), we may come to think that it is directed towards the interiorization (the world's coming to consciousness of its own nature in human being) and personalization (the world's taking responsibility for its own future) of the physical, and that humans stand at one crucial point in this development.

Such a hypothesis puts a question mark against Sartre's assumption of complete lack of purpose in the cosmos. If human ontological description does provide insight into the nature of being itself, some explanation is required, however hesitant, of how the personal world relates coherently to the physical world, which might ameliorate Sartre's tragic conjunction of total freedom and total purposelessness.

AUTHENTICITY AND RELIGION

The fact, movingly described by Sartre, of virtually universal human moral failure and incapacity is also problematic. Part of any adequate human phenomenology must be the recognition, not only of a sense of moral demand and moral failure, but also of a widespread sense of forgiveness, acceptance, and reconciliation. Not everyone possesses such a sense, just as not everyone has a strong sense of moral demand or of moral incapacity. But it is widespread enough to be important in any phenomenological description of what it means to exist as a human person. It is, in a broad sense, a religious impulse or feeling.

For a religious sensibility, there is not only being-in-itself (the being of objects), being-for-itself (the being of personal consciousness, oriented towards objects), and being-for-others (the being of conscious subjects in relation to other such subjects). There is also being-for-God or for a transcendent Other, the being of a subject oriented towards a reality transcending all finite objects and subjects, but providing an ultimate ground within which and in relation to which they all exist. One view of religion is that it is, as J.S. Mill supposed, the direction of the emotions and desires towards such an ideal object, recognized as of supreme value, and as rightfully authoritative over all objects of egoistic desire.

The question of whether such a reality exists cannot be settled by empirical investigation. Like our relation to other subjects, it is primarily a matter of immediate apprehension, a sense of being confronted by a totality which is mind-like or in some sense personal, and known to us (not only but primarily) in moral demand, judgement, forgiveness, and liberation.

This makes a huge difference to the analysis of human being. For it sees human being as existing in relation to a wider and deeper reality, which sets before us an objective possibility of intrinsic value, and which is able to liberate us from the condition of alienation in which we find ourselves.

Such an analysis helps to clarify the sense in which morality is related to metaphysics and to religion. Morality can be based on, for instance, an ordinary rational recognition of the importance of social feelings and the need for social co-operation. We do not have to see morality in terms of an objective demand to realize the authentic possibility of human being. But reflection on the nature of morality, as it is experienced in human consciousness, can lead to an ontology which sees the moral life as the realization of an ideal or authentic possibility for human existence – and I have suggested that Sartre, despite his disavowal of moral seriousness, was in fact morally serious about this. This in turn can lead to a metaphysical (explanatory) view of the physical cosmos as purposively directed towards generating moral consciousness. The recognition of human moral inauthenticity and failure can lead to a search for some form of liberation from this condition, a search which is often met by religious assertions that God (or Brahman, or the teaching of the Buddha) reveals – shows and makes possible – a way to authentic life, and to acceptance if not to moral perfection. A religious person is then able to see moral experience, from the first, as an encounter with a transcendent reality of supreme value, which places before humans the ideal of a morally just society of mutually self-realizing persons, and which promises its realization.

Sartre might say that he has no perceptions of objective value, though there is a human ideal of living in total freedom, and most people have fallen away from it. By contrast, Christianity – to take the religion most influential in the history of Europe – advocates a view of human existence as created to love God, as corrupted by pride and egoistic self-will, and as in need of deliverance from this corruption by some power greater than that of our conscious (and 'fallen') selves. Within the self, it says, there is a power beyond the self, from which the self has turned away, but which can reorient the self to empower it and free it from inner slavery to passion and egoism.

Those who reject the Christian view might regard the religious life as self-serving, sanctimonious, and deluded. There is no way to avoid such basic evaluational differences, but that is what they should be seen to be – formally undecidable perspectives on human existence, types of human self-understanding that underlie the most basic moral commitments.

For religious believers, morality is not autonomous and independent, even though there can usually be meaningful conversations about morality with those outside particular communities of faith. Morality is part of a way of life that is claimed to open up an authentic human possibility, to enable people to live well and in accordance with their ideal nature in the face of the imperative demands of goodness and the anguish of moral incapacity. One lesson of existentialist philosophy (taught, ironically, by Sartre, who opposed religion because he saw only the religion of bad faith, guilt, and anguish, but whose own philosophy of freedom points to the need for a power that can liberate humans from despair and enable them to be truly free) is that religious morality is not a matter of unquestioning obedience to a set of divine commands. It is a personal commitment to a transcendent moral ideal, which holds out the hope of a free, creative, and joyful life for all personal beings. Such a religiously based morality is not a matter of obedience to restrictive rules. It is a matter of aspiration to a more authentic life.

I have called Nietzsche, Marx, and Sartre 'anti-moralists', because that is how, at least sometimes, they describe themselves. They see that both morality and religion can be life-denying, socially complacent, and oppressive. But what they also help to make clear is that positive morality should aim at life, at liberation, and at authentic freedom. If it is to do so, then something more than mere morality is called for, something that can set the moral life in the context of a life-enhancing, liberating, creative understanding of human existence. That will be a metaphysical view, and I have argued that it may, despite what they say, be in some sense a religious one.

14

PHILOSOPHICAL IDEALISM AND RELIGION

WELL-BEING AND PURPOSE

It is, for theists and atheists alike, reasonable to make the welfare and flourishing of human beings the centre of an ethical system. Nietzsche, Marx, Sartre, contemporary humanists, and many Christians tend to agree on this. But, when one asks what such flourishing consists in, though there is, thank goodness, much common ground, answers can still differ considerably. I suspect that the common ground is there because modern liberal humanism is living on the borrowed capital of an overtly renounced Christian theism. I also suspect that, having renounced its theistic basis, humanism becomes more like a very reasonable and not too demanding morality for comfortable members of a fairly secure and wealthy society. Appreciating poetry and going to art classes does indeed make for a pleasant life. But is that all there is to morality in a patently unjust and violent world?

The ethics of Aristotle is probably the first major written exploration of what may be called a humanist approach to morality that exists, and it may be no accident that the virtues he lists are those of a small leisured and wealthy elite who have no difficulties about owning slaves and regarding non-Greeks as barbarians. He lists a set of distinctive human excellences (the virtues), which go to make up human flourishing and happiness. Aristotle was not, however, a humanist in the typically modern sense. He had an essentialist and purposive view of human nature, and a belief that physical reality was oriented by nature towards one supreme Good. God, for Aristotle, is not the efficient cause of reality, but is the ultimate final cause. God is an Ideal of fully realized value, which attracts the physical universe 'by love' or desire. The nature of this Ideal is intellectual contemplation or abstract intellectual thought (*theoria*), and so the highest sort of activity for humans is to imitate God by pursuing a life of contemplation. Other virtues are ways of realizing the final cause of human nature, actualizing the potentialities of that nature, that for the sake of which human nature exists. If you give up the Aristotelian ideas of essential nature, final causes, and a supreme good, what remains of his ethical system?

Suppose that there is no supreme final cause of all things, no God. There will be no final causes, no purposes at which humans ought to aim. Could we then continue to speak of morality in terms of the full realization of distinctively human capacities? We could, but what we say would have lost most if not all of its moral force. It could be queried whether there are any distinctively human capacities, or, if there are, whether that has any moral relevance. It could be asked why we should realize them, and, even more, why we should realize them fully, especially if we do not particularly want to. Of course, we would want to be prudent, and use reason to obtain a fairly secure and successful and happy life. But would this mean that we had to know as fully, feel as deeply, will as creatively, and sympathize as broadly as we possibly could?

It seems to me that Aristotle's view of ethics only took on a fuller plausibility when it was incorporated into the ethical system of medieval Christianity, especially as formulated by Thomas Aquinas. In that system, there is a God who has purposes for created things, including human beings. God would presumably want intelligent creatures to realize the capacities God has given them, insofar as they contribute to individual and general good. So, there is a good intellectual background for seeing morality in terms of the realization of distinctive human capacities.

The introduction of a creator God, which provides the divine mind in which final causes can objectively exist, which demands that they be realized, and which is capable of realizing them in the world, already changes Aristotle's system to some extent. The Christian God is said to love humanity and to create and redeem the world, and so is more actively involved in the world than Aristotle's God. The ideal of moral perfection will therefore not solely be contemplation. It will also include love and compassion, and especially, if the life of Jesus is anything to go by, compassion for the weak and the dispossessed. Distinctive human capacities will certainly include contemplation. But they will also include practical love and service of others, and a sort of 'ontological humility', that follows from seeing everything as given freely and undeservedly by

God. In addition, since God is love, there is good reason to obey God out of love and gratitude for what God is and for what God has done, and that will add a powerful motivation to moral conduct (which will be conduct that God desires).

Thomas Aquinas' God is also unlike Aristotle's God in offering an afterlife in which individual persons will experience the just consequences of their earthly actions, and in offering the promise of eternal life with God to all who accept God's offer. Thus it is that the Thomist adaptation of Aristotelian ethics changes the character of the virtues and adds incomparably stronger levels of motivation for moral conduct.

Nevertheless, Aristotle formulated his ethics without belief in an actively loving God or a fully personal afterlife, and it may be thought that it is all the stronger for that, since it does not depend on contentious beliefs. My point is that Aristotle did have a purposive worldview, and did see the human virtues as oriented towards, and attracted by, the idea of a supremely good, if rather self-contained, God. It is in fact influenced by a background metaphysical worldview, and it would be wrong to ignore that.

The meta-ethics can be abstracted from the metaphysics. We could just say that realizing distinctive human excellences is worthwhile for its own sake, and makes overall for a happy life. I think this is importantly true. It would be disastrous if only the religious had a firm ethical basis for conduct, while the rest of the world had no reason to be virtuous. But, of course, separating off ethics from theistic metaphysics in this way itself depends upon adopting a particular metaphysical stance – namely, that there is no creator God who has a purpose for humanity and for the cosmos, and who cares about its realization. In addition, what exactly one thinks the virtues (human excellences) are may be rather different if one denies the existence of one objective ideal of human nature. It is more likely that one might deny the existence of any essential human nature at all, or that, like Sartre, one might embrace an idea of total freedom to be whatever one decides to be.

A wholly secular version of Aristotelian ethics is possible, and aiming at the realization of distinctive human capacities probably does make for a satisfying life, especially for those who have the leisure and opportunity for it. There is enough agreement between a secular view of self-realization and a more metaphysical view like that of Aristotle or Aquinas to enable them to find many things in common. But there will be important differences, and, for a secularist, self-realization is only one possible approach to the moral life. An Epicurean pursuit of pleasure, a Utilitarian concern for universal happiness, or a Humean concern for social utility and extended sympathy will probably always continue to exist.

In this sense, self-realization is quite strongly rooted in a particular sort of theistic view like that of traditional Christian moral theology. Saying that using distinctive human capacities will in general produce a happy life is very different from saying that there is a God whose nature is love (compassion, concern, co-operation and delight), who created human lives for a purpose, who desires that humans should realize their distinctive capacities, who will help them to do so, who will ensure there are serious consequences for not doing so, but will forgive those who genuinely acknowledge their failure and try to seek the good, and who will ensure that the realization of human purpose is in the end assured.

If you do not think there is such a God, this will not appeal. But perhaps one reason inclining to belief in God is a sense that morality is a matter of self-realization, that humans are distinctively rational as well as social and passionate creatures, that there is a goal for each human life, that humans are doomed to almost inevitable moral failure, but that one needs to have hope for the future if moral effort is to be intelligible. Belief in the nature of the ultimate facts (metaphysics) and belief in the nature of ultimate values (meta-ethics) are closely intertwined. For that reason, it is misleading to say that ethics is completely distinct from metaphysical or religious and ideological worldviews. How you think you should act in the world will depend upon how you see the world. How you see the world will depend upon the values upon which you think you should act. Both aspects are necessary to the fully examined life.

ABSOLUTE IDEALISM

In expounding a theistic morality, I have concentrated on the idea of self-realization as a moral imperative. The idea of self-realization, however, may have misleading connotations. For a theist, such realization must be of the 'true' self, the self as it exists as an archetype in the divine mind, the essential individual nature of a human life. This does not mean that there is a preconceived plan of exactly how each life should go in detail. But it does mean that there are specific capacities and dispositions that are to be developed in specific ways by free individual choices, and that are to be oriented towards actualizing the basic personal values of understanding, compassion, sensitivity, and creativity. I have also stressed that God cares for all individuals, so that self-realization cannot be purely an individual or self-centred thing. It must be concerned with the realization of many selves in society, whose co-operation is an essential part of any individual realization.

There is a paradoxical sense, therefore, in which true self-realization requires an element of self-sacrifice. Jesus said, 'If any want to become my followers, let them deny themselves and take up their cross and follow me' (Mark 8: 34). It might be better to speak of the realization of object-ive goodness in us and in all humanity. This requires severe discipline of many natural desires and egoistic impulses. The point of speaking of self-realization is to stress that moral conduct is aiming at human fulfil-ment and flourishing. But it does so in a world that is so corrupted by hatred, greed, ignorance, and pride that the path of virtue will probably be hard and may well end in tragedy. It may seem a strange sense of self-realization that it may lead to conflict and death. This fact introduces a new dimension of moral action, which is the way that the individual self that is to be realized must first be transformed. It may be transformed by a concern for a profound unity with other selves. It must also, for a theist, be transformed by a concern for union with the Self of all, with God. Idealist philosophy, best known in the writings of Hegel in Germany and probably of Bradley in early twentieth-century Britain, sheds new light on this aspect of morality.

The philosophy of idealism is not very fashionable at the beginning of the twenty-first century, and is often ignored. It is a development from the philosophy of Kant, though not in a way of which he particularly approved. I do not want to consider it for its own sake, which would be a major enterprise in itself. But I do think it can add something to an understanding of the relationship between morality and religion, and I want to show how this is so. I think what it does is to stress the way in which moral action requires a change in the way of seeing things, rather than just a commitment of the will. To show this, I will consider some of the writings of one who is perhaps the major English Idealist of the early twentieth century, F.H. Bradley. In *Ethical Studies*, he argues that in moral action we are taken beyond the finitude of our empirical self. Indeed, 'in morality the existence of my mere private self . . . has already ceased' (1927, p. 80), and 'The will of the whole knowingly wills itself in me'.

When we adopt the moral point of view, we are not merely trying our best to be impartial. We are dying to self, as isolated, almost inevitably self-interested, individuals. We are making-present in the world, at least in part, a unitary reality (Hegel calls it '*Geist*' or Absolute Spirit), which is realized progressively in time and history, partly by working in and through us insofar as we are open to it.

This is not an alien will, over against me. It is my own true self, since I am its expression in time, and to know myself truly would be to know this to be so. My moral endeavours are attempts to let this be manifest, to let that reality that is the true centre of my, and of every other, being be expressed: 'the self is identified with, and wills, and realises a concrete universal, a real totality' (Bradley, 1927, p. 81) (a 'concrete universal' is a whole or unity that is more than the sum of its parts, and yet it only exists in its parts, not as a separate reality).

The ultimate aim of morality is indeed self-realization. But 'The self to be realised is . . . made what it is by relation to others', and it is essentially part of 'a system of selves, an organism of which I am a member, and in whose life I live' (ibid., p. 116). Of a truly moral person we can say, 'He has found his life in the life of the whole' (ibid., p. 172), and 'the self-consciousness of himself is the self-consciousness of the whole in him' (ibid., p. 183).

For such a view, morality is a way of seeing as much as a way of acting. It sees that one's individual life as an atomistic and self-sufficient entity is an abstraction or illusion. The truth is that we are parts of a wider social reality, and our selves are constituted by relationships with others. When we see all things and experiences as parts of one interconnected whole, we lose our ego-centredness, for in reality there exists no separate ego to be centred on. It is when we experience the inner unity of all things that we cease to think of individual self-interest even as a real possibility. We see that the moral life is 'to realise oneself by realising the will which is above us and higher than ours' (ibid., p. 159).

Bradley did not think that there was, or that it was important to think that there was, any objective personal God whose will humans obey. Indeed, such a notion could undermine morality by turning it into obedience to external commands. The 'objective will' is wholly expressed in the community of personal wills, and in the progressive series of moral advances that is human history. In Bradley's words, 'History is the working out of the true human nature through various incomplete stages' (ibid., p. 192), and the highest moral vocation of the individual is to play a part in this historical process.

There are some moral problems about this way of putting things. All who have seen the rise of Fascism, and of the philosophy of a 'Leader' who identifies his will with the moral spirit of the Aryan race, and tramples on individual rights in the name of the 'good of the nation', may tremble at Bradley's words. When individuals are reduced to functions of the social organism, and that organism is taken as the sole criterion of unquestionable moral goodness, some basic moral beliefs are seriously threatened. It may be important to hold that individuals have inherent moral worth, and that societies must be judged by higher standards than their own.

The unity that moral agents seek must be one that preserves individual freedom and that is wider than that of any family, tribe, or nation. If so, individual persons should not be reduced to being appearances of a wider purely social whole, and the moral ideal should not be reduced to being identical to, or being wholly expressed in, a historical process, however progressive that process is thought to be. That is to say, there is a real moral point in distinguishing individuals from 'the cosmic Whole', and in distinguishing any moral Ideal that actually exists from the temporal universe in which it may well be (partly) expressed.

When Bradley considers the nature of religion, in the final chapter of *Ethical Studies*, he at least partly responds to these points. He says that, whereas in morality the ideal is always to some extent a 'not yet', and the higher will is never completely realized, in religion we postulate 'the ideal self considered as realised and real' (1927, p. 319). This may seem a clear concept of God as self-conscious, self-complete, and distinct from the cosmic Whole. But it is not quite that, because this 'Ideal Self' is also described as the 'all and the whole reality', and, though it is existent in reality, it is yet to be realized in the world of appearance. The Absolute Ideal is not distinct from the cosmos, as the creator of something other than itself. It is what appears as the cosmos, and finite persons, like everything else, are parts of this appearance. This creates a major problem of how a perfect and changeless Ideal can also appear as a multiplicity of constantly changing, imperfect, and even evil wills.

In a passage from *Appearance and Reality* that is often quoted by hostile philosophers as typical Idealist nonsense, Bradley says that the Absolute Reality 'enters into, but is itself incapable of, evolution and progress' (1893, p. 499). I do not think it is such obvious nonsense, for what he is saying is that there is an unchanging and wholly perfect state of the Absolute, which, being perfect, is incapable of progress. But there is also a temporal aspect of the Absolute, which is its appearance in time, its reality as striving and self-realizing Will. Nevertheless, his way of putting it is problematic, for, if we do not distinguish God (the personal form of the Absolute) from finite individuals, it must be God, appearing in many finite wills, who does evil. Despite his claim that this evil will be transformed in the Absolute itself, it seems contradictory to say that a perfect being can do evil acts in any form whatsoever. That is a good reason for thinking that individual wills must be distinguished from the divine will more sharply.

PERSONAL IDEALISM

Bradley insists that the Absolute includes every finite appearance, but in a non-temporal way: 'Reality consists . . . in a higher experience, superior to the distinctions which it includes and overrides' (1893, p. 195). The Absolute is one and perfect, has the nature of experience, and somehow includes and yet transforms all appearances. For instance, 'the Absolute is timeless, but it possesses time as an isolated aspect which, in ceasing to be isolated, loses its special character' (ibid., p. 210).

One reason why this form of Idealism virtually disappeared from British philosophy was that such language seemed incoherent, even self-contradictory, and its basic assumption of one perfect timeless Absolute, which yet included time, pain, and evil, in an 'over-ridden' way, seemed both meaningless and gratuitous. Why should the Absolute in itself exclude all relations and all temporality? If pain and evil are necessary appearances of a perfect reality, does that mean that they are somehow to be accepted and embraced as good? And is the Absolute the only experient of completed perfection, while all finite selves know only imperfection and struggle?

I find these problems very severe, even though I am in sympathy with the idea that all the reality we experience is an appearance of a deeper spiritual reality. The problems are considerably eased if we deny that the Absolute in itself needs to be wholly without temporality or relationships. Absolute Mind can then be conceived as a supreme and self-existent creative and experiencing subject. God will be the most powerful possible source of all beings, the experiencer of all that is, or may be, changeless in that it is always the same unoriginated, uncausable, and indestructible subject of action and experience. Precisely as a subject of action and experience, it will be temporal and changing, in that it both experiences and relates to all temporal beings and events. Its nature is necessarily creative, wise, compassionate, and blissful. Yet it is not a wholly change-less reality that in a mysterious way includes all finite appearances in a completely non-temporal way. It will change and be changed by all temporal and finite events. It will not be a supreme instantiation of a completely changeless and timeless perfection. It will rather generate and be aware of a maximal number of intrinsically worthwhile temporal states to a maximal degree.

The idea of God as instantiating supreme perfection is a fairly standard view of God from Aristotle and Anselm to Leibniz and Kant. But many modern philosophers take creativity, temporality, and relationship to be desirable perfections, as most classical philosophers did not. In a revised temporalist context, 'supreme perfection' is read as meaning, 'possessing a number or degree of intrinsically worthwhile properties which will always be greater than is actualized in any other actual being'. The Supreme Subject will necessarily and changelessly be in this sense supremely perfect. But the properties that constitute its perfection will continually change, as the Supreme relates to events in a temporal, creative, and responsive fashion.

As such, the Ideal is distinct from the developing cosmos of struggle and suffering in which finite persons originate. It is ideal in that it presents a supreme case of truth, beauty, and goodness that attracts finite minds precisely by its absolute value. In itself, it is fully realized, and yet that 'fully' is never statically complete. It realizes itself by endlessly creating and appreciating new values, while always remaining the same agent and experient of those values. If the existent ideal is infinitely creative, then it is never a finally completed whole, beyond further change.

The Supreme Mind experiences all that finite beings experience, and does so in a transformed way, for which pain and suffering take on a very different character in the light of the total experience of which they are part. So far, Bradley is right. But, for Bradley, it is only the Absolute that experiences that transformation of pain by a wider joy. Finite persons remain stuck with unrelieved pain. If we grant immortality to all beings who have a sense of continuing identity, it is possible to suppose that they too will be able to share in such a transformation in some future form of their lives.

If God is supremely powerful, and always knows all that has ever been, such a supposition is plausible. Bradley is disparaging of any thoughts of personal immortality. But, if there is truly to be a realized end and goal of moral striving such that it can be called wholly good, it is a moral requirement that it must be a goal that can be realized by all sentient beings, not a goal that such beings can never hope to experience personally. The end need not be an end such that, once attained, nothing else ever happens. It may rather be a continuation of creative and blissful experience, but in which finite minds are fully united to the divine Mind and Will, in such a way that moral striving is ended, evil abolished, and the creative union of divine and human wills is realized.

The object of religious faith, says Bradley, 'is the inseparable unity of human and divine' (1927, p. 330). This is 'an organic human–divine totality; as one body with diverse members, as one self which, in many selves, realises, wills, and loves itself, as they do themselves in it' (ibid., p. 331). This, though it uses the vocabulary of theism, does not seem quite right. The object of theistic faith is God, perfect Mind, not the community of minds that are in union with God. In the world in which humans now exist, union with God is a future hope, but reverence for the Good, which remains distinct from finite wills, is the object of present consciousness. God does not realize, will, and love *itself* in many selves. God creates other selves, at least partly autonomous or self-shaping. God wills that they should attain their end by their own efforts, in co-operation with the divine. And God does not love God only in finite persons, though God may realize a specific sort of love – redemptive, compassionate, love – in relation to and even through finite persons. Moreover, if finite persons are to love and realize themselves in God, there must be more to finite consciousness than the often painful and always inadequate sense of union with the divine that is apparent in ordinary human lives. In all these ways, an affirmation of personal theism seems more consilient with Bradley's perspective on morality, and more coherent than Bradley's view of an all-including timeless Absolute. It is better able to account both for our sense of an objective moral demand and our hope for the realization of a desirable goal of moral endeavour.

Bradley's form of Absolute Idealism attempts to find the divine–human unity actually realized, but in a higher form, which is not accessible to any finite consciousness. For a properly theistic or personal Idealism, however, the existent Ideal is never fully realized in this world; human and divine are not yet fully one; and God is not 'an organism which realizes itself in its members', and is conscious of itself only in them (so that they become necessary to the divine self-consciousness). It may be true that God realizes and expresses the divine love in relation to finite persons, but the full union of human and divine wills is a future hope and goal.

Many forms of theism would wish to speak of a real future divine–human union of wills, and therefore would, with Bradley, see any divine-command theory of morality as one-sided and inadequate. Such theisms would see morality as a longing and aspiration for an inward union with the divine, in which the self could be truly fulfilled, and would become truly an expression or image of the divine. Religion will, as Bradley says, add to the moral ideal precisely the hope for union with the Ideal as existent. This will never undermine moral duties, and the divine will must always be conceived by us as harmonious with our highest moral perceptions. Yet religious hope may well add something to our purely moral duties, since it is concerned with establishing a certain sort of relationship with the Ideal. Bradley insists on thinking of God (the Absolute) as changelessly and fully expressed in its appearances, and therefore denies its distinct existence as a perfect Good, which is now a demand of morality, but will become a union of love in a form of being other than this. For a more fully personal Idealism (which is what, I think, theism really is), God, the cosmos, and finite persons remain distinct realities, but their destiny is to become a communion of embodied persons existing within one unitary spiritual reality.

THE END OF MORALITY

There is, for personal Idealism, a distinction between the actualized perfection of the divine being itself and the future perfection of many societies of finite beings in union with the Absolute (a perfection and a union that is not static, but is a continuing series of creative and cognitive acts). In that future, as Bradley says at the conclusion of *Ethical Studies*, 'morality is removed and survives in its fulfilment' (1927, p. 341). That is, on achieving full union with the divine will, the 'ought' that presupposes a 'not yet united' disappears, while at the same time the goal of moral striving is achieved. So, 'our morality is consummated in oneness with God, and everywhere we find that "immortal Love", which builds itself for ever on contradiction, but in which the contradiction is eternally resolved' (ibid., p. 342). Moral striving, which presupposes a contradiction or at least partial opposition between finite wills and the divine will, is consummated in union. I suggest that it is more coherent to suppose that the consummation includes all sentient beings in the future than that it holds only for the timeless Absolute itself, in which all sentient beings are effectively dissolved.

God as a will that is (partly, I would say) realized in the world is what is known in morality, and to realize this might help to liberate some idealist views from their tendency to promote nationalistic or totalitarian ideologies. But perhaps it would also be helpful to stress that God's will, which is always for good, and is therefore not fully realized in the world, is often opposed by created wills. In that sense, though the world does realize the divine ideal, it does not do so completely or in every respect. The full realization of the divine will, which is the completed end and ideal of the cosmos, requires a final eradication of evil and a future renewal of the world. A distinction thus appears between the future realization of the ideal in finite reality and the perfection of the Ideal in itself. Religion, in a developed state, requires both of these.

Bradley blurs this distinction, or even denies it, for he regards any form of immortality as highly improbable. There will, it seems, be no future state in which the Absolute as unconditionally good is fully expressed in appearance. There will certainly be no such state in which all finite minds can share. Instead, 'Every element of the universe, sensation, feeling, thought and will, must be included within one comprehensive sentience' (1893, p. 159), but in a way that transfigures their natures, uniting them in one harmonious whole that we cannot imagine. This state of the Absolute is not accessible by any finite mind, and so there seems to be a huge gulf between the experiences of finite minds, often miserable or painful in the extreme, and the perfect experience of the Absolute. It seems very odd to say that many minds, existing in suffering, are the appearances of a Reality of perfect experience. Religion requires some greater possibility of liberation from suffering than this. 'Ugliness, error, and evil, all are owned by, and all essentially contribute to the wealth of the Absolute. The Absolute . . . has no assets beyond appearances, and again, with appearances alone to its credit, the Absolute would be bankrupt' (ibid., p. 489). But, if many finite minds experience only the evil, and that evil is only transmuted in the experience of the Absolute, it hardly seems plausible to say that the appearances are genuinely of a perfect Absolute.

Idealist philosophy offers a view of morality that integrates it fully with a spiritual view of reality, and makes it clear that morality is as much a matter of how you see and interpret human life as it is a matter of sheer commitment of the will. If it is true that morality, taken in itself alone, carries the sense of a higher will and goal to which the self should be subordinated, and which is of supreme worth, then it is true that morality can plausibly incline the mind to the 'religious' view that there objectively exists such a will and goal, union with which is possible, and is the completion of moral endeavour.

In *Appearance and Reality*, Bradley defines religion as 'devotion to the one perfect object which is utterly good' (1893, p. 400, footnote). 'Our morality is consummated in oneness with God' (ibid., p. 342), and true religion exists 'only when the divine will, of which for faith the world is the realisation, reflects itself in us' (ibid., p. 341).

The positive point he makes is that such a divine will should not simply be considered as external to human personhood. It is when our wills are in union with the higher will, so that it acts in an inward co-operation with us, that we realize our own greatest potential and happiness. If the higher will is the will of God, then God must be considered as in active and inward relationship to us, and as realizing the divine nature as love precisely in this relationship. The particular, temporal, and social is not an illusion or irrelevant or external to the being of God. It is part of God's self-expression, but that self-expression is in relation to the finite, not one that eradicates difference and finite individuality. Individuals are constituted by their relationships, and they see themselves truly when they see themselves as parts of one organic whole. But that organic whole is not simply identical to God. It is certainly wholly dependent upon God, and constituted by its relation to God, but it is in itself a cosmic process that is yet to be brought to completion and purged of imperfection beyond the history of this ambiguous universe. Morality merges into metaphysics if and when it is seen as involving a dying to the egoistic self, while at the same time being true to the self in some deeper sense. For such an understanding of morality, it is not just a matter of following some rules about how to treat others. It is a matter of understanding the self in its innermost relation to the greater reality of which it is part.

MORALITY AND WORLD RELIGIONS

For religious believers, the 'greater reality' of which, in morality, we seek to be part is not just of physical nature, ruled by chance and necessity, or of human society, replete with greed and conflict, but of something beyond the natural world that is fully real and of objective value. What is at stake in morality is a free orientation of the self either towards egoistic desire or towards the realization of intrinsically worthwhile states for their own sake. It is a matter of enslavement or liberation. The enslaved self loses its being by negation, by becoming subject to passionate attachments that are illusory or empty. The liberated self also loses its being, but by positive enhancement, by becoming one with an objective good that endures, and in which the self is fulfilled by playing its own creative part in the realization of the intrinsically good.

The major world religions construe this objectively good reality in various ways. Bradley's Absolute Idealism is nearest to the *Advaita* (non-dual) *Vedanta* of the eighth-century Indian sage Sankara. For Sankara, all finite phenomena, including all finite selves, are illusory appearances, and are parts of *Brahman*, one absolute Self of intelligence and bliss. Sankara sees the devotional and ritual practices of religion as means to achieve knowledge of *Brahman*, and holds that, once it is attained, egoistic desire will cease to exist, the sense of a separate ego will be destroyed, and, realizing that we are one with the Self of all, we will naturally attain a supremely impartial and compassionate viewpoint that transforms our moral outlook. Morality may begin as obedience to rules and principles. But its heart is the realization, through meditation and moral practice, that the finite ego is not ultimately real, and that to realize our own true natures we must realize our identity with the Self of all. Moral practice is a way to religious insight, and that insight, once attained, transforms moral practice.

Other religious traditions that originated in India see things slightly differently, while being in broad agreement about the relation of morality to what may be called metaphysical insight. Some (like the *Vishist Advaita* of the twelfth-century sage Ramanuja) have a more personalist view of the Self of all. Finite selves are not absorbed into *Brahman*, but they have their being in *Brahman* as separate souls. This allows a more positive view of the world of appearance. It is not just illusion, but may play a positive role in expressing the nature of the Absolute Self. The basic insight, however, is the same – that the ultimate aim of morality is to pass beyond the sense of the isolated ego, and find the true self in conscious dependence upon the Self of all.

Buddhist traditions tend not to think of the ultimately Real as personal (though many *Boddhisattvas* are regarded in practice as personal beings). The religious path, however, is here also one of transcending any sense of ego, with its attachments to 'things possessed by the ego', and attaining mindfulness, a harmony with a wider unity, manifest perhaps in society, perhaps in nature, but more often in an indescribable state (*Nirvana*) where all selfish desires have been extinguished, and there is only one unbounded ocean of intelligence and bliss.

Semitic religious traditions are more overtly theistic, positing a Supreme Mind that has a positive purpose for the world and creates relatively autonomous persons through whom that purpose may be realized in various concrete situations. There are objective values to be realized in history, and we can play a part in realizing them. We can see how the

Hebrew idea of one moral will for a society of justice and peace arose out of this sense of moral objectivity and historical purpose. The idea of God is a natural objectification of this sense, capable of giving it a metaphysical basis, a view of how things ultimately are.

The idea of God could be a wish-fulfilling projection, or it could license the authoritarian imposition of commands said to have been made by a vengeful God. Religion is not free from ambiguity and corruption. That is a good reason for insisting that religious views should always be qualified by attention to moral requirements, and should never conflict with such requirements. But we can think positively of God as an objective will for good, which offers the possibility of a fulfilling personal union with that will, and of the final realization of our highest moral goals.

Idealist philosophies, among which Bradley's is only one, offer a number of different ways of providing views of the self and of ultimate reality, which will support moral endeavour, seen as an inner reorientation of the self towards objective good. I have defended a more personal form of theism than Bradley's Absolute Idealism. But the aim is the same – to provide a view of the self in relation to ultimate reality, which will make sense of our natural feeling that moral commitment requires both self-sacrifice (of the self-concerned ego) and self-realization (of the higher self), and that in such commitment something like an authentic human way of life is to be found.

THE BEATIFIC VISION

Bradley rejects what he sees as an orthodox Christian view of God and immortality, but, in fact, he is much nearer to an orthodox viewpoint than he thinks. When Thomas Aquinas wrote about morality, he pointed out that, for a believer in God, there are not only natural goods at which humans by nature are set to aim. There is also the all-important super-natural good, a supreme goal of all positive desire, knowledge of and union with which is supremely fulfilling. That goal is God, conceived as the changeless and perfect creator and redeemer of the world. 'Our ultimate end is uncreated good, namely God, who alone can fill our will to the brim because of his infinite goodness' (Aquinas, *Summa Theologiae*, 1a2ae, 3, 1).

Perfect happiness lies in knowledge of the essential nature of the first cause. This is only fully possible by the supernatural divine gift of grace, since only God can fill us with the knowledge of his essential beatitude (*beatitudo*). To know God fully is to be made like God, and only God can make us like God. Beatitude, and the path towards final beatitude which begins in this life, is thus infused by God, and is not attainable by human effort. The Spirit must fill human lives with God's own love.

This uniting of human to divine is partially manifested by specific theological virtues, the 'infused virtues', infused into the soul by God, the virtues of faith, hope, and love. Faith is the virtue of desiring God. It is the beginning of sharing in God's knowledge and love of himself. As such, it can only be produced in us by God, as the beginning of a new way of life, a 're-birth in the Spirit'. 'Faith is that habit of mind whereby eternal life begins in us' (Aquinas, *Summa Theologiae*, 2a2ae, 4, 1).

It is much more than the acceptance of a set of propositional beliefs, but, for Thomas as a Dominican monk, it does entail the acceptance of the propositional beliefs of the orthodox Christian creed. That is because the creed sets out what God has done for human salvation, and thus God's nature as redemptive and unitive love. There can, of course, be non-Christian faith in God, and subsequent Roman Catholic teaching has carefully set out the view that, while belief in Christ as the revelation of God is ultimately necessary for union with God, people can have a true faith in God if they cannot, for good reason, see what Christ truly is. God will, according to this doctrine, lead them to see the fuller truth of Christ in the world to come. This may sound slightly arrogant, until one realizes that virtually all systems of belief, theistic or not, must say much the same thing – though, if there is no life after death, most people will never find out the truth.

Faith is not knowledge, and when we attain perfect knowledge of God faith will fade away. Faith is more like firm attachment to a belief, because on hearing about God we are attracted to this vision of goodness, by the prospect of deliverance from moral failure and ignorance of truth, and by the hope of a better life, the beginnings of which we seem to feel in the encounter with God. The belief must have a fairly high degree of probability, though it cannot be conclusively established, and it must be seen as of great value.

William James wrote a classic article on 'The Will to Believe' (1896), in which he held that faith is justified when it presents a living option, when there is no way of establishing conclusively either the belief or its alternatives, when one is forced to believe something about the issue in question, and when belief would make a great practical difference for good. I think that Thomas would agree with this, but would probably add that faith arises from encounter with Christ, which moves the heart, and which is a response to an active moving of the heart by God (a gift of grace). Faith is already a sort of love, the beginning of the love of God, by which God begins to disclose the supreme desirability of the divine life.

To use a faint analogy, it is like falling in love with a person whom one may have known for some time. But suddenly that person is seen in a new light, as irresistibly attractive and beautiful. Such a discernment evokes trust (the New Testament word for faith, *pistis*, can mean 'trust'), and it involves a personal commitment and loyalty that may go well beyond the evidence, and yet not be thought irrational. So, having heard of God, or of the life and teaching of Jesus, a person may seem to feel a disclosure of God's love and beauty that is irresistible. That is the apprehension of the grace of God. If there is a God, it is the most natural and obvious way of evoking a reasonable belief in God, for which the heart generates a commitment that is not confined by the rigid canons of quasi-mathematical demonstration.

Faith carries with it the theological virtue of hope, hope for eternal beatitude, which only God can provide. It goes without saying that such hope can only exist in those whose hearts are ready to turn to God, and hope for something that is not the fulfilment of selfish desire, but of a passion for the realization of objective goodness. But hope too will fade when knowledge comes, leaving the one unfading virtue of love. This is not humanly generated love. It is the divine love itself, placed in the human heart, and so it is a sharing in God's own love.

Such love, says Thomas, can be called *amicitia*, friendship, which loves another for its own sake, and by which God's happiness is communicated to us. For Thomas, God loves and finds happiness in the contemplation of his own being, which is supreme perfection. It is in this divine self-contemplation that we share in beatitude, and so participate in eternity. Yet in this life our love for God (and, insofar as we have it, God's love in us) necessarily involves love for the world God has made, for the other beings that God has made, and for ourselves as creatures called into being to share in the divine love. The love of God does not exclude love of finite things, but mandates such love, since God's love is infinite. In this way, the doctrine of one God who actively creates and loves the cosmos develops considerably beyond the Platonic concept of the Good, which neither acts nor loves, but is simply an unchanging ideal.

Eastern Orthodox theologians emphasize the doctrine of *theosis*, or sharing in the divine nature (derived from 2 Peter 1: 4), and see the ultimate goal of human life as being a real union with the divine being.

Western Christians tend to be more cautious with such talk of union, but there can be little doubt that there is a sense in which the union of human and divine in Christ, and also in those who are 'in Christ', is a central theme in the Christian view. It is also found in Sufi forms of Islam, and adds another distinctive strand to theistic morality, with a strong connection to a metaphysical belief.

The conception of the beatific vision, of the theological virtues, of the work of divine grace, and of union with the divine transforms a secular view of morality. Something like it forms part of many theistic worldviews. It sets out a view of an ultimate moral purpose, of a supreme object of devotion, and of a way of seeing the moral life as one of disclosure, response, dependence, deliverance, and union, which is quite distinct from almost any secular view of morality. Such a morality cannot be autonomous, for it depends upon seeing the object of morality as an independently existing reality, belief in which requires a metaphysical commitment. It can, however, insist upon the freedom of humans to make their own moral decisions and to work out by rational reflection what is morally right and good. It can insist that moral considerations are irreducible and most often of overriding importance. It can insist that religious beliefs must be consistent with the highest moral standards we can conceive. Thus, there are important senses in which religious morality is autonomous, and in which religious beliefs are subject to moral criticism. Yet religious moralities, in quite a distinctive way, depend essentially upon metaphysical beliefs in spiritual reality, and they cannot be simply assimilated to one allegedly universal and independent moral base.

15

SOME CHRISTIAN DOCTRINES

SIN AND ATONEMENT

I have defended the view that certain wholly reasonable, but not overwhelmingly obvious, conceptions of morality depend in important ways upon belief in God. I have most often referred to Christian ideas of God, because most of the philosophers I have talked about have done so themselves. But the idea of God defended here is not necessarily or exclusively Christian, and most of the philosophers I have discussed – most notably Plato, Aristotle, Kant, Mill, and Bradley – have not been Christians.

I want to conclude, however, by referring to a number of problems concerning the nature of morality that arise specifically with regard to some distinctively Christian doctrines. I will consider four such problems, which some have regarded as morally dubious: belief that morality depends on divine commands; belief in original sin; belief in atonement; and belief in Hell.

Some contemporary philosophers think that the special character of religious ethics lies mainly and perhaps solely in the fact that it sees duty as obedience to divine commands. Simon Blackburn characterizes it thus. There is such a religious morality, but Professor Blackburn omits to mention that Christian moralists have usually condemned it (or one main form of it) as founded on a mistake. The mistake is to think that God commands obedience to a set of rules (perhaps rules for which no independent reasons can be found), and punishes us if we do not obey them. Or, even worse, God commands obedience to rules that we are unable to obey (because of 'original sin'), and then arbitrarily forgives some people, but not all, and exempts them from what should be their due punishment. Worse still, God punishes an innocent man (Jesus) in their place, and then regards them as innocent, even though they are not. To cap it all, God gives a few chosen souls an eternity of happiness, for no particular merit of their own, while millions are condemned to eternal fire for not doing what they were unable to do anyway. On this view, people are free to ignore morality altogether, and may still achieve an eternal happiness through no merit of their own. So divine commands become totally irrelevant – except for the fact that they license the punishment of an innocent victim to balance the strange equation of crime and punishment – every crime requires punishment, but it need not be of the criminal – that God requires.

There are many strands of thought to unravel here. I would not deny that some religious believers may hold views very like this. But even those views need to be stated in a much more sympathetic way to convey an understanding of how such believers think and feel. And most Christians have not held such views, as I hope to show now.

First, there is something right, but also something odd, in the notion of 'divine commands'. For most Christian views of God, it would be wrong to think of God as issuing arbitrary commands to which God requires strict obedience. God is necessarily good, and divine commands will issue from the necessary (not the arbitrary) nature of God. God's purpose, in the words of the Westminster Confession, is that humans should know God, and enjoy God for ever. Humans are created to know God, to share in the divine nature, to become one with the divine goodness, and thereby to find their fulfilment. Divine commands are 'for our good'. That is, they map out the way to our final fulfilment in God.

This does not make moral rules merely means to a prudential good. They depict a way of life oriented to the universal good of all creatures. The beginning of true morality is to see myself as I truly am – a creature made to participate in God through the exercise of virtue (of distinctive human excellences). Christians must learn to love, and they must do so by learning to share in the divine love. They can only do that by seeing and coming to know God. When one sees God truly, one will respond appropriately – in reverence and adoration, which is the appropriate love for God.

Thus it is that the most important commandment of divine law is to 'love God'. No one can conjure up love to order. But you come to love God insofar as you come to see God truly. So the command is to learn to attend to God, the supremely good, and respond appropriately. This is no arbitrary command. It is an instruction to learn to see appropriately, and that requires purity of heart. Obedience or disobedience to God's commands does involve reward and punishment. But the reward is not one that would appeal to the unreformed heart. It is simply the vision of God itself, in which vision all desires are at once transformed and fulfilled. And the punishment is not some fixed penalty. It is the loss of the knowledge of God, and a life of increasing inability to love and of enslavement to self-destroying desires.

If this is so, one can see that speaking of a 'divine command' morality is apt to be misleading. It might be better to speak of an 'objective ideal' morality (though that too, taken on its own, will be one-sided in being unduly impersonal), where an ideal of moral perfection is instantiated in the personal reality of God, and draws things to itself by desire for the good. Knowledge of it is in itself fulfilling, and the lack of such knowledge is in the end self-negating. Perhaps a range of metaphors for God is needed. John Hare, in his historical survey of philosophical ideas on God and morality (2007), concentrates on four – God as 'magnet' (what I have called 'objective ideal'), God as sovereign commander, God as lover, and God as model or exemplar. There will be others also, none adequate on its own, but each presenting some aspect of the divine being that is important to an understanding of human morality and human nature.

What of the 'original sin' that makes moral obedience impossible, and requires free divine grace to take the place of moral success? Not all Christians believe in original sin (the Eastern Orthodox churches do not), and those who do interpret it in different ways. But it can be thought of as a basic moral weakness or inability to love God fully and to be the sort of person God intends us to be. As such, it is just a fact of life. This fact probably originates in repeated failures to choose the good in the early history of humanity, which led to the institution of a culture of greed, hatred, and egoism throughout the human race. So it is a form of 'sin', of responsibly caused alienation from God. It is 'original', in that it is a weakness and predisposition with which individuals are now born. But it does not mean that moral effort is irrelevant. It teaches that humans are flawed and imperfect beings, who cannot do what is right in our own strength. John Hare quotes St Augustine: 'God bids us do what we cannot, that we may know what we ought to seek from him' (Augustine, *On Grace and Free Will*, 16, 32). In this situation, forgiveness and divine empowerment are necessary means to fulfilment. But they are not given by God arbitrarily (God does nothing arbitrarily). For most Christians, they are given freely to all who accept forgiveness and empowerment.

It is true that some Christians seem to limit God's forgiveness to those who have heard of and accepted Jesus as the vehicle of divine grace. But most Christians prefer to think that God's grace is unlimited, and offered to all without exception, though we cannot tell the form in which it comes. They would add that such grace does come through Jesus, but that people do not have to realize this, or even to have heard of Jesus, to receive the gift of God's love (Roman Catholic documents from Vatican II make this clear, though they stress that it must make sense to say that such people would have desired baptism, if they had seen what it truly represented).

As for those who say that God requires the death of an innocent man to pay the price of human sin, a more sympathetic statement of that doctrine is needed if one is to be fair to it. In the mainstream Christian view, Jesus is not an innocent man tortured by a vengeful God. Jesus *is* God in human form. It is God who suffers and dies for human sin – which is to say, perhaps, that God shares in the suffering that human corruption causes. There are various attempts in Christian history to understand how the death of God in human form could 'pay the price of sin', and none has achieved universal acceptance among Christians. It is worth looking at this belief in slightly more detail, though I will only discuss it so far as questions of moral acceptability and insight are relevant to it. I am concerned to sketch a view of atonement that is both morally accept-able in itself and that arguably provides deep insight into the moral life.

Richard Swinburne (1989) picks out four conditions of forgiveness for wrong-doing. These are repentance, apology, reparation, and penance. It is important, I think, to add that penance, though it should involve self-sacrifice, should not be just some sort of self-flagellation. It must be related in some intelligible way to the offence, and bring about some positive good. For instance, it could be helping children in need, if the offence was against a child. Also, reparation will often not be possible. You cannot make adequate reparation for murder, though you can for stealing.

This is relevant to the question of divine forgiveness for human wrongdoing. You may well have offended God (though God cannot be harmed by human action, and a morally good God would not just take offence, as Anselm's account implies that God does). But there is no reparation you can make to God. To that extent, I am not convinced by Swinburne's argument that God gives us the means (the death of Jesus) to make reparation that we are unable to make on our own. That seems to me to amount to God making reparation to God, which hardly makes sense.

John Hare, commenting on this (1996, ch. 10a), suggests that a more traditional Christian view is that it is not we who 'offer' Jesus' life and death as a reparation to God. It is Jesus who offers his own life, culminating in the ultimate self-sacrifice of suffering and death, as an act of perfect obedience to the divine will. Since, on the Christian view, Jesus still lives and is present in a special way in every Eucharist, it is he who offers himself and his completed earthly life and death to the Father. This is not best represented, I think, as a reparation made to God. It is, however, a perfect self-offering, which justly results in Jesus' entrance into the life of eternity – the new resurrection life, which is inseparably connected with the sacrifice of the cross.

A 'reparation' account assumes two elements that are problematic for morality. First, we have to say that some punishment must be exacted for each act of wrongdoing. That does not consort well with Plato's insight that a good person will never cause harm unduly. God is good by definition. So, though God might punish (cause harm) in order to try to bring someone to repentance, it is unlikely that God will require the full extent of punishment for every offence. That would seem to render forgiveness impossible, and it seems essential that God should punish only the offender, and then do so in ways and to the extent that punishment should have a reformative intent.

That thought introduces the second morally dubious element, that punishment can be justly transferred to an innocent person (so that Jesus literally takes the punishment that was due to us). It would be a morally heroic thought to accept a punishment in someone else's place, but that would not make it a just thing for a judge to permit. Of course, if the judge took the punishment himself, that might seem better (that would fit the Christian case). But, if the judge has full discretion, we might ask why he should require a punishment at all in such a case, why he needs to punish himself instead of just forgiving the offender and remitting any punishment.

It would take a whole book to discuss this fully. Fortunately, I believe we can avoid this issue, and take a different approach – which could be consistent with the 'substitutionary' account if that account was carefully stated. We can, as John Hare suggests, draw attention to the idea of humans 'participating in the life of God' as the goal of salvation, instead of focusing on the 'transfer of punishment and death' from a guilty person to an innocent one.

When Christ offers his life (in the Eucharist) as a perfect self-sacrifice to the Father, he includes us (Augustine says, 'the congregation and fellowship of the saints') in that offering. We are thus included both in his self-giving and in his resurrection life. We are sinners, wrongdoers. But, by our repentance and by our faith (our commitment to be united with Christ), we are made sharers in his perfect offering and in his resurrection life. The life of God is one of both *kenosis* (self-giving) and of *theosis*, of beatific joy. Jesus expresses this life in human history, in his sacrifice on the cross and his ascension to Paradise. This expression continues in the community of the Church, and humans can share in the divine life by hearing and responding to his call, and becoming inwardly united to him as we are moved by the spirit that filled his earthly life. This unity of human and divine is the atonement (the making-one of human and divine), a progressive death to sin and growth in union with the divine life. We do not need to talk of a 'transfer of punishment'. We only need to speak of a divine life of sacrifice and resurrection that is able to unite us to itself insofar as we acknowledge our estrangement from God and receive the power of divine healing and reconciliation.

The early Christian theologian Athanasius expressed this by saying that God entered into the human situation, sharing human nature and enduring the worst it contains, in order that humans could share in the divine nature. Christ endured suffering – he paid the price of sin in that he suffered because of the sins of others, though he did not have to do so – and his love was unbroken. It is that enduring and victorious love in which humans can share, through the gift of the Spirit that ruled his life and is meant to rule all human lives. However exactly it is interpreted (and all interpretations may well be inadequate), the doctrine of the atonement is meant to show that God's love is unlimited, and can bring humans out of the deepest darkness of sin and self to share in the life of God. Of course, this doctrine should be framed in terms of the highest morality of which we can conceive. It should be possible for anyone to see how talk of a love which shares in suffering with compassion, and is capable of bringing all humans out of their suffering and self-concern to a greater joy, life, and love, meets and transcends the highest moral standards we might otherwise have. The insight it brings is that duty is swallowed up in love, though love must be constrained by and expressed in the demands of duty. Even if one thinks such an account of ultimate reality is false, it would be an unfair caricature that saw it as immoral or morally infantile.

It is a regular complaint against Christians that they believe that only a few are 'saved', given eternal happiness, and then purely by the arbitrary choice of God, while millions suffer torment in Hell through no fault of their own. This is not a majority Christian view. It is perfectly orthodox to believe that all will be saved who freely turn to God, and that no one will suffer torment unless they obdurately refuse to turn to God, and are consumed by hatred and anger. It is a very widely held view that God's love will not allow any who wish for union with God, and sincerely try to achieve it, to suffer loss. What is called 'Hell' is the suffering of those who wholly reject love and who destroy their own integrity and wholeness by giving way to self-centred passions, to greed, hatred, and arrogant pride. If there are any such – and perhaps there are not – they may ultimately pass into nothingness, leaving a world without evil and without suffering, illuminated by the full awareness of the all-embracing reality of God.

It would be quite wrong to see such a Paradisal state as a prudential reward for good conduct, or perhaps for trying very hard. Only those who have come truly to love good for its own sake, and to love all things for the sake of good, will inherit that happiness, which derives only from love. Of course, there may be no God, and then there will be no such Paradise. But, for those who believe themselves to experience something of a God of love, the hope of Paradise is the hope of closer knowledge and love of God, not just a hope for more personal pleasure. The hope of heaven is entailed by belief in a God of love. Those who have learned the lessons of love will say that, even if their belief, that upon which they have based the whole of their lives, turns out to be false, they would still have made the same moral commitment, and have lived with the same faith and hope. In a world where so many things are disputed, perhaps the most reasonable course, and certainly the most honourable course, is to choose the best way of life of which we can conceive, commit ourselves to the hope that the beliefs that embed this way are true, and live with a passionate commitment to what is theoretically uncertain but practically imperative. That is the life of moral faith.

A THEISTIC MORALITY

What is the relation between God, goodness, and moral obligation? The lesson of Plato's Euthyphro should be clear, that things do not become good or obligatory just because God says so. What is good is what is objectively worth choosing by any fully rational and impartially attentive being. God is such a being, and, as all possible truths are contents of God's mind, God knows what is good in knowing Godself. If God creates anything, it will be for the sake of its distinctive goodness (or will be a necessary, or a contingent, though necessarily unpreventable, consequence or unavoidable condition of that goodness).

It follows that created intellects are capable of knowing what is good without believing in God. They can know created goods without realizing that they are instantiations of the contents of God's mind, and without even believing that there is such a mind. Nevertheless, one who believes in the existence of God will believe that there is an actual case of supreme goodness that has created the world for the sake of good. This may affect what one takes to be good (if there is reason to believe, for instance, that God instantiates self-giving love (*agape*) as a supreme form of goodness). It may affect the specific goals at which it would be best to aim, if God intends that certain future goals would be best for a specific human being, given their situation and previous choices. It will make love for God morally obligatory (it is appropriate to respond to supreme value with reverence and gratitude). It will imply belief in the final triumph of goodness and the possible fulfilment of all created moral agents. It will introduce the possibility of divine help for human moral weakness and failure. And it may, on some views of God, raise the possibility of some form of union of divine and human as the ultimate goal of human life.

These are all elements that will radically affect the way morality is seen. Morality will be part of a journey towards participation in the divine–love. It is because of this that, though God does indeed command some things, and although all goods are commandable, the expression 'divine-command theory' can give an inadequate idea of theistic morality. It picks on just one element of a complex totality, when other important elements are such things as divine necessity, perfection, attraction, and union. Perhaps it is better just to speak of 'theistic morality'.

Will goodness depend upon God? Perhaps that question poses too simple and binary a choice. There are many ways in which goodness can be, and is, seen. It could be seen as a matter of personal preference. It could be seen as what an imagined impartial spectator would choose for beings of a specific nature. It could be seen as what is objectively worth choosing for its own sake. It could be seen as a participation in some transcendent, eternal, and necessary reality, the 'Good-and-Beautiful'. These are just some of the ways of conceiving of 'goodness'. There is not one universally agreed idea of goodness that is to be related to just one agreed idea of God.

Moral obligation is related to moral goodness. It would be odd to say that what one ought to do has nothing to do with what is good. But again there are different ways of construing this relation. Perhaps one could construct a continuum of possibilities, some being close to each other and some being rather far apart. A crude expressivist view that moral assertions simply express personal feelings is far from a theistic view that there are objective moral goods that we are obligated to pursue, others that it would be good to pursue, and some objective evils that we should not pursue. A view that there are objective moral facts that evoke obligations when perceived is rather close to a theistic view that it is ideas in the mind of God that evoke obligations.

My view is that moral goodness consists in something being intrinsically worth choosing, and intrinsic worth is a property of some ideas that exist necessarily in the mind of God. God does not arbitrarily make some things good. Goodness is a necessary part of the being of God. Robert Adams holds that 'goodness' is 'resemblance to God' – 'to be good is to be like God in a way that could serve as a reason for God to love it' (1999, pp. 34–6). It is hard to see how this could apply to the statement 'God is good', for it is empty to say that God resembles God. I have to say that I do not find it very helpful with regard to human goodness either. For, if we resemble God, we do so, as Adams admits, only in very partial, fragmentary, and defective ways. I do not think I choose x because it resembles God. I choose x because I consider it to be intrinsically good. If x is worth choosing, then of course God would choose it, if it is something which it is appropriate for God to possess, in an appropriately divine and unlimited way. But some goods are not appropriate for God to possess. For example, the goodness of a cow is no doubt fitting for a cow, but it would not be appropriate for God to resemble a perfect cow, and I do not admire a good cow because it is like God.

Adams concedes that 'resemblance' is a very slippery concept. But I am not convinced by his attempt to say that good cooks resemble God, not in their culinary excellence, but in respect of their creativity. This sounds to me like a desperate attempt to find resemblance where the idea would be better dropped. What seems to be happening is that features are picked out that could resemble God, precisely because we have a prior idea of what God's excellences are like. But God's excellences are very unlike ours. We humans are finite sensual beings with moral duties and prone to many moral failures. It is good for us to do our duty, to repent of our sins, to be temperate, courageous, diligent, reverent, and grateful to God. None of these excellences belongs to God, and I see little point in trying to find some respect in which something Godlike could be found in them.

In any case, I am not sure that resemblance to God would give God a reason to love something. That sounds, if anything, rather egocentric of

God ('the more something is like me, the more I admire it'). God loves everything, in the sense of caring for its well-being, unless and insofar as it harms the well-being of other things in avoidable ways. I even think it is possible for things very unlike God to be loved by God, partly because they are unlike God. For example, Mozart's Fortieth Symphony may be admired by God, even though God did not personally write it, and it may be unlike what God might have written, and good partly because it is a product of a creative activity other than God's.

It seems to me better to say that objective goodness or value exists as an idea in the mind of God, so forms of goodness would resemble, and indeed be identical to, not God as such, but ideas in God's mind. Of course, whatever we do, good or bad, would, on this view, resemble some idea in God's mind, so that is no test of what is good or bad. Resembling an idea in the mind of God is not the same as resembling God's actual character.

Since God is, *ex hypothesi*, the supreme case of all compossible values, it will be true that many human goods will resemble divine goods in some, very faint, respects. This will be what Robert Audi (2011) calls an ontic, not a semantic, resemblance. The term 'good' will not *mean* the same as 'resembling God', and goods can be known independently of belief in God. More importantly, we will decide what it is for God to be good by asking what sorts of things are good, rather than discovering what is good by asking what God's independently known nature is.

Plato, it is true, speaks of good things being like, or participating, in the Good. But that is precisely because Plato thinks of the Good as the impersonal and intelligible reality in which all things participate, as the pattern for the natures of all things, in which they share. If, however, we place the intelligible realm in the mind of a personal God, then we can indeed say that our goodness, and our very being, is patterned on archetypes in the divine mind, which God chooses to actualize in the phenomenal world. God's own nature is not identical without remainder to the archetypes in the divine mind, and what God chooses to actualize is not simply an emanation of or instantiation of the divine nature, but is due to a creative and contingent act of the divine will. We can say that to be good is to instantiate a divine archetype of intrinsic value, one which God wills us to bring to full actualization by our own free action. It is not, in Absolute Idealist fashion, just a necessary self-expression of the divine nature itself, which does not involve free finite creativity. Presumably, God wants us to be good in a way that is proper to our own natures, and perhaps to be free to actualize those natures in a uniquely creative way.

Christians do think that there is a human nature that in some way (very difficult to spell out) resembles and is identical with God – the nature of Jesus. And Christians think that we may all, by grace, share in the nature of Jesus (we are 'in Christ'). I would not hesitate to say that, for Christ, to be good is to resemble God, and that we may all come to be like and participate in Christ. So what is my problem? It is, I think, that this is a work of divine grace, not of human morality, and it is largely a hope for the future more than a completed reality in the present. Using a very traditional distinction, I would feel happier saying that to be naturally good is to actualize the virtues proper to our created natures, whereas to be supernaturally good is to be raised by God's power to share in the very nature of God, as it has been disclosed in the person of Jesus Christ. Only the former is within our own power, but we may hope that the latter will be the completion and fulfilment of our human lives. That is a significant addition to many moral and many religious views, and it would certainly transform a naturalistic view of morality in ways that seem to me fully rational, though not based solely on general considerations of reason without appeal to revelation.

Mark Murphy speaks in this way of the moral life as a 'participation in God'. This means sharing God's own actual properties, and only God could bring that about. Actualizing an idea that exists in God's mind (being good in one's own unique way) is different from sharing in an actualized state of the divine nature. So, natural morality and virtue is distinct from the morality of grace, which yet fulfils and completes natural morality. Even in natural morality, we can think of God's supreme perfection luring or attracting us towards realizing values appropriate to our created natures (Murphy, 2011, p. 162). There is such a natural attraction, arising from the just perception of God's perfection. But natural goodness itself is not a sharing in God's actual perfection, nor is obligation generated by such sharing. Goodness is grounded in God's thoughts, and obligation is generated by apprehension of values, as proper goals for beings with a human nature.

That humans exist with the natures they have may be contingent. But that, if they exist, their fulfilment consists in the actualization of specific goods, is necessary. So, it is possible for humans to come to know their objective obligations by knowledge of human nature, especially if that nature is seen as having an inherent teleology or fulfilment. Perhaps, however, even such a naturalistic morality points beyond itself, to a fulfilment of human life in union with the life of God.

On the continuum of views of morality, some other views share many features of theistic morality, especially views that stress the objectivity and binding authority of moral claims. Thus, I have tried to move progressively from an analysis of widely held views of morality in largely secular Western societies towards proposing that fully theistic views deepen and make explicit a metaphysical grounding for what may seem at first to be a wholly secular morality. This grounding, in turn, may draw attention to a fully theistic morality for which God is the origin, object, and goal of a fulfilled and happy human life.

For such a morality, moral goods and obligations are founded in a supremely good God on whom I completely depend for my existence and who has a good purpose for my life, which God can bring to fruition, despite the many evils in the world and my own moral weaknesses. It would be irrational not to fulfil such obligations, and it would be an expression of reverence, gratitude, trust, and love to fulfil them. If there were such divine ideals and goals, this would be significantly different from simply having good, naturally based reasons to do something, even if there was wide agreement on what ought to be done.

A non-theistic morality need not be less obligatory than a theistic one. But theism provides a metaphysical context that gives moral claims a different character, a clearer objectivity and authority, and a distinctive form of motivation (love for the supreme perfection of a personal God) that is rarely found in non-theistic views. Theism, in other words, will support and complement but not replace the normativity of moral obligation and the objectivity of moral goodness.

CONCLUSION

I have argued that there is a natural affinity between a commitment to morality and a commitment to religious practice. That such an affinity sometimes seems strained in the modern world is partly brought about by interpretations of religion that make it a matter of believing lots of improbable facts that fly in the face of scientific findings, of accepting moral conclusions based solely on unquestioned authority rather than on rational debate, and of being prepared to accept moral attitudes expressed in ancient texts that license violence and discrimination. It is a matter of moral importance to find a fully rational belief system about human nature in relation to the wider reality of which it is a part, to formulate a fully sympathetic morality that takes universal human fulfilment seriously, and to seek ways of overcoming human tendencies to violence and dominance.

It is possible to do this while regarding morality as a purely human invention, which is somehow self-supporting without reference to any wider metaphysical justifications. But such moral commitments may also be taken as evidences of a wider rationality, purpose, and value that is essentially built into the structure of being.

For us to regard ourselves as free rational agents, morally obliged to realize our potentialities in creative, just, and compassionate ways, may come to seem an almost irrational option if we also regard ourselves as accidental by-products of a morally indifferent and directionless cosmic mechanism. It may come to seem a matter of taste or subjective preference whether or not we give moral endeavour a central place in our personal lives. If our lives have no objective meaning and significance, why should morality have some sort of ultimate and decisive importance?

The fact is that for many of us it does. But that may lead us to see the cosmic process as essentially oriented towards the emergence of mind, purpose, and value. The challenge is to frame a coherent conception of the relation between the necessities of nature and the ideals of morality. Some would hold that this cannot be done, and we must simply live with the 'absurdity' of moral obligation in a morally indifferent universe.

A more positive possibility is to postulate a reality, God, which is itself of supreme value, and in the mind of which exist all the possibilities of finite being, good and bad. Many, perhaps all, possibilities that can generate unique and otherwise unobtainable goods are known and can be intentionally realized by God, the intention being that many varieties of goodness should be realized and perhaps shared and even created by many finite minds.

This is a metaphysical postulate that seems to me, as it has seemed to many philosophers throughout history, to be coherent, plausible, and attractive. It may be affirmed without reference to moral experience in particular, but it gives to moral experience an objectivity, authority, and effectiveness that would immensely strengthen the motivating force of morality and its consilience with a more general worldview. It may be affirmed without reference to revelation. Yet it is one interpretation of some central doctrines of the great religious traditions of our planet. Most revelations disclose a God, or a compassionate Mind, which creates for the sake of goodness or which is itself supremely good, and which offers a way of liberation from self-centred egoism, and a prospect of attaining true human flourishing and well-being ('salvation'). In this way, morality, metaphysics, and religion may converge on a view of reality and a practice of morality whose elements are mutually supportive.

Moral experience itself may contribute important strands of support for such a moral viewpoint. We interpret our sensory experience as an encounter with a world of external physical objects, and we interpret our interaction with other people as encounters with hidden personal worlds of thought and feeling that are never fully open to us. So, we may interpret our moral experience as an encounter with something external to us that encounters us as demand and inspiration, as judgement and acceptance. It demands our commitment, often to our own personal disadvantage; it also inspires us to new moral insights and challenges to conventional opinions. It causes us to acknowledge moral failures and inadequacies. And it holds out hope for a fuller realization of the moral goal to which we are called.

The phenomenology of moral experience is *sui generis*, and should not be too easily assimilated to prior notions of a personal God. But there is no doubt that for many people that experience is felt to be an encounter with an objective aspect of reality, and that some notions of God, as a quasi-personal presence, capture the nature of that encounter in positive and helpful ways. Moral experience is one of the data of consciousness that need to be explained by inclusion in a general metaphysical view, if we are impelled to adopt such a thing. If we have a sense that there is a sort of person we should be, that we find it hard to be by our unaided efforts, and that sets before us the goal of a good society that often seems empirically unlikely ever to exist, then we may feel that in moral experience we encounter a reality that is more than empirical or sensory, that is not just invented, and that makes demands on us that only it could fulfil. That is one part, and a very important part, of the idea of God.

My argument has been that moral views presuppose metaphysical theories of human nature. Some metaphysical theories are not consilient with theism, and for them morality must be explicated without reference to any transcendent grounding. I have suggested, however, that it is difficult for them to avoid covert reliance on beliefs in objective moral values and goals that sit uneasily with their explicit philosophies. Many, perhaps most, metaphysical beliefs do try to include that sense of objective value and purpose, and there are various ways of doing so. Among such ways, theistic morality is importantly distinctive, and is not merely an add-on to some universally establishable secular morality. Theism provides morality with an objectivity, authority, and hope for realization of a moral goal that it is very difficult for a secular morality to match. And moral experience is one major root of and evidence for a theistic worldview. It is equally important to see, however, that theism itself must be developed in such a way that it supports and reinforces our best insights into what makes for the moral flourishing of human life.

It is in the union of a morally sensitive theism and a transcendentally grounded morality that we may sustain a sense that the highest business of life is to live well in a just and compassionate society, and to see that living well consists in seeking the true, the good, and beautiful for its own sake, in realizing as fully as possible our positive human potentialities, and in working for a society and a world in which that is a real possibility for all without exception.

BIBLIOGRAPHY

Adams, Robert, *The Virtue of Faith* (OUP, 1987)

Adams, Robert, *Finite and Infinite Goods* (OUP, 1999)

Aquinas, Thomas, *De Veritate*

Aquinas, Thomas, *Summa Theologiae*, 1a2ae, questions 90–4 (On Natural Law), 1a2ae, questions 1–5 (On Beatitude), 2a2ae, questions 1–33 (On the Theological Virtues)

Aristotle, *Nichomachean Ethics* (trans. J.A.K. Thomson, Penguin, 1955) and *Politics* (trans. T.A. Sinclair, Penguin, 1962, p. 283)

Audi, Robert and Wainwright, William, *Rationality, Religious Belief and Moral Commitment* (Cornell University Press, 1986)

Audi, Robert, *Rationality and Religious Commitment* (Clarendon, 2011)

Augustine, St, *On Grace and Free Will*

Blackburn, Simon, 'Rule Following and Moral Realism', in *Wittgenstein: To Follow a Rule*, ed. Steven Holtzman and Christopher Leich (Routledge, 1981)

Blackburn, Simon, *Essays in Quasi-Realism* (OUP, 1993)

Blackburn, Simon, 'Realism, Quasi or Queasy?', in *Reality, Representation and Projection*, ed. John Haldane and Crispin Wright (OUP, 1993)

Bradley, F.H., *Appearance and Reality* (Allen and Unwin, 1893)

Bradley, F.H., *Ethical Studies* (Clarendon Press, 1927)

Clarke, Samuel, 'A Discourse Concerning Natural Religion' (1706)

Cottingham, John, *The Spiritual Dimension* (CUP, 2005)

Crisp, Roger, 'Naturalism and Non-naturalism in Ethics', in *Identity, Truth and Value, Essays for David Wiggins*, ed. Sabina Lovibond and S.G. Williams (OUP, 2000)

Crisp, Roger and Hooker, Brad (ed.) *Well-Being and Morality: Essays in Honour of James Griffin* (Clarendon, 2000)

Dignitatis Humanae, 'Declaration on Religious Liberty' [1965], in *Documents of Vatican II*, ed. Austin Flannery (Dominican Publications, 1992), p. 799

Dworkin, Ronald, *Justice for Hedgehogs* (Harvard University Press, 2011)

Ellis, Fiona, 'God, Value, and Naturalism', *Ratio*, 2011, vol. 24, issue 2, pp. 138–53

Finnis, John, *Natural Law and Natural Rights* (OUP, 1980)

Foot, Philippa, 'Morality as a System of Hypothetical Imperatives', 'Moral Beliefs', and 'Virtues and Vices', reprinted in *Virtues and Vices* (Blackwell, 1978)

Griffin, James, *Well-being* (Oxford, Clarendon, 1986)

Griffin, James, *Value Judgment* (Clarendon, 1998)

Griffin, James, 'Replies', in *Well-Being and Morality: Essays in Honour of James Griffin*, ed. Roger Crisp and Brad Hooker (Clarendon, 2000)

Haldane, John and Wright, Crispin, *Reality, Representation and Projection* (OUP, 1993)

Hare, John, *The Moral Gap* (OUP, 1996)

Hare, John, *God and Morality* (Blackwell, 2007)

Hare, R.M., *Moral Thinking* (Clarendon, 1981)

Hume, David, 'An Enquiry Concerning the Principles of Morals' (1751)

Hume, David, 'Treatise of Human Nature' (1739)

Huxley, T.H., 'Evolution and Ethics' (London, Pilot Press, 1947)

James, William, 'The Will to Believe' [1896], in *Essays in Philosophy*, ed. Frederick Burkhardt, Fredson Bowers and Ignas K. Skrupskelis (Harvard University Press, 1978)

Kant, Immanuel, *Critique of Practical Reason* (1788; quotations from Lewis White Beck, Bobbs-Merrill, 1956)

Kant, Immanuel, *Critique of Pure Reason* (1781; quotations from Kemp Smith, Macmillan, 1952)

Kant, Immanuel, *Critique of Teleological Judgment* (1790; quotations from J.C. Meredith, Clarendon, 1952)

Kant, Immanuel, *Groundwork to the Metaphysic of Morals* (1785; quotations from T.K. Abbott, Longmans, 1959)

Kant, Immanuel, *Lectures on Ethics* (from student notes, circa 1782; quotations from Louis Infield, Harper, 1963)

Kant, Immanuel, *Metaphysic of Morals* (1797; quotations from Mary J. Gregor, Harper and Row, 1964)

Kant, Immanuel, *Religion within the Limits of Reason Alone* (1794; quotations from Theodore Greene and Hoyt Hudson, Harper and Row, 1960)

Korsgaard, Christine, *Creating the Kingdom of Ends* (CUP, 1996)

Korsgaard, Christine, *The Sources of Normativity* (CUP, 1996)

Lenin, N., 'The State and Revolution' [1919], in *The Essential Left* (Unwin Books, 1960)

MacIntyre, Alasdair, *After Virtue* (Duckworth, 1985)

MacIntyre, Alasdair, *Whose Justice? Which Rationality?* (Duckworth, 1988)

Marx and Engels on Religion (Moscow, Progress Publishers, 1972)

Marx, Karl, *Karl Marx: Selected Writings*, ed. T.B. Bottomore and Maximilien Rubel, Penguin, 1963)

Marx, Karl, with Engels, Friedrich, 'The Manifesto of the Communist Party', in *The Essential Left* (Allen and Unwin, 1960)

McDowell, John, *Mind and World* (Harvard University Press, 1994)

McDowell, John, 'Are Moral Requirements Hypothetical Imperatives?', in *Mind, Value and Reality* (Harvard University Press, 1998)

Mill, John Stuart, *Three Essays on Religion* [1874] (published, among other editions, by Amherst, NY, Prometheus Books, 1998)

Mill, John Stuart, 'Utilitarianism' [1861] (many reprints; quoted here from *Utilitarianism, Liberty and Representative Government*, in Everyman's Library, Dent, 1960)

Moore, G.E., *Principia Ethica* [1903] (5th edition, CUP, 1951)

Murdoch, Iris, *The Sovereignty of Good* (Routledge, 1970)

Murphy, Mark, *God and Moral Law* (OUP, 2011)

Newlands, George, *Christ and Human Rights* (Ashgate, 2006)

Nietzsche, Friedrich, *Thus Spoke Zarathustra*, trans. R.J. Hollingdale (Penguin, 1961)

Nietzsche, Friedrich, *Beyond Good and Evil*, trans. R.J. Hollingdale (Penguin, 1973)

Nietzsche, Friedrich, *A Nietzsche Reader*, trans. R.J. Hollingdale (Penguin, 1977)

Plato, *Symposium*, trans. Walter Hamilton (Penguin, 1973)

Plato, *The Republic*, trans. Desmond Lee (Penguin, 1986)

Putnam, Hilary, *Ethics without Ontology* (Harvard University Press, 2004)

Quinn, Philip, *Divine Commands and Moral Requirements* (Clarendon, 1978)

Raphael, David Daiches, *The British Moralists 1650–1800* (Clarendon, 1969)

Ratzinger, Cardinal, *Instruction on Certain Aspects of the Theology of Liberation* (1984)

Ritchie, Angus, *From Morality to Metaphysics: The Theistic Implications of our Moral Commitments* (OUP, 2013)

Ross, W.D., *The Right and the Good* (Clarendon, 1930)

Ruse, Michael, *Evolutionary Naturalism* (Routledge, 1995)

Sartre, Jean-Paul, 'Existentialism and Humanism' (lecture delivered in 1945), trans. Philip Mairet (Methuen, 1989)

Sartre, Jean-Paul, *Being and Nothingness*, trans. Hazel Barnes (Routledge, 2000)

Shafer-Landau, Russ, *Moral Realism* (Clarendon, 2003)

Strawson, Peter, *Freedom and Resentment and Other Essays* (Methuen, 1974)

Sutherland, Stewart, *God, Jesus, and Belief* (Blackwell, 1984)

Swinburne, Richard, *Responsibility and Atonement* (OUP, 1989)

Teilhard de Chardin, *The Human Phenomenon* [1938–40] (Brighton, Sussex Academic, 2003)

Tennant, F.R., *Philosophical Theology*, esp. Vol. 1 [1929] (Cambridge University Press, 1968)

Thornton, Tim, *John McDowell* (Acumen; Philosophy Now Series, Chesham, 2004)

Timmons, Mark, Greco, John and Mele, Alfred (ed.) *Rationality and the Good* (OUP, 2007)

Veritatis Splendor (Catholic Truth Society, 1993)

Wainwright, William, *Religion and Morality* (Ashgate, 2005)

Ward, Keith, *Ethics and Christianity* (Allen and Unwin, 1970)

Ward, Keith, *The Development of Kant's View of Ethics* (Basil Blackwell, 1972)

Ward, Keith, *The Divine Image* (SPCK, 1976)

Ward, Keith, *The Philosopher and the Gospels* (Lion/Hudson, 2011)

Wielenberg, Eric, *Value and Virtue in a Godless Universe* (CUP, 2005)

Wigner, Eugene, 'The Unreasonable Effectiveness of Mathematics in Natural Sciences', *Communications in Pure and Applied Mathematics*, vol. 13, no. 1 (February 1960)

Wilson, E.O. *Consilience* (Little Brown, 1998)

Wittgenstein, *Lectures on Aesthetics, Psychology, and Religious Belief* (Blackwell, 1970)

Wittgenstein, *On Certainty*, ed. G.E.M. Anscombe and G.H. von Wright (Blackwell, 1979)

Wolterstorff, Nicholas, *Justice: Rights and Wrongs* (Princeton UP, 2008)

INDEX OF NAMES

Adams, Robert 104–106, 209
Aquinas, Thomas 65f., 184, 197–199
Aristotle 41f., 183
Athanasius 206
Audi, Robert 105, 210
Augustine 107f., 203

Blackburn, Simon 48, 76–79
Blake, William 89
Bradley, F. H. 187–195

Clarke, Samuel 21, 23–34
Cudworth, Ralph 27

Dworkin, Ronald 3

Ellis, Fiona 97

Finnis, John 66
Foot, Philippa 35–39

Griffin, James 5, 16, 61–63
Gutierrez 165

Hare, John 119, 123f., 129, 136, 203, 205
Hare, R. M. 82, 116, 119, 128
Hobbes, Thomas 19, 72
Hume, David 22–34, 43
Huxley, T. H. 69

James, William 198

Kant, Immanuel 115–140
Kohlberg 137

Lenin, N. 167

MacIntyre, Alasdair 72–75
Mackie, J. L. 76
Marx, Karl 164–172

McDowell, John 21, 46–58
Mill, J. S. 141–147
Moore, G. E. 80–86, 109
Murdoch, Iris 16, 60f., 88–96
Murphy, Mark 68, 106, 211

Nagel, Thomas 11
Nietzsche, F. 157–163

Penrose, Roger 86
Piaget 14
Pindar 14
Plato 59, 87, 89f., 107
Putnam, Hilary 78

Quinn, Philip 104

Ramanuja 196
Ratzinger, Joseph 170
Ritchie, Angus 57
Ross, W. D. 84
Ruse, Michael 18

Sankara 196
Sartre, J-P 173–182
Shafer-Landau, Russ 86
Shaftesbury, Lord 19
Smith, Adam 30
Strawson, Peter 13
Sutherland, Stewart 90–92
Swinburne, Richard 204

Teilhard de Chardin 70
Tennant, F. R. 70
Tennyson 70

Wigner, Eugene 87
Wilson, E. O. 6–9, 11f.
Wittgenstein, Ludwig 13m 48f.
Wolterstorff, Nicholas 147–149

INDEX OF SUBJECTS

Absolute Idealism 186–190
Advaita Vedanta 19
Alienation (in Marx) 168–170
Aristotelian categoricals 52f.
Atonement 204–206
Authenticity (in Sartre) 177–182
Autonomy: as irreducible moral discourse 17,
    20, 40, 135
  and metaphysical foundations of ethics
    3, 17, 71, 111, 135, 200
  as self-determination (free choice of
    good and evil) 4f., 37, 102f.,
    131, 136
  as thinking for oneself 138–140
  as creating moral law 131, 138
  as working out moral principles for
    oneself 131
  as recognising what is right 137f.
  in Kant 136f.
    and revelation 139f.

Bad faith 174, 178
Beatific vision 197–200
Being-for-God 180
Buddhism 146, 196

Categorical imperative, the 116, 121f.
Critical Idealism (Kant) 116, 122f.

Declaration on religious liberty (Vatican II)
    171
Devotion, moral 36–39
Dionysian morality and Christ 159, 162f.
Dipolar nature of God 103
Divine command theories 31f., 60, 68,
    103–108, 201–203, 208
Divine perfection 107f., in Aristotle and
    Aquinas 183–185
Divine–human union 192f., 198–200, 211

Enlightenment project, the 71–75
Epicurean morality 120f.
Epigenetic rules 6, 11
Error theory of morality 76

Essential human nature 66
Eucharist, the 205
Euthyphro dilemma
Evil (moral) 55–58, 62–64, 132 cf. Suffering
Evolution as open and emergent 70f., 102
Evolutionary Psychology (Sociobiology) 18f.
Existentialism and Humanism (Sartre)
    173–177
Explanatory gap, the 57f.

Faith, Kant's definition of 116, 127f., in
    Aquinas 198f., moral 207
Feelings, as the basis of ethics 23f., 30f.
Fitness 21, 24, 36
Flourishing, human 43, 52–64, 65–67, 110,
    183–186
Forms of life 49f.
Freedom, in Kant 130, in Sartre
    173–177, 179, and indeterminism 102f.
Free-loading 33

God as impartial spectator 60
God as supreme objective ideal 91, 110, 154,
    180, 203
Good, the 88–90, 96, 99
Goodness as a non-natural property 80–84
Goodness and beauty 89f., 94–96, 89f.
Goodness as resemblance to God 209–211
Grace 134

Happiness (*eudaimonia*) 42, 53–55, 121
Happiness in accordance with virtue 55,
    120–128
Hell 151, 161, 178, 206f.
Holy will, in Kant 130
Humanism, in Aristotle 183f., transcendental
    144, 147, 215
Human rights 147–149
Hume's Law 82
Hypothetical imperatives 35

Ideal goal morality 72f.
Immortality: see Life after Death
Intuition in morality 47, 83–85

222   Keith Ward

Ionian Enchantment 6–9, 111
'Is'–'Ought' argument 23f., 25f., 39f., 81f.

Jesus (and Nietzsche) 161f.
Just perception in morality 13–17, 38, 46–51
Justice and desert 150–153

Kingdom of God 143

Liberation theology 170–172
Liberation/salvation 133f., 161, 181, 195
Life after death 148–150, 152f., 162, 170,
    191f., 207
Love of God (*amicitia*) 199
Love of the Good 44f., 55, 57, 59–61, 90

Marx on religion 167–172
Mill's idea of God 144–147
Mill's 'religion of humanity' 141–147
Moral argument for God, Kant's
    115–128
Moral facts 68, 77–79, 86, 97, 157
Moral gap, the 119, 129
Moral realism 67, 76–79

Natural law 65–71
Naturalism 4f., 35, 43; expansive 5, 16;
    enriched 46–51, 65–71, 97–100
Naturalistic Fallacy 23, 80–82
Necessary and eternal truths 104, 209
Nirvana 196
No Exit (*Huis Clos*) 178

Objective and reactive attitudes 13–16
Objective and subjective moral properties
    47, 61
Objective moral truth 20, 176f.
Obligation, moral 105
Obligations and divine commands 105f.
Ontology and ethics 78f.
Option for the poor 170
Original sin 203–204

Perception and taste models of value 61
Personal Idealism 190–193
Perspectivalism 11, 158f., 174f.
Pity (*mitleid*) 157f.
Plato and the closed society 59
Platonic Enchantment 9–12, 111
Possible worlds 98–101, 102f., 104

Predisposition to evil (in Kant) 119
Presuppositional argument for basic human
    virtues 40–42
Prima facie obligations 85
Prudence 26
Punishment, retributive and reformative
    151–153
Purpose and morality 88–94, 103, 115,
    179, 184
Purposes of nature 68–71

Quasi-realism 76–79

Rationalists and sentimentalists in morality
    31–34
Rational rule morality 72f.
Reason and inclination in morality
    25–28
Reason and passion in Hume 28–31
Reason as creative rational will (in Kant) 117
Reason as the slave of the passions (Hume)
    29
Reasons for action 36–39
Reductive Naturalism 5–10
Revelation 154f., 214
Radical evil 131–133

Self-realisation 183–186 and self-sacrifice
    186–197
Sin and evolutionary theory 132f.
Stoic morality 120f.
Sub specie aeternitatis 91
Suffering 100f. Cf. Evil.
Summum bonum, the 122–128
Superman (*Ubermensch*) 158f.

Teleology in the cosmos 69–71, 87f., 179
Temporality in God 102f., 190–192,
Theosis 199f.
Transcendental morality 75m 91m 215

Utilitarianism 53f., 141

Veritatis Splendor 67
Virtue, vice, and happiness 152f,
Virtues and human flourishing 39–40m 153f,
Virtues, intellectual and moral 41f.
Virtues, theological 198

Will to power, the 157